ADVANCING CHILDREN'S RIGHTS IN DETENTION

A Model for International Reform

Ursula Kilkelly and Pat Bergin

With a Foreword by
Ann Skelton

BRISTOL
UNIVERSITY
PRESS

First published in Great Britain in 2023 by

Bristol University Press
University of Bristol
1-9 Old Park Hill
Bristol
BS2 8BB
UK
t: +44 (0)117 374 6645
e: bup-info@bristol.ac.uk

Details of international sales and distribution partners are available at bristoluniversitypress.co.uk

© Bristol University Press 2023

British Library Cataloguing in Publication Data
A catalogue record for this book is available from the British Library

ISBN 978-1-5292-1321-8 hardcover
ISBN 978-1-5292-1322-5 paperback
ISBN 978-1-5292-1323-2 ePub
ISBN 978-1-5292-1324-9 ePdf

Cover design: Clifford Hayes
Front cover image: a mechanical model made by a young person in an activities workshop in Oberstown Children Detention Campus (photo: Keith Atkins, Dublin, 2019)

Bristol University Press uses environmentally responsible print partners.

Printed in Great Britain by CMP, Poole

Contents

List of Cases and Instruments

Cases

B v Director of Oberstown [2018] IEHC 601.
B v Director of Oberstown [2020] IESC 18.
Byrne v Director of Oberstown [2013] IEHC 562.
MG v Director of Oberstown Children Detention Centre & ors [2019] IEHC 275.
M v Director of Oberstown [2020] IECA 249.
SF v Director of Oberstown [2017] IEHC 829.

International instruments

League of Nations, Declaration on the Rights of the Child 1924 (the Geneva Declaration), adopted by the Assembly of the League of Nations on 26 September 1924.

United Nations Convention on the Rights of the Child, adopted by General Assembly resolution 44/25 of 20 November 1989.

United Nations Declaration of the Rights of the Child, adopted by General Assembly resolution 1386 on 20 November 1959, A/RES/1386(XIV).

United Nations General Assembly Resolution 62/141. *Rights of the Child*, 22 February 2008.

United Nations Guidelines for the Prevention of Juvenile Delinquency (the Riyadh Guidelines), adopted and proclaimed by General Assembly resolution 45/112 of 14 December 1990.

United Nations Rules for the Protection of Juveniles Deprived of their Liberty (the Havana Rules), adopted by General Assembly resolution 45/133 of 14 December 1990.

United Nations Rules for the Treatment of Women Prisoners and Non-custodial Measures for Women Offenders (the Bangkok Rules), adopted by General Assembly resolution 65/229 on 21 December 2010.

United Nations Standard Minimum Rules for the Administration of Juvenile Justice (the Beijing Rules), adopted by General Assembly resolution 40/33 of 29 November 1985.

European instruments

European Convention for the Prevention of Torture and Inhuman or Degrading Treatment or Punishment, ETS No. 126, Strasbourg, 26 November 1987.

Guidelines of the Committee of Ministers of the Council of Europe on Child-friendly Justice (the European Guidelines), adopted by the Committee of Ministers on 17 November 2010 at the 1098th meeting of the Ministers' Deputies.

Recommendation CM/REC 2008 of the Committee of Ministers to member states on the European Rules for Juvenile Offenders Subject to Sanctions and Measures (the European Rules), adopted by the Committee of Ministers on 5 November 2008 at the 1040th meeting of the Ministers' Deputies.

Irish legislation

Children Act 1908.
Children Act 2001.
Children (Amendment) Act 2015.
Children First Act 2015.
Criminal Justice Act 2006.
Criminal Justice (Community Service) Act 1983.
Health and Social Care Professionals Act 2005.
Ombudsman for Children Act 2002.
Prisons Act 2007.
Prison Rules 2007, S.I. No. 252/2007.

List of Figures

About the Authors

Ursula Kilkelly is Professor of Law at the School of Law, University College Cork, Ireland, where she teaches international children's rights and juvenile justice. Ursula has authored nearly 100 publications, including several monographs, edited collections, journal articles and book chapters on children's rights and youth justice, and is currently co-editor of *Youth Justice: An International Journal*. Ursula has consistently sought to use her international research and her leadership roles to bring about progressive change in the implementation of children's rights. In 2016, Ursula was a government-appointed chair of the Board of Management of Oberstown Children Detention Campus and she was re-appointed for a second term in 2019.

Pat Bergin was the first Director of Oberstown Children Detention Campus 2013–20. During this time he used his skills, knowledge and experience to develop and integrate Ireland's national detention facility for children, expanding the service, modernizing social care practices and bringing about enormous change as part of an evolving youth justice system. Pat took up the post as Head of the National Forensic Mental Health Service with the HSE in November 2020. He has qualifications in social care and management (EMBA) from Waterford Institute of Technology, and has worked in social care and social care regulation for more than 30 years.

Acknowledgements

This book is an account of a process of change undertaken while we held leadership roles in Oberstown Children Detention Campus, where we sought to fulfil the goal of advancing children's rights in detention. Viewed from our different perspectives, bringing together the theory and practice of advancing children's rights in detention has truly been a learning experience for us both. While the goal was clear and simple, its completion was complex and daunting at times, demanding vision, trust, skills, partners, resources and time. Throughout the process of writing this book, we recalled the support we received from many individuals and organizations in our respective worlds. So many people helped us to respond to the challenges, to shoulder the responsibility, to continuously imagine what was possible.

At the heart of the Oberstown journey was the passion we share – and shared with others – for young people and their right to be treated with dignity and respect, wherever they are. So, to all those young people who trusted and challenged us over the years, thank you for helping us to shape detention for young people in Ireland, now and into the future.

We hope this book will provide an insight into the theory and practice, the policy and legislative requirements and the skills and resilience required to put in place a child-centred model of care in detention, in line with a children's rights approach. We are grateful to Bristol University Press for their interest in this project from the beginning, and to Helen Davis for her enthusiasm throughout. The book was only made possible with the generous support and solidarity of the wider Oberstown family, Ursula's academic colleagues at University College Cork and beyond, and the stellar research assistance of Rose Wallace, Chelsea Carr and especially Laura Lanigan.

Foreword

Ann Skelton
Professor of Law, University of Pretoria, member of the United Nations
Committee on the Rights of the Child and Chair of the Advisory Group
of the Global Study of Children Deprived of Their Liberty

"We are safe here physically, everything is well, but we have stress all the time because every minute we have a dream that is being out of here with our families and friends" (Nowak, 2019, p105). These words of an adolescent boy, interviewed during the Global Study on Children Deprived of their Liberty, remind us that no matter how good the conditions of confinement might be, freedom remains the perpetual dream for every detained child. Manfred Nowak, who led the Global Study, equated children's deprivation of liberty with deprivation of childhood and he recommended that states 'make all efforts to reduce the number of children held in places of detention and prevent deprivation of liberty before it occurs' (Nowak, 2019, p 668). The Global Study accepts that in 'rare' cases, deprivation of liberty remains unavoidable, and if it is used, then it 'should be in conditions and circumstances that ensure respect for the human rights of children' (Nowak, 2019, p 257).

This book by Ursula Kilkelly and Pat Bergin gives a detailed account of how Ireland has grappled with developing a child-rights-compliant approach to caring for children deprived of their liberty. The authors acknowledge that, until a few years ago, Ireland's detention practices fell short of good practice, with inadequate standards of care, high levels of restrictive practices and ineffective responses to children's complex needs. The book explains how Ireland has made important changes during the past five years to bring its youth justice detention practices in line with international human rights standards pertaining to children. The story of Oberstown Children Detention Campus is a narrative of transformation that provides insights into the relevance of a purpose-built facility. It demonstrates the vital importance of professionalizing the workforce, and reshaping the way that they work with children, which in turn has a significant impact on outcomes for children.

Article 40(1)) of the United Nations Convention on the Rights of the Child (CRC) requires that children in the youth justice system must be 'treated in a manner consistent with the child's sense of dignity and worth'. This requirement is both profound and simple, but it is not always easy to achieve in practice, particularly in places of detention where imposed communal living in confined and impersonal spaces seems to pull in the very opposite direction. The wording indicates that it is the child's own subjective sense of dignity and worth that matters. This underscores the importance of giving children a chance to say how they feel, really listening to them and making changes accordingly. The authors underscore that a commitment to child participation and listening to children has been embedded into the model at Oberstown, in individual, unit and campus decision-making, as well as in the complaints procedure.

The United Nations Committee on the Rights of the Child, which monitors compliance with the CRC, provided guidance in its General Comment 24 (2019) on children's rights in the child justice system. It elaborates on the requirements of Article 37(c) of the CRC – that children should be treated with humanity and respect for inherent dignity of the person, and in a manner that takes into account the needs of a person of his or her age. The General Comment emphasizes that detained children should be provided with an environment that is conducive to the reintegrative aims of residential placement. The book explains that the ratification of the CRC was a catalysing event, which triggered law and policy reform. The government of Ireland's commitment to establish a child-centred model of detention was a crucial platform for the intricate work that followed. The decision to create a single, national facility for Ireland progressed along a bumpy and sometimes difficult path, reminding us that change is not easy and that change-makers must be in it for the long haul. The resolute efforts of the reformers have paid off, and the last four chapters of the book present evidence that children's lived experience while in detention has improved.

Progress to date is summarised in Chapter 10, which explains that child-centred care has been achieved through a consistent approach to the individual assessment of need on admission, personalized placement plans and an integrated model of care through multidisciplinary services and supports. This work continues through the monitoring of the goals of each child's placement plan in a manner that is inclusive of children and their parents. Therapeutic services are carried out on site. All of this is supported by an electronic case management system that promotes good record-keeping and evidence-based decision-making.

The authors also identify the complex range of measures that were taken to advance children's rights in detention. These include the grounding of the work in international and domestic law standards and the improvement of the quality of care through recruitment, training, supervision and support for the staff who carry out the complex work with children. Other important factors were accountability through independent oversight, ongoing scrutiny, awareness-raising among the public, political leadership and support. Crucially important was the constant learning during this planned process of change, and how that was fed back into the design. Documenting the various steps as the journey unfolded also provided a bedrock of information from which the authors have drawn in presenting the detailed analysis of the process of change that this book offers.

The microcosm of Oberstown has been an incubator for ideas about how to work in a rights-compliant way with detained children. Kilkelly and Bergin have contextualized this within international human rights standards, and in so doing, have provided an action research exemplar that may serve as a blueprint for other reformers around the world.

Introduction

Child detention is a global phenomenon and, according to the United Nations Global Study on Children Deprived of Liberty, up to 250,000 children are deprived of their liberty in the justice system globally every day (Nowak, 2019, p 251). Despite the minimum standards set by the United Nations Convention on the Rights of the Child (CRC) (Liefaard, 2008), the Global Study reports that children in detention are exposed to breaches of their rights, as a result of little or no education or healthcare and poor regard for their development. While overcrowding and inadequate material conditions are experienced by children in poorer countries, children's rights everywhere are challenged by the deprivation of liberty, with minority children and children living in poverty disproportionately impacted. The gravity and complexity of the issues documented in the Global Study also highlight a failure – for multiple complex reasons – to protect the rights of children in practice. Despite numerous international instruments setting out children's rights standards in detention, real challenges in their implementation continue to persist.

In Ireland, significant progress has been made in improving the treatment of children in detention in line with international standards, and the past five years in particular have witnessed the reform of child detention, with a child-centred and rights-based model becoming the standard for everyone aged under 18 years in detention. To enable this process, the national facility – Oberstown Children Detention Campus – has undergone substantial change, developing a modern, purpose-built facility, professionalizing the workforce and embedding new ways of working to ensure that the children enjoy their rights to care and education, healthcare and programmes that prepare them for their return home or for transition to prison on reaching 18 years. The adoption of a new Children's Rights Policy Framework, which places the child at the centre of the decision-making process, is a milestone in advancing children's rights in detention. The transformation has not been without difficulty, however. Resistance to change and severe operational challenges threatened the viability of the reforms at times. However, the adoption of a range of strategic, policy and practical measures have now combined to deliver a changed environment, in which the rights of children are emerging centre stage.

Aims of this book

It is the central aim of this book to document and analyse the Irish change process, to identify the steps taken to achieve positive outcomes and to share the learning from what has been a remarkable, if challenging, transformation process of advancing children's rights in detention. Identifying the key elements of a children's rights approach to the deprivation of liberty, we present an analysis, informed by theory and practice, of how they can be made a reality. The book aims to situate the Irish experience in its international context so that the relevance of the learning can be shared by other jurisdictions.

The book does not purport to make a case for decarceration or for the abolition of child detention. It accepts, however flawed the argument, that there is a place for the detention of children in exceptional cases, including where no other option would constitute an appropriate response, especially where children are convicted of serious, violent offences. That is not to say that a case cannot be made for abolition (Goldson, 2005) or, more persuasively, for the reduction in the use of detention defined by the Annie E. Casey Foundation to be 'dangerous', 'ineffective', 'wasteful' and 'inadequate' (Mendel, 2011). Put simply, however, that is not the aim of this book. Legitimate or otherwise, in many jurisdictions the public demand for accountability, especially where children have caused great harm, is currently served by detention, among other measures. Assuming that detention will, in some form, remain part of youth justice for the foreseeable future makes it even more important that it meets the highest standards required by international children's rights.

We acknowledge the limits of what even progressive and rights-based approaches to detention can achieve. The landscape is complex and poverty, disadvantage and racial and ethnic disparities have dominated youth justice for decades if not centuries (Bishop and Feld, 2012; Junger Tas et al, 2012; Mallett, 2018; Goldson et al, 2021; Zane 2021). Dowd and others have called for 'total reform' of a 'broken system' (Dowd et al, 2015); and similarly, Feld (2017, p 280) notes with regard to the historical problems of racism, poverty and community disadvantage, that 'no justice system can remedy these conditions'. Although they cannot be remedied by detention either, it is vital nonetheless that children's care in detention ameliorates rather than compounds their difficult circumstances.

With this in mind, we set out to identify how detention can achieve greater compliance with children's rights. We outline how those responsible for detention can be held to account, providing insights from experience of how the various challenges and obstacles to a rights-based approach to detention can be overcome. In this way, the book draws on both the theory of international children's rights and the practical experience of giving them effect. In doing so, we do not suggest that child detention in Ireland is now children's rights compliant, that the work is complete. There are clear areas where gaps remain, where progress has been slow or where work remains to be done to fully embed the progress made into practice. We draw attention to these issues throughout the book. Nor can we do justice to all the issues or concerns that are prevalent in Ireland or indeed elsewhere. For instance, due to the characteristics of the Irish context, where youth detention is not dominated by race, unlike the experience of many other jurisdictions, there is relatively little consideration given to this factor here. What we argue, however, is that a robust child-centred approach should be sufficiently adaptable to respond to the needs of every individual child, regardless of their circumstances or background. Moreover, drawing attention to the important connections between detention and broader child welfare and justice systems, we recognize that the issues of disproportionate impact on children in detention that arise as a result of racism, poverty and gender discrimination, among others, cannot be 'solved' by considering detention in isolation. Indeed, they are dependent on rights-based approaches elsewhere in the wider child justice system, addressed here and in the work of others.

Methodology

This book uses a number of different methodological approaches in its analysis of children's rights in the practice of detention. There are parts, based on desk-based research, where we draw on academic literature and legal standards and the approach is interdisciplinary, including material from law, the social sciences and health sciences, with some references to change management literature. Significant emphasis is placed on the children's rights standards in international law, including legal instruments and their interpretation by treaty bodies including the Committee on the Rights of the Child (the CRC Committee), on which the model of advancing children's rights in detention is based. Our analysis of how these standards have been implemented in practice is based mainly on the reports of national inspectorates and international human rights bodies, while accounts of recent developments and events are based on Oberstown's annual reports, presented to the Houses of the Oireachtas (Parliament). We are also grateful to the management of Oberstown Children Detention Campus for permission to use some data not otherwise available that help to enrich the book and to the Council of Europe Development Bank for their permission to use an unpublished report on the design of Oberstown. The reflections on the learning from the process, although they draw on children's rights and other literature, are our own and a certain subjectivity is therefore to be expected.

In relation to terminology, both the CRC and Irish law define a child as anyone under the age of 18 years. For this reason, we use the term 'child' throughout.

Chapter outline

The book is divided into ten chapters. Chapter 1 introduces the international children's rights standards and identifies the rights to which children are entitled generally and with specific reference to youth justice and detention. Measures required to implement those rights are set out before the model to advance children's rights in detention is introduced. Chapter 2 presents an analysis of the challenges documented internationally in the protection of children's rights in detention. Stark evidence of the breaches of children's rights is presented along with emerging optimism regarding the reform of detention as a result of research, litigation and advocacy. Chapters 3 and 4 begin to set the scene from an Irish perspective, by tracing the evolution of the Irish youth justice system both generally (Chapter 3) and with regard to detention (Chapter 4). These chapters highlight the longstanding commitment to a child-centred model of detention and explain how this became embodied in national law and government policy, setting the scene for the change that is outlined in the chapters that follow. Chapter 5 traces the development of Oberstown Children Detention Campus from 2015 to the current day, using inspection reports to illustrate the improvements made in advancing children's rights. Chapters 6 and 7 document the extent to which children's rights standards are met in practice, meeting the key elements of child-centred care, and the child's rights to provision, participation, preparation, partnership (Chapter 6) and protection (Chapter 7). Chapter 8 considers two critical elements necessary to advance children's rights in detention, namely staffing and communications, while Chapter 9 considers the issue of public scrutiny and accountability, in identifying the role played by national and international bodies in bringing about change. The final chapter – Chapter 10 – presents an overview of the process of reform, summarizing the key areas where progress has been made in the advancement of children's rights in detention and the gaps that remain. The book concludes with reflections on the key enablers for the introduction of a rights-based approach, the barriers and how they might be overcome. An Afterword offers some final words of advice in the pursuit of reform everywhere.

1

Children's Rights in Detention

Introduction

The United Nations Convention on the Rights of the Child (CRC) was adopted in 1989 and is the most highly ratified instrument in human rights law, setting the minimum standards to which children are entitled across their childhood (Tobin, 2019). The Committee on the Rights of the Child (the CRC Committee) has played an important role, interpreting the CRC in its General Comments and helping to improve implementation at a national level through the state party reporting process (Sloth-Nielsen, 2019). Over the years, the CRC's standards have been supplemented by instruments adopted at international and regional levels, producing a now comprehensive framework for the legal protection of children's rights.

Children who come into conflict with the law were an early concern of the international community, resulting in two substantial provisions in the CRC – Articles 37 and 40 – that address the child's rights in youth justice and detention (Liefaard, 2020). Article 40(1) of the CRC recognizes the right of children in conflict with the law to be treated in a manner consistent with their sense of dignity and worth, reinforcing the child's respect for the rights and freedoms of others and which takes into account the child's age and the desirability of promoting their reintegration into society. It requires states to have regard to the child's due process rights and prescribes measures of specialization and diversion as key to the rights-based approach to youth justice. Article 37 recognizes that children deprived of liberty are entitled to respect for dignity and age-appropriate treatment and requires states to ensure that detention is 'a measure of last resort', used for 'the shortest appropriate period of time' (Article 37(b), CRC). Children must be separated from adults in detention, have the right to maintain contact with family through correspondence and visits, and the right to prompt access to legal and other appropriate assistance (Article 37(c) and (d), CRC). It is implicit in Article 37 that detention can cause children harm in light of their vulnerability and stage of development. In order to minimize this harm, and to prevent the child from reoffending, international instruments set out the rights to which children in detention are entitled and the measures that states must take to ensure those rights are protected. Building on the legal obligations set out in the CRC, international and regional bodies, like the United Nations and the Council of Europe, have adopted guidelines and recommendations that seek to protect children's rights in detention. And yet, despite the range and detail of these instruments, the Global Study on Children Deprived of Liberty concluded in 2019 that 'millions of children of all ages are suffering in many different types of detention in violation of international law' (Nowak, 2019, p 13). The reasons for this gap between international children's rights standards and the children's enjoyment of their rights are complex and the challenge of translating international standards into practice is not well understood.

This chapter aims to introduce the relevant international children's rights standards in order to set out the key benchmarks of detention from a children's rights perspective. First, the chapter introduces children's rights, with specific reference to the principles and provisions of the CRC. It then considers the international standards on youth justice, before focusing on standards specific to children deprived of liberty. The next section considers the measures that states must adopt to ensure those standards are enjoyed in practice. Bringing this together, the chapter concludes by identifying the key elements of rights-based child detention, introducing an original model to advance children's rights in detention. The learning from the application of this model in Ireland is explored in the chapters that follow.

Introducing children's rights

International standards on youth justice and detention have their basis in international human rights law, specifically the body of law that sets out the rights of the child. In 1924, the League of Nations adopted its first instrument in this area, the Declaration on the Rights of the Child 1924 (the Geneva Declaration), which recognized that 'men and women of all nations, recognizing that mankind owes to the Child the best that it has to give', declared and accepted it as their duty to meet the needs and rights of the child to development, protection and welfare. Even at this time, in acceptance that children in conflict with the law deserved special attention, the Geneva Declaration explicitly referred to the 'delinquent' child as a child that 'must be reclaimed' (Liefaard, 2020, p 280). This instrument, which focused on the child as a subject in need of protection, was followed by the United Nations Declaration on the Rights of the Child in 1959, which recognized for the first time that children, like adults, were rights holders entitled to the protection of the state. In its Preamble, the 1959 Declaration acknowledged that 'the child, by reason of his physical and mental immaturity, needs special safeguards and care, including appropriate legal protection, before as well as after birth'. In a shift towards a rights-based approach, the 1959 Declaration recognized the rights of the child in 'Ten Principles' while also calling on parents and voluntary organizations, but also crucially local authorities and national governments, to recognize the rights in the Declaration and 'strive for their observance'. This approach reflected human rights law, which recognizes that individuals are entitled to have their rights vindicated by the state. For children, long since considered the property of their parents, this was a significant recognition of their status as autonomous rights holders, with the protection of their rights no longer a private, family matter. Significantly, the 1959 Declaration contained the first international expression of the best interests principle and recognized the child's rights to education, development, healthcare and special protection. Although it mentioned children without family care, the Declaration did not specifically address the rights of children in conflict with the law.

Nearly 30 years later, the United Nations concluded a decade-long process of drafting its first binding legal instrument on the rights of the child. The CRC was adopted unanimously by the General Assembly of the United Nations in 1989 and in a groundswell of international support it came into force in rapid time, becoming the most highly ratified instrument in international law, with only the United States failing to join (Doek, 2019). As a comprehensive legal instrument, the CRC sets out the rights to which children are entitled in all areas of their lives, while making specific provision for the rights of children in particular settings and circumstances, including refugee children (Article 22), children in armed conflict (Article 38) and children in conflict with the law (Article 40). The Committee on the Rights of the Child (the CRC Committee), established to monitor progress in the implementation of the CRC, identified four provisions as 'general principles' to guide implementation of the CRC (CRC Committee, 2003, p 4). These are:

- the requirement that all children enjoy their rights equally without discrimination (Article 2);
- the best interests of the child are a primary consideration in all actions concerning children (Article 3);
- the child's right to life, survival and development (Article 6); and
- the child's right to have their views taken into account in all matters affecting them, with those views given due weight in accordance with the child's age and maturity (Article 12).

These provisions are considered to have additional weight, as a lens through which all CRC provisions are to be interpreted and applied (Peleg, 2019).

Intended as a direct remedy to children's invisibility from decision-making about them and their lives, Article 12 is particularly significant 'not only for what it says, but because it recognizes the child as a full human being with integrity and personality and the ability to participate freely in society' (Freeman, 1996, p 37). Like Article 3, the best interests principle, which has served to promote child-centred decision-making (Sutherland and Barnes MacFarlane, 2018), Article 12 has inspired a movement to bring about greater involvement of children in decisions made about them inter alia through Lundy's model of space, voice, audience and influence (Lundy, 2007).

The CRC is comprehensive and detailed, recognizing the rights that apply to children everywhere, while making special provision for children who are particularly vulnerable or require special care (Tobin, 2019). It recognizes the rights of the child to healthcare (Article 24), education (Articles 28 and 29) and an adequate standard of living (Article 27), while giving expression to the child's rights as a citizen, including freedom of expression (Article 13), freedom of religion (Article 14), freedom of association (Article 15) and the right to privacy (Article 16), along with the child's right to enjoy their own culture (Article 30) and play, rest and leisure (Article 31). Every child's right to special protection from abuse, harm and ill-treatment is recognized in Article 19, along with the right to investigation and recovery in Article 39, with extensive protection from exploitation set out in Articles 32 to 36. Uniquely in the CRC, children are entitled to information about their rights under Article 42.

The CRC clearly recognizes the important role of the family in providing the child with protection and care. The Preamble highlights the family as the 'natural environment for the growth and well-being of all its members and particularly children', providing that the family should be afforded 'the necessary protection and assistance so that it can fully assume its responsibilities within the community'. It recognizes 'that the child, for the full and harmonious development of his or her personality, should grow up in a family environment, in an atmosphere of happiness, love and understanding'. This concern for the child's right to family care appears throughout the CRC in:

- Article 5, which recognizes the role of parents to support the child's exercise of their rights;
- Article 18, which recognizes the primary responsibility that parents have for their children;
- Article 7, which provides for the child's right to know and be cared for by their parents; and
- Article 9, which has regard to the child's right to have contact with their parents in circumstances of separation.

Children without family care receive special attention throughout the CRC too. Articles 9 and 10 highlight the importance to the child of family support and relationships and Articles 20 and 21 provide special protection to children whose protection must be found outside the family. For children in detention, contact with family is explicitly named as a right in Article 37.

The CRC defines the child as every human being below the age of 18 years (Article 1) and although states are entitled to prescribe that majority is reached earlier, Article 1 has put down a marker that the protective status of childhood and children's rights should, in the main, apply from birth to 18 years. This is at odds with the approach in some jurisdictions where children who come into conflict with the law are treated as adults, ending the protection of childhood through a low or no age of criminal responsibility or the application to children of adult sentencing or detention regimes (Lynch and Liefaard, 2020). Children's right to protection of their rights under the CRC can seem at odds with the fact that in some jurisdictions very young children are held fully accountable under the criminal law; in this situation, as in other areas of the child's interaction with the youth justice system, parental responsibility for all children under 18 years plays an important role (Kilkelly, 2020). In addition to the definition of age, the CRC underscores the entitlement of all children to dignity and respect as individual rights holders. In this way, children's rights are not earned or conditional and they apply regardless of the child's status, background or circumstances.

Implementation of children's rights

Article 4 of the CRC requires state parties to take 'all appropriate legislative, administrative, and other measures for the implementation of the rights' in the CRC and the CRC Committee has set out its guidance in this area in its General Comment No 5 (CRC Committee, 2003). These measures have been found to have an 'incremental and transformative' effect on the legal implementation of the CRC at a national level (Kilkelly, 2019) and, according to the committee, they include both legal and non-legal measures designed to give the CRC the force of domestic law and to shift the treatment of children from passive recipients of charity to holders of rights with legal entitlements against the state (CRC Committee, 2003, p 3). The committee recommends the review and withdrawal of all reservations to the CRC (CRC Committee, 2003, p 5) and promotes the incorporation of the CRC into domestic law, so that it can inform policy-making and be directly invoked before the courts (CRC Committee, 2003, p 6). The committee welcomes the inclusion of children's rights provisions in national constitutions and emphasizes that domestic law should reflect the CRC's general principles (CRC Committee, 2003, p 7). Consolidated 'children's rights statutes' are welcomed, but it is equally important that relevant sectoral laws (on education, health, justice and so on) reflect the CRC's standards (CRC Committee, 2003, p 7). In this way, enshrining the CRC's provisions and principles in national law is key to their effective implementation (Kilkelly et al, 2021).

In addition to the measures that support the CRC's standing in domestic law, the committee recommends the adoption of non-legal measures to further implementation at the national level. Its key advice for state parties is to ensure cross-sectoral coordination, as well as regular monitoring of implementation, with the involvement of national human rights institutions, non-governmental organizations (NGOs) and others (CRC Committee, 2003, p 8). In recognition of the important role of national policy, the committee has strongly recommended the adoption of a unified, comprehensive national strategy or action plan, rooted in the CRC, highlighting that developing such a strategy must take account of the views of children, including those heard less often (CRC Committee, 2003, p 8). The committee advocates a process of child impact assessment, to evaluate the impact of proposed policy and budget decision-making on children, and promotes self-monitoring and evaluation as a government obligation but one in which others – parliamentary committees, academic institutions, NGOs and independent human rights institutions – should also participate (CRC Committee, 2003, p 11). Importance is attached to the impartial scrutiny of government policy by NGOs and national human rights institutions (CRC Committee, 2003, pp 14–15), while the media is identified as a 'valuable partner' in the implementation process (CRC Committee, 2003, p 14).

The child's right to information about their rights in Article 42 draws a unique connection between children's awareness of their rights and their effective realization, and by extension, the CRC Committee has consistently recommended that the training and capacity-building of those who work with and for children should be systematic and ongoing, emphasizing the status of the child as a holder of rights and encouraging active respect for the child's rights (CRC Committee, 2003, p 13).

Children's rights and youth justice

Although many CRC provisions apply to children in conflict with the law, there are two substantive provisions that are especially relevant to this context. Article 37(a) prohibits torture and other cruel, inhuman or degrading punishment, including capital punishment and life imprisonment without the possibility of release, and Article 37(b) requires that arrest, detention and imprisonment must be in conformity with the law, used only 'as a measure of last resort' and 'for the shortest appropriate period of time'. The remainder of Article 37 recognizes the rights to which children are entitled when deprived of liberty. Article 37(c) requires that every child deprived of liberty is treated with humanity, respect and dignity and in line with the child's needs. It provides that children must, in most circumstances, be separated from adults in detention and have the right to maintain contact with family through correspondence and visits, recognizing the importance to children of retaining contact with family. Finally, Article 37(d) recognizes the child's right to prompt access to legal and other assistance as well as the right to a prompt challenge of the legality of their detention before a court.

Article 40 sets out the detailed due process rights to which children are entitled when they come into conflict with the law. Most importantly, Article 40(1) provides that every child alleged as, accused of or recognized as having infringed the penal law has the right:

> to be treated in a manner consistent with the promotion of the child's sense of dignity and worth, which reinforces the child's respect for the human rights and fundamental freedoms of others and which takes into account the child's age and the desirability of promoting the child's reintegration and the child's assuming a constructive role in society.

Article 40(1) sets down a marker as to how children in conflict with the law must be treated, setting expectations as to the national approach to youth justice. Article 40(2) sets out the specific rights and safeguards to which children are entitled, such as: the right to be innocent until proven guilty; to be informed of the charges against them; not to be compelled to give testimony or confess guilt; and to have free access to an interpreter. Of particular importance is the right of the child, in Article 40(2)(vii), to have their privacy respected at all stages of the proceedings. Article 40(3) of the CRC highlights the importance of specialization, requiring state parties to promote the establishment of 'laws, procedures, authorities and institutions specifically applicable to children alleged as, accused of, or recognized as having infringed the penal law'. In particular, the CRC requires states to establish a minimum age of criminal responsibility and to put in place 'whenever appropriate and desirable, measures for dealing with such children without resorting to judicial proceedings, providing that human rights and legal safeguards are fully respected'. Article 40(4) requires states to make available a 'variety of dispositions, such as care, guidance and supervision orders; counselling; probation; foster care; education and vocational training programmes and other alternatives to institutional care', in order to ensure that children are dealt with 'in a manner appropriate to their well-being and proportionate both to their circumstances and the offence'.

The CRC Committee adopted a General Comment on Children's Rights in Juvenile Justice in 2007 on the basis of its work reviewing state party implementation in this area (CRC Committee 2007). Recognizing that many state parties have 'a long way to go in achieving full compliance with

CRC', the General Comment sought to provide 'more elaborated guidance and recommendations' on how to ensure the administration of juvenile justice complies with the CRC (CRC Committee, 2007, p 3). In addition to providing insights on the interpretation of Articles 37 and 40, General Comment no 10 clarified the application of the CRC's general principles in juvenile justice, contained guidance on setting the age of criminal responsibility, and addressed the right of the child to participate in justice proceedings and have their rights protected when deprived of liberty. In 2019, the committee took the unusual step of revisiting this General Comment, revising it in light of 'the promulgation of international and regional standards, the committee's jurisprudence, new knowledge about child and adolescent development, and evidence of effective practices, including those relating to restorative justice' (CRC Committee, 2019a, p 2). The decision to adopt General Comment no 24 reflected the committee's concerns about 'the minimum age of criminal responsibility and the persistent use of deprivation of liberty' (CRC Committee, 2019a, p 2) and its new title – Children's Rights in the Child Justice System – is an important reminder that even when in conflict with the law, children retain their status as children and remain rights holders under the Convention.

A number of detailed instruments have been adopted by the United Nations and other regional bodies in the area of youth justice. At an international level, these include the United Nations Standard Minimum Rules for the Administration of Juvenile Justice (the Beijing Rules) adopted in 1985, the United Nations Rules for the Protection of Juveniles Deprived of their Liberty (the Havana Rules) adopted in 1990, and the United Nations Guidelines for the Prevention of Juvenile Delinquency (the Riyadh Guidelines) also adopted in 1990. The United Nations Rules for the Treatment of Women Prisoners and Non-custodial Measures for Women Offenders (the Bangkok Rules) are also relevant insofar as they recommend special provision for girls in detention. At the regional level, the Parliamentary Assembly of the Council of Europe has adopted multiple recommendations on the treatment of children in conflict with the law and the Committee of Ministers has adopted two major instruments in this area. In particular, the European Rules for Juvenile Offenders subject to Sanctions and Measures (the European Rules) were adopted in 2008 to set specific rules for the protection of the rights of children subject to custodial and community-based sanctions, and the Guidelines of the Committee of Ministers of the Council of Europe on Child-friendly Justice (the European Guidelines) were adopted in 2010 to provide guidance on the effective participation of children in justice proceedings (Liefaard and Kilkelly, 2018).

These instruments are varied in depth and focus. Taken together, they constitute a substantial and detailed body of guidance designed to inform national approaches to youth justice and detention in line with children's rights standards. Not susceptible to the vagaries of public opinion, these minimum standards have 'credibility' and 'a sense of timeless value' as the 'common language of youth justice' (Kilkelly, 2008a, p 1919). The guidance is extensive in reach and detail, meaning that it is applicable to the variety of national approaches to youth justice that exist around the world (Muncie, 2006). Indeed, 'the world has witnessed the emergence of a comprehensive international legal framework of human and children's rights standards relevant to juvenile justice', which has given rise to law reform and an increased awareness and understanding about the rights of children in justice systems (Liefaard, 2020, p 283). Although the overlapping and at times contradictory nature of these instruments has been highlighted (Hespel et al, 2012), their principal value lies in the extent to which they capture 'best practice' across the youth justice system, along with a consistent commitment to 'age-appropriate treatment, the importance of diversion and the imperative of rehabilitation' (Kilkelly, 2008a, p 188). Underlying these instruments is a key assumption that children in conflict with the law must be treated in a child-specific manner, which is fair and respectful of their inherent dignity and rights. Liefaard observes that this requires 'a specific justice system for children', pedagogical in orientation, and specialist in approach, with key principles incorporated in law, policy and practice throughout the wider justice system (Liefaard, 2020, pp 284–8). These principles, and the detailed instruments that underpin them, form the basis of a rights-based approach to youth justice.

Children's rights in detention

The fact that children deprived of liberty are singled out for specialist treatment in the CRC and in related international and regional instruments is a measure of the serious concern that exists around the world regarding the treatment of children in detention (Goldson and Kilkelly, 2013). This is reflected in the standards themselves. As the European Rules explain, for instance, their purpose is to 'uphold the rights and safety of juvenile offenders' and promote their 'physical, mental and social well-being', including when deprived of liberty. More pointedly, Rule 3 of the Havana Rules explains that its standards are designed to '[counteract] the detrimental effects of all types of detention', fostering children's reintegration into society.

International monitoring work has highlighted the challenges in the implementation of children's rights in secure settings, and bodies such as the European Committee for the Prevention of Torture and Inhuman or Degrading Treatment or Punishment (the CPT), which visits places of detention under the eponymous Convention, has identified a range of deficits in how children are treated (Kilkelly and Casale, 2012). In response, the CPT has recommended that 'juveniles who are deprived of their liberty ought to be held in detention centres specifically designed for persons of this age, offering regimes tailored to their needs and staffed by persons trained in dealing with the young' (CPT, 2015c). The CPT has highlighted the importance of robust inspection and complaints mechanisms and training and specialization among staff as key measures to promote better standards of protection in this area.

The CRC Committee's General Comment No 24 also advocates a specialist system of child detention, envisaging 'separate facilities for children', 'staffed by appropriately trained personnel' that 'operate according to child-friendly policies and practices' (CRC Committee, 2019a, p 15). It sets out clear direction regarding the kind of conditions children should enjoy when deprived of their liberty and the priorities for state authorities in ensuring that children's rights are protected in detention. The main requirements are that:

• The physical environment should be conducive to reintegration, with opportunities for peer interaction, social and leisure activity and privacy.
• The child has a right to education suited to their needs and abilities and designed to prepare them for return to society. Every child should receive vocational training in occupations likely to prepare them for future employment.
• The child has a right to a health assessment on admission and adequate healthcare throughout their stay.
• The child should have frequent communication with the wider community, with friends and family, and the opportunity to visit home. There should be no restrictions on communication with the child's lawyer.
• Restraint or force should only be used when the child poses an imminent threat to themselves or others and should never deliberately inflict pain or be used as punishment. Staff should receive training on the applicable standards and use of restraint or force and violation of the rules and standards should be punished appropriately. All incidents of restraint or force should be recorded, monitored and evaluated and reduced to a minimum.
• Discipline should be consistent with upholding the inherent dignity of the child, and measures in violation of Article 37 of the CRC must be strictly forbidden, including corporal punishment, placement in a dark cell, solitary confinement or any other punishment that may compromise the physical or mental health or wellbeing of the child concerned. Discipline should never deprive the child of their basic rights, such as visits by legal representatives, family contact, food, water, clothing, bedding, education, exercise or meaningful daily contact with others.
• Solitary confinement should not be used and any separation of the child from others should be for the shortest possible time and used only as a measure of last resort for the protection of the child or others. Where it is deemed necessary to hold a child separately, this should be done in the

presence or under the close supervision of a suitably trained staff member, and the reasons and duration should be recorded.

- Every child should have the right to make requests or complaints and be informed of the response without delay. Children need to know their rights and to know about and have easy access to complaints mechanisms.
- Independent and qualified inspectors should conduct inspections on a regular basis, including unannounced inspections. They should place special emphasis on holding conversations with children in the facilities, in a confidential setting.

These standards provide important benchmarks for how child detention is organized and managed, and for the provision of quality care to children, in line with respect for children's rights.

Implementation of children's rights in youth justice and detention

In addition to the general measures of implementation for children's rights, which highlight the requirement to incorporate the CRC into domestic law and policy, the CRC Committee has also highlighted the measures that must be taken to ensure the implementation of children's rights in youth justice and detention (CRC Committee, 2019a). Its principal recommendations in this regard concern specialization, effective interagency coordination and the importance of taking an individual and multi-disciplinary approach to assessing and meeting children's needs. The committee reiterates the importance of involving NGOs in the development and implementation of child justice policy (CRC Committee, 2019a, p 18) and highlights the obligation to raise awareness about the rights of the child with specific reference to youth justice. In doing so, it highlights that 'children who commit offences are often subjected to negative publicity in the media, which contributes to a discriminatory and negative stereotyping of those children', noting that this 'negative presentation or criminalization of children is often based on a misrepresentation and/or misunderstanding of the causes of crime' (CRC Committee, 2019a, p 18). The committee recommends that state parties seek the 'active and positive involvement of Members of Parliament, non-governmental organizations and the media to promote and support education and other campaigns to ensure that all aspects of the Convention are upheld for children who are in the child justice system'. According to the committee, it is 'crucial' for children, in particular those with experience of the justice system, to be involved in these awareness-raising efforts (CRC Committee, 2019a, p 18).

The committee also highlights the importance of specialized training for those working with and for children in the justice system, noting that 'the quality of the administration of child justice' requires that all the professionals involved receive appropriate multi-disciplinary training on the content and meaning of the Convention' (CRC Committee, 2019a, p 19). This training should be 'systematic and continuous' and extend beyond information on national and international law to include:

- 'established and emerging information from a variety of fields' including 'the social and other causes of crime';
- 'the social and psychological development of children, including current neuroscience';
- disparities that may amount to discrimination against certain marginalized groups, culture and trends relating to young people;
- the 'dynamics of group activities'; and
- 'available diversion measures'. (CRC Committee, 2019a, p 19)

The committee notes that there should 'be a constant reappraisal of what works' and stresses the importance of collecting and analysing disaggregated data concerning children who come into conflict with the law (CRC Committee, 2019a, p 19). It recommends regular evaluations of child justice systems, with a focus on the effectiveness of the measures taken, and in relation to discrimination, reintegration and patterns of offending, noting that these should 'preferably' be undertaken by 'independent academic institutions'; they should also involve children, especially those 'who are or who have previously had contact with the system' (CRC Committee, 2019a, p 19).

A model for advancing children's rights in detention

What is clear, therefore, is that the detailed and wide-ranging international children's rights standards both recognize the rights to which children deprived of liberty are entitled while pointing to the duty on state parties to respect, protect and fulfil those rights. Although any summary of these standards is likely to be incomplete or insufficiently sophisticated to cater for the complex needs of every child, fundamentally they can be presented in the form of a rights-based model of detention, as follows. In particular, a children's rights approach prioritizes child-centred care for all children under 18 years, while assuring to every child the rights to protection from harm, participate in decision-making and enjoy provision of their basic needs. Their rights to be prepared for when they leave detention are integral both to continued enjoyment of their rights, and to their right to healthy development. The fulfilment of these rights requires partnership – with the child's family, with multi-disciplinary professionals and with agencies, both in detention and in the community – so that the rights-based approach is holistic, integrated and system-wide.

Figure 1.1: A model for advancing children's rights in detention

The model to advance children's rights in detention thus has five interconnected elements. At its core is the child-centred approach, which must be applicable to all children under 18 years, supported by regard for the child's rights in the five thematic areas of provision, protection, participation, preparation and partnership. The model assumes that detention will only be used within the confines of the law, its use limited to being a measure of last resort and the shortest appropriate period of time. The final section sets out these elements in more detail.

Child-centred care

At the core of the model (Figure 1.1) is the requirement, in line with the fundamental principle of children's rights, that all actions, measures and approaches to children deprived of liberty must be child-centred. This requires a commitment at all levels to treat children deprived of liberty as children regardless of their background, their age or their circumstances, or the reasons for their detention. It recognizes that children deprived of liberty are entitled to quality, individualized care that is developmentally appropriate, in line with their assessed needs. All children have a right to be treated in a manner that ensures their rights are fulfilled. The child-centred approach is based on the requirement to ensure that all actions that affect children – day-to-day decisions, actions and practices – should be guided by what is in children's best interests both individually and as a group. Recognizing that some children, including girls, transgender children or children with disabilities for instance, may have additional needs, and that certain groups of children, such as those from migrant or minority ethnic backgrounds, may also require special care, reinforces the importance of treating each child individually and holistically.

Building on the requirement to be child-centred, the international children's rights standards require that child detention advances children's rights in the five areas of provision, protection, participation, preparation and partnership. These five Ps, which are interconnected and indivisible from each other and from the child-centred approach, can be explained as follows:

- **Provision.** All children are entitled to have their basic needs met, and detention must thus provide for the child's fundamental rights to development, to education and to healthcare. Detention presents an important opportunity to address deficits in meeting those needs to date, by providing intensive care for the child's mental and physical health, providing healthcare and interventions that address the factors that may have contributed to the child's offending. Education must be provided to every child in line with their needs and interests, balancing an academic curriculum with the skills and vocational training that will improve the child's life chances on release.
- **Protection.** The child must be protected from harm while in detention, and receive treatment and care for previous trauma, ill-treatment and exploitation. The child has a right to feel safe and have adults they can trust to address their concerns. Any limitations on the child's exercise of their rights – through physical intervention or separation from their peers for instance – must be safe and ensure the child's right to protection from harm.
- **Participation.** Every child has the right to express their views in all matters that affect them and it is fundamental to child-centred care that children have a right to participate in decision-making. Children deprived of liberty have the right to be active agents in their own care and have their views taken into account in decision-making on all matters that affect them. They have the right to information about their rights, and about their care, and to access effective complaints mechanisms in respect of their treatment.
- **Preparation.** Successful reintegration and rehabilitation requires that every child has the right to have their needs met in a holistic and multi-disciplinary manner, which places their offending in its wider social context, with access to services, supports and mechanisms designed to prepare each child for successful return to the community. Rights that prepare the child to leave detention, to an onward placement or back to their community, are of fundamental importance.
- **Partnership.** Acknowledging the importance of the child's relationship with their family, the child deprived of liberty has the right to regular contact and visits from family, so that this relationship is maintained and

strengthened. Regular contact with community-based agencies and services should take place in a manner designed to fulfil the child's rights and promote their reintegration in a system-wide approach that meets the child's needs. Approaches to child detention must be connected to national policy on children and strong linkages between detention and community-based services must be put in place.

Conclusion

Based on a comprehensive body of international children's rights standards, this chapter identified the key elements of the model designed to advance children's rights in detention. The model draws on a wealth of children's rights standards to articulate an integrated vision for child detention that is child-centred and designed to protect, promote and fulfil the child's rights to provision, protection, participation, preparation and partnership.

As subsequent chapters show, however, rights-based detention cannot be achieved without a number of supporting and inter-related actions, including:

- embedding children's rights in law and policy;
- ensuring staff are supported to provide rights-based care;
- monitoring and inspection systems in a rights-compliant manner to deliver accountability; and
- communications and engagement with the wider community, including national human rights bodies, parliament and the media, all of whom are vital to promote a wider understanding of the rights-based approach.

These supportive actions are explored in the chapters that follow.

2

An International Perspective

Introduction

Despite the proliferation of international instruments setting standards and expectations for the protection of children's rights, significant gaps remain between these standards and children's lived experiences of their rights in detention (Liefaard, 2008). The failure to adequately protect and fulfil the rights of children deprived of liberty is well documented (Nowak, 2019), while the disproportionate effects of detention on children from minority and disadvantaged backgrounds now dominate international discourse. While there is extensive literature – from academic and other sources – on children in detention, the aim of this chapter is to take a global view of children's *experiences* of their rights in detention. Accordingly, the chapter presents a global perspective not on children in detention per se, but on the implementation of international children's rights standards in detention. In this regard, it aims first to identify the main gaps that exist between children's rights in theory and their enjoyment in practice. Second, in considering some of the reforms taking place, the chapter details the advocacy and academic contributions that have helped to underpin these changes. Overall, the chapter seeks to provide the reader with a global lens through which the challenges of advancing children's rights in detention can be understood.

The chapter draws on a range of materials. First, it considers the observations of the international human rights bodies that examine state progress in the implementation of children's rights in detention. Particular use is made of the Concluding Observations of the United Nations Committee on the Rights of the Child (the CRC Committee) and the reports of the European Committee for the Prevention of Torture and Inhuman or Degrading Treatment of Punishment (the CPT) and other such bodies. Second, the chapter draws on reports by advocacy groups that identify key areas of concern nationally and internationally. Combined with the academic literature, the chapter considers the contribution of the Global Study on

Children Deprived of Liberty in an effort to draw together the international themes relating to children's rights in detention.

Key global concerns

The CRC Committee regularly raises the treatment of children deprived of liberty in its national dialogue with state parties about the implementation of the United Nations Convention on the Rights of the Child (CRC), and its Concluding Observations reveal serious concerns about the rights of children in detention across a number of jurisdictions. Drawn together with the reports of visiting committees, like the CPT, which inspects places of detention across the Council of Europe's 47 jurisdictions, and publications from international advocacy bodies such as Human Rights Watch, a grave picture emerges of the rights of children in detention around the world. This section presents a snapshot of these concerns relating to: conditions of detention, violence and ill-treatment and the use of solitary confinement and restraint. Additional problems highlighted include the absence of child-specific facilities and specialized staff, and the need for complaint mechanisms and more robust monitoring and inspection systems. This analysis aims to underscore the importance of the rights-based model of child detention introduced in Chapter 1.

Children's rights to education, health and family contact

Through its dialogue with state parties, the CRC Committee has criticized the inadequate conditions in which children are detained in many jurisdictions, highlighting the extent to which children are denied their rights to health, education, leisure and family contact. The committee has noted concerns about overcrowding, insufficient medical care and nutrition, lack of education and training, restrictions on communication and a lack of leisure and outdoor activities. For instance, living conditions in Argentina were noted to be 'appalling' due to 'overcrowding, poor nutrition, inadequate bedding and sanitation facilities, combined with a lack of education and training opportunities' (CRC Committee, 2018a, para 43), and in Bulgaria, the committee noted that 'a large number of children continue to be placed in juvenile correctional and educational facilities with inadequate living conditions' (CRC Committee, 2016a, para 58). The focus in Bosnia Herzegovina was on the need for measures to promote education to children deprived of liberty (CRC Committee, 2020a, para 47), whereas in Mozambique, the committee highlighted the importance of promoting access to health and education services (CRC Committee, 2020b, para 47). In Bulgaria, concern was expressed about the detention of children in conditions of isolation from the wider community, with limited contact with family (CRC Committee, 2016a, paras 58–60). The committee observed that in South Africa, children were detained in overcrowded conditions, with a lack of access to 'educational, health and other services, especially for those in pretrial detention' (CRC Committee, 2016b, para 71); and in Guinea, similarly, it expressed concern that child detention was 'characterised by overcrowding and poor nutrition, and by a lack of adequate health care, of adequate sanitation, and of education and training opportunities' (CRC Committee, 2019b, para 45). Overcrowding and 'extremely poor conditions' were a serious concern in Uruguay (CRC Committee, 2015a, para 29); and in respect of Fiji, the committee criticized 'deteriorating infrastructure and a lack of delivery of essential services' (CRC Committee, 2014a, para 71). These concerns have been documented by international human rights groups too. For instance, in Burundi, Human Rights Watch reported the failure to meet children's basic needs in detention, without access to adequate food, bedding or education, as well as physical and sexual abuse (Human Rights Watch, 2007). On the other hand, a report by Defence for Children International (DCI) into the conditions of detention in 13 countries highlighted the opportunity lost by failing to ensure children's access to appropriate education and made recommendations for greater compliance with international standards (Robinson and D'Aloisio, 2009).

Violence and ill-treatment

Violence against children in detention is clearly a global concern, with ill-treatment ranging from inhuman treatment to physical punishment and abuse. The lack of respect for the child's dignity, in breach of Article 37 of the CRC, has been highlighted by the CRC Committee in the case of several state parties. In the Republic of Korea, for instance, the committee noted the isolation of children in detention with HIV and the imposition of compulsory body checks and haircuts (CRC Committee, 2019c, para 46). In Australia, the committee noted that children in detention were frequently subjected to 'verbal abuse and racist remarks, deliberately denied access to water, restrained in ways that are potentially dangerous and excessively subjected to isolation' (CRC Committee, 2019d, para 47). The ill-treatment of children has also been highlighted as a serious concern in the case of Serbia (CRC Committee, 2017a, para 64), Nauru (CRC Committee, 2016c, para 56) and Bahrain (CRC Committee, 2019e, para 43). In the cases of Brazil and Honduras, the committee noted reports of violence, including gang violence leading to death, and sexual abuse (CRC Committee, 2015b, para 87, 2015c, para 83). It expressed concern that children in detention in the West Bank and in the Gaza Strip are reportedly ill-treated (CRC Committee, 2020c, para 58), and in Rwanda, it noted reports of 'ill-treatment and beatings of children during pretrial detention' (CRC Committee, 2020d, para 47).

Accounts of violence against children in detention have also been documented extensively by international advocacy organizations such as Human Rights Watch and DCI. For instance, in 2006, Human Rights Watch reported that street children in Hanoi were detained and suffered physical and verbal abuse, routine beatings and were locked up for more than 23 hours per day in very poor conditions, often with adults. There were no educational and rehabilitative measures in place, and children had no access to medical or psychological treatment or mechanisms through which they could challenge their detention (Human Rights Watch, 2006). DCI, similarly, reported very significant concerns regarding the treatment of children in detention in Latin America in 2014, highlighting, in particular, the torture, inhuman and degrading treatment experienced by children in countries such as Argentina, Bolivia and Uruguay (Regional Juvenile Justice Observatory, 2014).

In 2006, the United Nations published the World Report on Violence against Children, documenting the harm experienced by children in secure and other settings (Pinheiro, 2006). According to the Study, children deprived of liberty face violence, harm and ill-treatment from staff and other children as a result of poor and unsafe conditions, punishment and harmful practices, and the Study made recommendations to address the reasons for the reliance on detention and promote alternatives to its use. In addition to enshrining diversion and detention as a last resort in legislation, it recommended measures to improve the protection of children in detention, including improved staffing, reporting and accountability with respect to incidents of violence. It also recommended that guarantees should be set out in legislation that 'the voices of children and their families will be heard', as well as providing 'simple, accessible, independent and safe complaint mechanisms' and appeal processes to which children and their representatives should have access (Pinheiro, 2006, p 205). In 2009, following a recommendation of the General Assembly of the United Nations, the Secretary General appointed a Special Representative on Violence against Children (United Nations, 2008) whose mandate includes the elimination of violence against children, including in detention, giving the issue profile at the highest international level.

In a follow-up to the Global Study on Violence against Children, DCI developed a set of indicators to monitor violence against children in the justice system, including detention, with a view to improving the protection of children deprived of liberty (Detrick et al, 2008). The indicators aim to promote better data collection and create a baseline with regard to the number of children in detention and incidents of death in detention, solitary confinement, incidents of self-harm and contact with parents. It also identified policy indicators in relation to inspections, complaints, use of restraint and specialized procedures.

Separation, solitary confinement and restraint

The use of restrictive measures in child detention through separation, solitary confinement and physical or other restraints is also a global concern. The CRC Committee has criticized the use of solitary confinement in the United Kingdom (UK) (CRC Committee, 2016d, para 78) and noted its prolonged use in Estonia (CRC Committee, 2017b, para 48). In Portugal, the fact that the law provides for 16- and 17-year-olds to be separated for up to 30 days in detention was criticized by the committee in 2014 (CRC Committee, 2014b, para 65) and in 2020, the committee recommended that Portugal abolish the practice as a punishment and urged the 'immediate' removal of all children from solitary confinement (CRC Committee, 2020e, para 44). In relation to Costa Rica, the committee recommended the 'enforcement of legislation prohibiting corporal punishment, collective sanctions and isolation, and prevent[ing] practices of prohibition of family visits to children deprived of liberty' (CRC Committee, 2020f, para 24).

Multiple campaigns in the United States (US) have sought the abolition of solitary confinement in child detention and, in 2012, Human Rights Watch worked with the American Civil Liberties Union in a major initiative to highlight the practice. Their report, based on interviews and correspondence with more than 125 young people in 19 states who had spent time in solitary confinement while under 18 years of age, as well as with jail and/or prison officials in ten states, addressed the harm that solitary confinement causes children and made recommendations as to how to end the practice (Human Rights Watch, 2012). The report noted the important role played by better behaviour management approaches and specialized facilities in minimizing the practice (Human Rights Watch, 2012). Others have also argued for the statutory regulation of the use of segregation, proposing that limitations and procedures are put in place to limit and regulate its use (Gallagher, 2014). Public interest litigation has also targeted the use of this practice, with varying success (Dale, 1998; Singer, 2012).

The call for the reduction in the use of restrictive practices has also been made in the UK, connecting them to wider systemic reform. For instance, the Howard League for Penal Reform commissioned a report into the use of physical restraint, solitary confinement and forcible strip-searching of children deprived of liberty, which made 45 recommendations targeted at resolving conflict, reducing violence and improving practice (The Lord Carlile of Berriew QC, 2006). Its recommendations for a wide range of systemic, policy and practice measures were aimed at policy-makers, inspectors, administrative authorities and the facilities themselves. The use, duration and conditions of segregation have also concerned the English Children's Commissioner who in 2018 observed increased use of the measure in frequency and duration (Children's Commissioner, 2018, pp 5–6) due to gang involvement, staffing levels and an absence of specialist mental health facilities to address children's acute needs. The HM Inspectorate of Prisons for England and Wales has also observed the use of segregation as punishment and criticized inadequate oversight arrangements, concluding that they 'do not safeguard children's well-being', that managers and leaders have 'failed to prevent children from being subject to harmful regimes for extended periods of time' (HMI Prisons, 2020, p 8), ultimately recommending that the current model is replaced with 'a new system' (HMI Prisons, 2020, p 9). A UK parliamentary inquiry by the Joint Committee on Human Rights (2019) into solitary confinement and restraint in youth detention has also expressed concern about the use of the pain-compliant method of restraint to maintain good order, which, it noted, is not compliant with international human rights standards. In response, the report recommended that government take steps to ensure that children deprived of liberty are treated with 'appropriate care'. Like other reports, it highlighted: the need to address the suitability of placements to ensure such decisions are needs-based; the need to appoint sufficient numbers of appropriately trained staff; and the importance of effective complaints and redress. In particular, the Joint Committee recommended a series of measures that would: improve transparency relating to detention; increase the participation of children and their parents in decision-making; and improve the accountability of staff for any harm or breach of the child's rights.

Absence of specialist staff, facilities and approaches

The CRC Committee has drawn an important connection between respect for the rights of children in detention and the need for specialist staff, facilities and approaches. In France, for instance, the committee noted the absence of trained staff with regard to providing quality education, healthcare and psychiatric care (CRC Committee, 2016e, para 81), and this was also a noted concern in Jamaica (CRC Committee, 2015d, para 64). According to the CPT, specialization and staff training must be a priority and there is a need to ensure mixed-gender and multi-disciplinary staff recruitment (Kilkelly and Casale, 2012).

The absence of a child-centred approach has been highlighted in numerous states around the world. For instance, the committee noted that a punishment regime was still in place in Barbados (CRC Committee, 2017c, para 60) and noted a lack of rehabilitation programmes as a common concern in many countries, including Iraq (CRC Committee, 2015e, para 86), Hungary (CRC Committee, 2014c, para 56) and the Russian Federation (CRC Committee, 2014d, para 69). In Venezuela, the use of a military training programme for children in detention, which frequently gave rise to riots and injury, was criticized (CRC Committee, 2014e, para 74), and in Kyrgyzstan, the prison-like conditions were the subject of concern (CRC Committee, 2014f, para 66). Where reform was mentioned, it was criticized as being too slow. In Mauritius, for instance, the committee was concerned about the 'lack of progress in restructuring institutions for the rehabilitation of minors in conflict with the law, and in properly training rehabilitation personnel' (CRC Committee, 2015f, para 69). In the case of Rwanda, the committee recommended that 'services for the psychological counselling and social reintegration of children released from transit centres or from prison, including access to education, vocational training and family-based alternative care', are continued (CRC Committee, 2020d, para 24).

Connected with this, the committee has highlighted concern about the failure either to separate children from adults in detention or alternatively to put in place specialist facilities for children deprived of liberty. For instance, this was raised as a concern in the case of the Congo (CRC Committee, 2014i, para 80), Kenya, (CRC Committee, 2016f, para 75), Malta (CRC Committee, 2019f, para 44), Angola (CRC Committee, 2018b, para 37), Pakistan, (CRC Committee, 2016g, para 79), France (CRC Committee, 2016e, para 81) and Hungary (CRC Committee, 2020h, para 40). The CPT shares the concern, following its visits to places of detention, about children being detained with adults, considering that it places children at risk of violence and ill-treatment. It has also highlighted inadequate regimes, especially for children on remand, noting that even in countries with good conditions for child detention, the situation of children on remand can be poor (Kilkelly and Casale, 2012). Reflecting the widespread concern about the treatment of children on remand, DCI reported in 2010 on the overuse of pre-trial detention in many countries, highlighting the particularly detrimental conditions experienced by children in such settings (Volz, 2010).

Absence of complaints and oversight

The CRC Committee regularly highlights the absence of complaints or oversight mechanisms. For instance, the lack of a complaint mechanism has been noted in several states including Chile (CRC Committee, 2015g, para 85), whereas in Croatia, the committee criticized the fact that detention centres are not regularly visited by judges, despite their legal obligation to do so (CRC Committee, 2014g, para 58). In Côte d'Ivoire, the committee recommended that 'regular inspections' be carried out (CRC Committee, 2020g, para 53). While law reform was under way in Jordan, the committee criticized that it did not address the consequences of, and follow-up to, the inspection of detention facilities where children are placed (CRC Committee, 2014h, para 63). The State of Palestine was recommended to introduce child-friendly complaints mechanisms for children deprived of liberty (CRC Committee, 2020c, para 59).

Concerns relating to the safety of children in detention in Brazil have been highlighted by Human Rights Watch, where the absence of a complaint mechanism (Human Rights Watch, 2003) and independent effective monitoring (Human Rights Watch, 2005) have been key concerns. The CPT has also noted the importance of robust inspection and complaint mechanisms to ensuring transparency and accountability with regard to children's rights in detention and it has highlighted the challenges that children experience accessing complaints mechanisms, especially with regard to their ill-treatment by staff (Kilkelly and Casale, 2012). According to the CPT, children should 'have avenues of complaint open to them, both within and outside' the detention environment and be entitled to 'confidential access to an appropriate independent authority … competent to receive – and, if necessary, act upon – their complaints' (CPT, 2008, para 139). It has found, however, that these mechanisms are absent in many Council of Europe states and even where they exist, children have no faith or confidence in them (Kilkelly and Casale, 2012, p 24).

Race and over-representation

According to Lynch and Liefaard (2020, p 100), 'the most pressing and difficult challenge for children's rights in the coming decades is the over-representation of certain groups of children in the criminal justice system. This is accompanied by disparity of outcomes of treatment'. In the US, not a party to the CRC, African American boys, in particular, are over-represented at every stage of the system, from arrest to detention (Zane, 2021), and are more likely to be detained in carceral conditions, either in prison or in prison-like restrictive conditions (Sawyer, 2019). While undoubtedly a contemporary challenge, Mallett (2018) describes disproportionate minority contact with the US justice system as a complex, historical problem going back 200 years. Nor is it confined to the US in that over-representation of minority – including indigenous – children is a feature of youth justice in Canada (Cesaroni, 2019), Australia (Cunneen, 2006), New Zealand (Lynch, 2019) and Europe (Webster, 2018). The over-representation of children from Traveller, Gypsy and Roma backgrounds in the UK has led to calls for a formal inquiry there (The Traveller Movement, 2016). Separately, the overlap with the child protection system, which results in care-experienced children 'crossing over' into the criminal justice system, including detention, has now also emerged as an international phenomenon (Baidawi and Sheehan, 2020).

Efforts to address the ethnic and racial disparities in US juvenile justice have been largely ineffective (Zane, 2021), and permanent and systemic change has so far been illusive (Leiber and Fix, 2019). Zimring (2014, p 184) concludes that '[t]he major positive reforms in juvenile justice over the past generation … have not had dramatic impact on the disproportionate involvement of minority youth in the deep end of the juvenile system'. Although it is recognized that addressing racial and ethnic disparities in detention cannot be achieved in isolation from those in the wider justice system or indeed in society, the scale of concerns about the treatment of children in detention has led some jurisdictions to focus reforms in this area. In the US, for instance, there is a growing trend towards closing or repurposing facilities along therapeutic lines – see initiatives in Massachusetts (Miller, 1991), Cook County (Roush, 2019) and California (Macallair, 2015) – as well as a more expansive approach to community-based interventions, diversion and the non-use of custody for low-level or status offences (Sawyer, 2019). In the US, Prison Policy Initiative notes the falling numbers of children in detention (Sawyer, 2019), with some noting that this contraction of the justice system offers the best hope for resolving the problem of disproportionate minority contact – as numbers in detention fall, the positive impact is likely be felt by over-represented groups (Zane, 2021). Despite the persistence of race as a concern in the criminal justice system of England and Wales (Lammy, 2017), however, the recent drop in the numbers of children in detention has not impacted Black and Minority Ethnic (BAME) boys as favourably as their non-BAME peers (Barn et al, 2018).

Gender

Girls have been identified as an especially vulnerable group in detention in light of their gender and their small numbers (Penal Reform International, 2014) and in 2006, this led Human Rights Watch to partner with the American Civil Liberties Union (ACLU) to campaign for better treatment for girls in detention (Human Rights Watch and ACLU, 2006). In addition to poor and abusive conditions reported in two juvenile facilities for girls in New York State, their report highlighted the absence of monitoring mechanisms and recommended, among necessary improvements, the need to improve transparency and accountability. The Annie E. Casey Foundation has also sought to raise awareness about the challenges faced by girls in detention, highlighting the systemic issues that result in their detention and drawing attention to the need for gender-responsive programmes (Sherman, 2005). In England, Goodfellow (2017, p 5) has highlighted the dilemma posed by the increasingly small number of girls in detention whereby their 'diminishing minority' in custody has exacerbated the marginalization of their needs. Rather than being overlooked because the number of girls in detention is small, she argues that their particular circumstances and vulnerabilities justify careful consideration from a gendered perspective (Goodfellow, 2017). The intersectionality of race and gender means that girls from minority ethnic backgrounds can be doubly disadvantaged (Stein et al, 2015) and in general it is clear that specific programmes that address family difficulties, sexuality and gender-specific health and reintegration needs should be prioritized (Zahn et al, 2009). International bodies have also recommended that girls receive special attention, including gender-specific policies, trained staff and separate detention from boys (Penal Reform International, 2014).

Reforming child detention

The picture of children's rights in detention painted by national and international human rights bodies, through monitoring, research and advocacy activity, is bleak. At the same time, and driven largely by relentless attention to these concerns including those documented here, many states are now focused on the reform of detention, making progress reducing the use of detention and improving children's enjoyment of their rights. Admittedly, in many instances, this is from a very low base, but it is important nonetheless that momentum has begun to build.

In the US, reform has been led by organizations such as the Annie E. Casey Foundation, whose research has highlighted the deeply problematic nature of youth incarceration (Mendel, 2011, p 4), while highlighting the successful reforms under way in several states reducing child detention and redesigning systems to better advance the rights of young people and the public. In addition to instituting mechanisms and approaches that divert children from detention, the Foundation supports the replacement of large institutions with small, treatment-oriented facilities for the limited number of young offenders engaged in serious and chronic offending, observing that such facilities should 'embrace this more constructive, humane, and cost-effective paradigm for how we treat, educate, and punish youth who break the law' (Mendel, 2011, p 49). Attention is also drawn in this context to the importance of using data to inform and support the reform of detention, measuring recidivism and monitoring conditions of detention in improving accountability. Separately, Campaign for Youth Justice (2007) has highlighted the detrimental impact on children of their detention in adult jails, especially pre-trial, and recommended legislative reform to end the practice, while Human Rights Watch has drawn attention to the conditions of detention experienced by children serving life sentences without parole in the US (Calvin et al, 2012). Here, through the powerful testimony of children, their families and a range of professionals across multiple states, the particular challenges faced by children serving such sentences are outlined, including their exposure to abuse, punitive isolation and self-harm, as well as limited access to development and educational opportunities as a result of being categorized as 'the least deserving' (Calvin et al, 2012, p 27).

In addition to the monitoring work of bodies such as the CRC Committee, there has been sustained campaigning by international organizations, such as Human Rights Watch and DCI, and national groups such as the Howard League for Penal Reform in the UK and the Annie E. Casey Foundation in the US on the treatment of children in detention. While advocacy has undoubtedly focused on the most grave children's rights violations, it has played an effective role in generating support for global action on the rights of children deprived of liberty. In 2003, DCI published a major report on the implementation of international children's rights standards around the world, with country reports from 22 countries (Meuwese, 2003). *Kids Behind Bars* documented the use of, and conditions in, detention in these countries and highlighted the need, in line with international children's rights standards, to promote alternatives to detention and improve conditions for those children who are deprived of liberty. Although the report contained some discrete recommendations, including that no child under 15 years of age should be placed in detention, its true value was as a campaigning tool. In this respect, the report recommended a series of actions to be taken at local, national and international levels by state parties, non-governmental organizations (NGOs) and international governmental organizations, to include, for instance, measures designed to increase the international visibility of children deprived of liberty and improved research and data collection on the issues. Following the DCI Study, an alliance of international NGOs was formed – comprising Amnesty International, Human Rights Watch, DCI and others – to launch a campaign for the full implementation of the CRC in the justice system, with particular reference to children deprived of liberty. The principal outcome of this campaign, several years later, was to gain the formal endorsement of the United Nations General Assembly for a Global Study on Children Deprived of Liberty. The Global Study, led by independent expert Manfred Nowak, was completed as a collaboration with NGOs, academics and others, published in 2019 (Nowak, 2019).

According to the Global Study, children are detained for multiple reasons and the trends in child detention have multiple causes (Nowak, 2019). A reliance on institutional care, excessive criminalization and the use of detention to address problems of armed conflict, national security and migration all reflect a dysfunctional dependency on detention, and for many children this comes at a huge cost to their rights. As the Global Study notes, around the world, children in detention suffer from overcrowding and poor sanitation, a lack of appropriate education and development, and breaches of their rights daily. Children in detention, who were consulted about their rights for the Global Study, expressed concern about their right to protection from harm, their right to access appropriate educational and vocational opportunities and their right to have meaningful contact with their families (Nowak, 2019, p 113). Many spoke about their experience of loss and trauma and of discrimination and stigma, although despite this, they displayed resilience and looked forward, with hope, to the future.

The Global Study noted that children deprived of liberty will almost universally be 'distinguished with a high burden of ill-health' due to the overlap between the social and structural drivers of detention with the determinants of health (Nowak, 2019, p 117). Children in justice-related detention, who use drugs or alcohol, may be at increased risk as a result of the nexus with offending behaviour, while at the same time risky substance use in young people is associated with poor mental health, injury and infectious disease. The Global Study noted a high prevalence of mental disorder and infectious disease among justice-involved children (Nowak, 2019, p 117), while at the same time highlighted that detention presents an opportunity to address children's healthcare needs achieving positive health outcomes (Nowak, 2019, p 120). The Study considers the disproportionately negative impact of detention on children with disabilities, and considers the gender dimension of detention where boys are disproportionately detained in the justice system, whereas girls suffer discrimination as a result of their involvement in trafficking and institutionalized care (Nowak, 2019).

According to the Global Study, more than seven million children are deprived of their liberty worldwide, while approximately one-and-a-half million children are detained annually as a result of a judicial or administrative decision (Nowak, 2019, p 659). The Study estimates that 410,000 children are detained in the justice system, 94% of whom are estimated to be boys and 6% girls (Nowak, 2019, p 662). Significantly, this is more than 50% lower than the one million children estimated by UNICEF to be in detention in 2007 (Nowak, 2019, p 666). Although there is no definitive evidence of this, the Study considers that the adoption by states of specialized procedures, including effective diversion from the criminal justice system, is likely to be the key driver in the decreasing use of detention in the justice setting.

The recommendations of the Global Study focus predominantly on methods to avoid, reduce and where possible eliminate the detention of children, by drawing attention to the root causes and pathways that lead to the deprivation of liberty. States are recommended to 'rigorously apply' the requirements of Article 37(b) of the CRC to ensure detention is a measure of last resort, requiring that children shall only be detained in 'truly exceptional cases' (Nowak, 2019, p 668). Where detention is unavoidable, the Study recommends that states apply 'child-friendly and gender-sensitive' conditions and protect children from abuse, neglect and exploitation. Children should have access to 'essential services aimed at their rehabilitation and reintegration into society, including education, vocational training, family contacts, sports, recreation, adequate nutrition, housing and health care' (Nowak, 2019, p 669). These recommendations reflect the observations of bodies such as the CRC Committee and the CPT, noted earlier. Given that it was the subject of extensive research, it is perhaps surprising that the Study highlights relatively few good practices. Surprising too perhaps is the absence from the Study of one of the global issues in youth justice, that of disproportionate representation in detention of children from minority backgrounds.

Campaigns for reform have taken root at a national level too. In addition to the US reforms highlighted earlier, for instance, momentum is building in the UK. In England, the Children's Commissioner has led a sustained campaign on child detention in recent years, highlighting the different settings in which children are deprived of their liberty for health, care and justice reasons (Children's Commissioner, 2019). In 2020, the Commissioner found that 'despite the high number of children in custody who have experienced trauma or who have mental health or other underlying needs, the custodial environment is neither inherently therapeutic nor child friendly' (Dempsey, 2020, p 11). Difficulties managing behaviour safely and an over-reliance on restrictive practices among a population with complex unmet needs are some of the main problems identified, and the difficulties attracting or retaining skilled and experienced staff have also been noted. The Commissioner's report highlights that during the COVID-19 pandemic, the conditions for children in detention were 'particularly bleak' (Dempsey, 2020, p 17), with children confined significantly to their cells, having limited time for daily outdoor exercise and inadequate access to education. The report welcomes plans for reforming child detention, including the agreement on a 'youth justice specialist' role to replace custody officers and the introduction of the Custody Support Plan (CuSP), an evidence-based model of care planning. However, implementation has been 'too slow' according to the Commissioner, and 'insufficiently radical' to develop a truly child-friendly system (Dempsey, 2020, p 20). While welcoming the introduction of a system of 'secure schools' with a greater emphasis on education and reintegration, in implementation of the recommendations of the Review of the Youth Justice System in England and Wales (Taylor, 2016), the Commissioner highlighted the need for the new system to be properly resourced, including a redesign of the physical environment and investment in specialist staffing, if it is to be truly child-centred.

Hearing the views of children in detention

While there has been increasing research *about* children's experiences in detention, there is still relatively little research *with* children in detention. Admittedly, such studies can be complex and challenging to undertake (Cox, 2017) and require both creativity and sensitivity to ensure children's views and experiences are documented in a rights-respecting manner (Lundy, 2007). At the same time, it is vital that children's experiences of their rights in detention are not documented without the incorporation of their views and perspectives, and this is even more important with regard to the experiences of marginalized or minority groups. Particularly acute gaps exist, for instance, around the experience of BAME young people in detention (Barn et al, 2018) and the experience of girls (Goodfellow, 2017).

Advocacy organizations increasingly involve young people in their work. The Howard League, for instance, has engaged young people directly in promoting awareness and advocating for reform (Howard League for Penal Reform, 2010). The evaluation of this programme – called U R Boss – highlighted that involving young people with detention experience in advocacy work strengthens the extent to which such campaigns are informed by their views and experiences, while it also builds their capacity to advocate for themselves and others on matters of importance (Fleming et al, 2014).

Significantly, the Global Study on Children Deprived of Liberty included the first global consultation with children deprived of liberty, by interviewing 274 children in 22 countries about their experiences of their rights in detention (Nowak, 2019). Among the issues highlighted by the children were concerns for their safety and protection, challenges accessing healthcare and appropriate education and vocational training and insufficient opportunity to maintain relationships with their family. For many, the detention experience was one of isolation, loneliness and fear, and the children described a sense of disempowerment and stigma, of not having their voices heard or their complaints or concerns taken seriously. At the same time, they described the camaraderie they enjoyed with their peers, their resilience in coping with the adversity in their lives and their hope that, with appropriate supports and services, their rights can be protected, enabling them to live a healthy life and make a contribution to society when they leave.

What is significant about the Study therefore is its recommendation that children in detention are heard and 'empowered to influence decisions relating to their treatment' (Nowak, 2019, p 670). It also recommends the establishment, through ratification of the Optional Protocol to the Convention against Torture, of National Preventive Mechanisms with particular expertise to conduct visits to places of detention where children are deprived of liberty (Nowak, 2019). National and international bodies play an important role in documenting the experience of the children they meet as part of their visits to and inspections of places of detention, but there is a need for greater capacity-building among these bodies so that their approach to consultation with children is itself rights-compliant (Kilkelly and Casale, 2012). Some inspectorates adopt a systematic approach to consultation with children, such as the HM Inspectorate of Prisons for England and Wales, which uses surveys to inform the inspection process (HMI Prisons, 2021). Others have partnered with children in detention to enable their views and experiences to be brought more directly to decision-makers in pursuit of detention reform (OCO, 2011; Kilkelly and Logan, 2021). What is clear, however, is that inspection bodies must not just speak directly to children about their experiences in detention; their inspection frameworks should also be consistent with children's rights, developed in partnership with children themselves.

Conclusion

This chapter provided a snapshot of the issue of child detention from a global perspective, drawing on the work of international treaty monitoring bodies, as well as international governmental organizations and NGOs focused on global and national reform campaigns. It offered a glimpse into the extensive advocacy and academic work on child detention from which a number of consistent and relevant themes emerge. The first is the obvious point that the treatment of children in detention is a global concern, both regarding the use (although in decline) of detention for children and the conditions in which children are held. The absence of child-centred care and the denial of children's rights to health, education and family contact are particularly serious concerns, along with the child's right to protection from violence, including as a result of restrictive practices such as solitary confinement and restraint. The absence of specialist approaches and specialized staff, along with the detention of children alongside adults or in prison-like conditions, are also global issues, as is the absence of effective complaints and independent monitoring mechanisms. The disproportionate impact on the rights of children from minority backgrounds is very clear.

Importantly, however, from these data have emerged a compelling case for the reform of child detention. Monitoring, research and advocacy that draws on the experiences of children and, increasingly, their voices, have raised the visibility of these issues, adding momentum to international developments such as the first Global Study on Children Deprived of Liberty (Nowak, 2019). Some national reform of child detention is also taking place and, while some jurisdictions continue to try to adapt child detention, others are reaching for more ambitious and transformative systemic change. While all impetus to improve children's rights in detention is to be welcomed, as this book argues, it is only through a deliberate and holistic system of reform, built on a rights-based foundation of law and policy, that the detention of children will truly meet the international children's rights standards. The next two chapters move on to explain how this is being achieved in Ireland.

3

Irish Youth Justice Law and Policy

Introduction

Article 4 of the United Nations Convention on the Rights of the Child (CRC) requires that state parties adopt all appropriate legislative, administrative and other measures to implement children's rights and research has shown that these measures combine to enhance children's lived experiences of their rights (Kilkelly et al, 2021). As the international children's rights standards make clear, child detention does not exist in a vacuum, but rather is part of the national response to children who come into conflict with the law. In this regard, this chapter traces the development of Irish law and policy in the area of youth justice, from a history of institutionalized care to a more progressive, rights-based approach. The chapter begins with a brief history of the Irish youth justice system, identifying the reforms that gave rise to the contemporary legislative framework. Administrative responsibility for youth justice is outlined and the policy developments and priorities are set out. The chapter ends with some conclusions about the nature of the Irish youth justice system, highlighting the importance of ensuring that the law and policy platform, on which detention is based, must itself be rights-based in order to advance children's rights.

Irish youth justice – a brief history of reform

By most standards, Ireland is considered to have a mainly progressive approach to youth justice that largely coheres with international standards of children's rights (Kilkelly, 2006). An overhaul of the legislative framework took place during the 1990s, coinciding with Ireland's ratification of the CRC in 1992 and following several decades of parliamentary review and inquiry into the child welfare, reformatory and industrial school systems (Sargent, 2016). The Children Act 1908, considered the beginning of Ireland's approach to youth justice, had endured for more than a century due to its 'enlightened' and 'flexible' nature (Kilkelly, 2006, p 25) and a recognition of the need to rehabilitate young offenders and avoid exposing them to the full power of the criminal justice system served Ireland well. The 1908 Act placed limits on the nature and length of custodial sentences, emphasized non-custodial punishments and provided for summary trial for most offences, with protections in place for the privacy of children in conflict with the law. Despite obvious shortcomings, including a reliance on the industrial and reformatory schools to which children could be referred on welfare as well as penal grounds, the 1908 Act provided a 'philosophical touchstone upon which many of the developments within the realm of youth justice were built' (Bradley et al, 2009, p 12).

Although the industrial school system was abolished in the United Kingdom (UK) in 1933, in Ireland it lasted into the 1960s, enduring well after the publication in 1936 of the Cussen Report, a commission of inquiry into the industrial and reformatory school system (Commission of Inquiry into the Reformatory and Industrial School System, 1936). The publication of the Kennedy Report on the Reformatory and Industrial School System in 1970 (Committee on Reformatory and Industrial Schools, 1970) marked the beginning of the end of the industrial school system (Kilcommins et al, 2004), with its recommendations to end institutionalized care and increase the age of criminal responsibility (Sargent, 2016). Although the Kennedy Report was largely credited with instituting a sea-change in Ireland's approach to 'delinquency', institutionalized care remained for decades under the management of religious orders in what was a significant and distinctive feature of the Irish approach (Sargent, 2016).

The Kennedy Report, published in 1970, was a catalyst for the reform of youth welfare in Ireland and, in 1974, the First Interim Report of the Henchy Committee, the Interdepartmental Committee on Mentally Ill and Maladjusted Persons (1974), built on its recommendations, suggesting the introduction of day and residential assessment services for young people interacting with the court system and proposing that probation and welfare officers be involved in their assessment (Sargent, 2016, p 29). The Second Interim Report, which considered the Provision of Treatment for Juvenile Offenders and Potential Juvenile Offenders, recommended that a high priority be given to the provision of resources for the treatment of young offenders in the community, including educational facilities, child psychiatric services and day centres (Sargent, 2016, p 30). The Report also suggested the introduction of a closed unit for young male offenders up to the age of 16 years who were deemed 'unmanageable' by the industrial and reformatory schools and who, the report considered, required a degree of 'physical containment and a more structured regime' to enable them to benefit from educational and therapeutic programmes (Sargent, 2016, p 30). In response, amid much opposition, a closed institution at Loughan House was established in 1978 for children aged between 12 and 16 years and, although it was closed in 1982, it was replaced with Trinity House, which began to receive children in 1983 (see later in this chapter), signalling a preference for detaining children whose behaviour could not be managed in other care services (Sargent, 2016, p 30).

In 1980, the Government Task Force on Child Care Services made numerous recommendations on child welfare and juvenile justice, placing emphasis on tailoring facilities to the needs of young people (Department of Health, 1980). The Task Force advocated for an approach to youth crime that would offer rehabilitation and development and it recommended that such facilities be governed by the Departments of Education, Health and Justice, signalling important interdepartmental responsibility for the area (Sargent, 2016). In parallel, the O'Sullivan Report (1980) outlined recommendations for the growth of youth work services, including additional financial support for voluntary youth organizations, encouragement for pilot projects in deprived areas, support for counselling services and additional training for youth workers and members of An Garda Síochána (the Irish police service). The rise in the delivery of community-based services for young people in the 1980s reflected growing support for accommodating young offenders within the community, where 'community service' – introduced in the Criminal Justice (Community Service) Act in 1983 – offered young people aged 16 to 21 years an alternative to a custodial sentence.

However, it was the highly influential Whitaker Report (Committee of Inquiry into the Penal System, 1985) that set a new imperative for modernizing the Irish youth justice system. The report advocated alternative methods to imprisonment, including the expansion of diversion, supervisory relationships, community penalties and the establishment of restorative programmes, and it recommended community involvement in the prevention of crime by introducing local projects to allow young people to become more active members in their society. Many of the ideas proposed by the Whitaker Report remain relevant today (Irish Penal Reform Trust, 2007).

Despite multiple reviews and inquiries, however, it was not until 1992 that a parliamentary committee recommended legislative overhaul in line with international standards on youth justice. The Report of the Dáil Select Committee on Crime, Juvenile Crime, Its Causes and Its Remedies, drafted by Professor Robbie Gilligan, made a series of enlightened recommendations, which for the first time advocated a graduated response to offending, varying from light (involving no prosecution) to heavy (detention) by introducing a range of options, such as cautions, conditional discharge, mentoring, victim-offender mediation and a range of probation orders involving supervision (Dáil Select Committee, 1992). The report also recommended an increase in the age of criminal responsibility to 12 years, from the common law age of seven, and made a case for specialization within youth justice among the police, prosecution and probation services, while advocating for the introduction of juvenile courts with specially trained judges. The Report recommended diversion to be placed on a statutory basis, local juvenile crime prevention committees to be established, and non-custodial and custodial measures to be rationalized. The Committee concluded that the imprisonment of children was abhorrent in any circumstances.

The Dáil Committee's recommendations reflected a commitment to meeting the standards laid down by relevant United Nations instruments including the CRC, recently ratified by Ireland, and other United Nations Recommendations and Rules including the Riyadh Guidelines, the Beijing Rules and the United Nations Rules for the Protection of Juveniles Deprived of their Liberty. According to the Committee, it was 'self-evident' that our claim to 'a valued place in the community of civilized nations depends heavily on our performance in this particularly sensitive area of civil liberties and public policy. Our provision must match the standards laid down by these documents' (Dáil Select Committee, 1992, unpaginated). Perhaps it was not surprising, then, that when legislative reform finally took place, the Children Act 2001 had many of the hallmarks of these international standards (Kilkelly, 2006).

The Children Act 2001

The Irish youth justice system is a justice-based model that promotes the welfare, rights and accountability of children in conflict with the law through the criminal justice system (Kilkelly, 2006). The Children Act 2001 came into effect on a gradual basis after its adoption, meaning that the system has continued to evolve. Following a review by the Department of Justice, Equality and Law Reform in 2005, the adoption of a series of legislative and administrative measures significantly enhanced its implementation in line with international children's rights standards (Department of Justice, Equality and Law Reform, 2006). Amendments to the legislation subsequently took place in 2006 (the Criminal Justice Act 2006) and 2015 (the Children (Amendment) Act 2015) and litigation has also prompted law reform in some areas. Although a commitment to review the Children Act is contained in the Youth Justice Strategy 2021–2027, by any standards, the system has proven to be remarkably stable in the 20 years since the 2001 Act was adopted (Department of Justice, 2021).

The Irish youth justice system operates on the basis of a child, defined as a person under 18 years (section 3), in line with Article 1 of the CRC, with some flexibility granted at the upper age for those who reach 18 years when before the Children Court or serving a detention order (Children Act 2001, section 155). The Act (section 52(1)), as amended, provides that a child under 12 years shall not be charged with an offence, effectively setting this as the age of criminal responsibility, with some exceptions for indictable crimes – murder, manslaughter and sexual assault – which require trial in the (adult) Central Criminal Court. An adapted regime for the treatment of child suspects by the police, largely in line with international standards, is also set out in Part 6 of the Children Act (Drislane, 2011). Section 55 of the 2001 Act requires the Garda Síochána to act with due respect for the personal rights of the child, the child's vulnerability due to their age and maturity and the child's special needs, including any disability they may have. Parents must be notified of a child's arrest and the child must be separated from adults in police custody insofar as practicable.

Diversion is at the cornerstone of the Irish system, represented by the Garda Diversion Programme to which all children who come into conflict with the law are referred (Berkery, 2018). The 2001 Act placed the youth caution scheme on a statutory basis (Brennan, 2012) and, under the Act, a child over 12 years who accepts responsibility and agrees to be cautioned for offending behaviour will be referred for admission to the programme (section 23). If the Director of the programme agrees to admit the child, they will receive either an informal or a formal caution, depending mainly on the seriousness of the behaviour, formal caution usually being accompanied by 12 months of supervision (section 27) by a special trained member of the Gardaí known as a Juvenile Liaison Officer (JLO). The JLO may also decide to convene a family conference (section 29) to bring together the child, their family and others to establish why the child became involved in the alleged behaviour, to discuss how the family and others can prevent the child from being further involved in such behaviour and where appropriate to review the child's behaviour since their admission to the programme. The conference also serves to mediate between the child and any victim of the child's offending and develops an action plan for the child to prevent further offending. Described as one of the 'most coherent and well managed' parts of the youth justice system (Kilkelly, 2006, p 94), and notwithstanding questions about the compatibility of the programme with the child's due process rights (Smyth, 2011), the Programme has continued to grow and develop in line with good practice. The implementation of the programme is monitored by a statutory committee whose annual reports provide a useful statistical snapshot of youth crime in Ireland. The most recent report of the committee from 2019 indicates that 9,842 children were referred to the Programme that year (Garda Youth Diversion Bureau, 2019, p 12). The Programme admits children from 12 years upwards, and in 2019, the majority of participants were aged between 15 and 17 years and 72% were male (Garda Youth Diversion Bureau, 2019, p 12). In 2019, 57% of children referred to the programme received an informal caution and 21% received a formal caution (with supervision). The main offence categories for which children were referred were: theft (31%), public order (19.7%), damage to property (8.1%), assault (9.5%) and drugs offences (9.6%) (Garda Youth Diversion 2019, p xi).

There is no detailed information published about the 16% of children 'deemed unsuitable' for the Programme (Kilkelly, 2011; Smyth, 2011), but given that all children who come into conflict with the law are referred to the Programme, this cohort is likely to include those who do not meet the criteria under section 24 of the 2001 Act (for example, they refuse to accept a caution or deny involvement in the behaviour in question). The Director of the Programme will usually have determined, in consultation with the Director of Public Prosecutions, that prosecution is more suitable for these children. There has been no longitudinal evaluation of the impact of the Programme but the 2017 report indicates that 64% of individuals who received an informal or formal caution as their first caution between 2013 and 2017 did not reoffend up to 2017. Those who received an informal caution for the first time over this period were less likely to reoffend than those who received a formal caution (66% compared with 49%) (Garda Youth Diversion and Crime Prevention Bureau, 2017, p 26).

The Garda Diversion Programme has been supplemented in recent years by a nation-wide network of community-based Garda diversion projects where youth justice workers work alongside JLOs and other community services to help young people stay out of trouble. Despite concern about the expansion of diversion projects that purport to intervene with 'at risk' youth (Swirak, 2016), the increased attention to community-based supports for young people has been important in strengthening the role of diversion in the Irish youth justice system. The Youth Justice Strategy 2021–2027 identifies further actions to strengthen diversion in Irish youth justice in line with children's rights principles (Department of Justice, 2021, pp 22–3).

Children referred for prosecution normally appear before the Children Court, which is a court of first jurisdiction in the Irish court system, with a wide jurisdiction (Children Act 2001, section 75). The 2001 Act (section 71) requires the Children Court to sit in a different building or room from that in which sittings of other courts are held, or on different days or at different times. Sittings of the court must be arranged so that children are not brought into contact with persons attending a sitting of any other court and, as far as practicable, the proceedings must be arranged so that the time that the persons involved have to wait to be heard is kept to a minimum. There is little formal specialism among the Irish judiciary, but according to the Act, judges of the District Court appointed after 1995 must participate in 'any relevant course of training or education' that may be required by the President of the District Court before transacting business in the Children Court (section 72). One national study of the operation of the

Children Court criticized the extent to which children enjoyed their right to participate in the process (Kilkelly, 2008b), although the adoption of a Practice Direction for the Dublin Metropolitan District in 2014 (District Court, 2014) and the development of a Children Court Bench Book in 2015 (District Court, 2015), updated in 2020, highlight the commitment of the judiciary to improving practice in this area. Most of the Children Act provisions concerning the operation of the courts in children's cases do not apply outside the Children Court, for example, in the Circuit and Central Criminal Courts where children are tried for more serious offences. While relatively little is known about how these courts operate in children's cases, it is notable that the trial of two children for murder in 2019 (Delahunt, 2020) involved clearly adapted proceedings in line with international best practice (Kilkelly and Forde, 2016). This is an area of evolving and increasingly progressive judicial practice in Ireland.

One area where practice has developed in line with international children's rights standards is the protection of the child's anonymity in criminal proceedings. According to the Children Act, as amended, cases in the Children Court involving children are to be held in camera, limited only to those parties directly concerned with the proceedings (section 94) and reporting that may identify a child accused appearing before any court is prohibited (section 93). This requirement can be dispensed with in certain limited circumstances, but the courts have been reluctant to allow media to publish a child's identity. In 2020, for instance, a number of people were prosecuted for naming a child accused on social media contrary to a court order and a journalist was fined for inadvertently referring by name to a child accused during a radio broadcast, indicating how seriously the courts take the duty to protect the child's identity in such cases.

Under the Children Act, the Children Court has at its disposal a range of measures and sanctions that it can choose from with regard to children who appear before it. New to the 2001 Act were two measures that aim to divert children from the Children Court. Section 77 provides for children to be transferred to social services (Tusla, the Child and Family Agency), providing a route out of the criminal justice system for children for whom criminal proceedings are inappropriate. Section 78 provides a similar mechanism whereby children suitable for a family conference can be diverted to the attention of the Probation Service for the purpose of developing an Action Plan to prevent the child from further offending. This is then submitted to the court for approval and if these measures are successful in keeping the child out of trouble, the court can order the discontinuation of the proceedings against the child. The take-up of both measures appears low for various reasons (Kilkelly, 2014).

If the court finds a child guilty of an offence, a Probation Report or a Victim Impact Report may assist it in choosing the most appropriate sanction. Under section 96 of the Act, detention is to be a measure of last resort and Part 9 of the Act sets out a wide range of community-based sanctions. These include:

- an order for fines, costs or compensation;
- an order imposed on parents, such as a parental supervision order or an order that a parent be bound over;
- a community sanction, such as a probation order, a day centre order, an order restricting movement or an order requiring supervision by a suitable person or mentor; and
- an order placing a child in detention or combining detention with a period of supervision in the community.

One notable development in recent years has been the emergence of mentoring, delivered by Le Chéile Mentoring on behalf of the Probation Service – a volunteer service whereby trained mentors act as a positive role model, adviser and supporter to young people. This has proven to be a very effective way to support desistance and improve young people's life chances (O'Dwyer, 2019).

When exercising their jurisdiction in children's cases, the courts may consider the child's age and level of maturity as mitigating factors and must ensure that the sanction imposed interferes as little as possible with the child's education, training or employment (Children Act 2001, section 96). Furthermore, in determining sanctions, the measure should take the form most likely to maintain and promote the development of the child and be the least restrictive form appropriate in the circumstances. Any court dealing with a child charged with a criminal offence must have regard to the principle that children have 'rights and freedom before the law equal to those enjoyed by adults and, in particular, a right to be heard and to participate in any proceedings of the court that can affect them' (section 96(1)). The courts must also take into account the principle that 'criminal proceedings shall not be used solely to provide any assistance or service needed to care for or protect a child' (section 96(1)). In the higher courts, sentencing practice can appear at odds with these laudable principles. For instance, where a child has reached 18 years in between the alleged offence and sentencing, losing the protections of the Children Act notwithstanding prosecutorial delay, they can be sentenced as an adult. While in such circumstances, the courts are free to mitigate the loss to the young person of the advantages of the Children Act, this discretion is not unlimited and recommendations have been made for the introduction of sentencing guidelines to ensure that the developmental factors are taken into account in such circumstances (McNickle, 2018). This area has also been flagged for reform in the Youth Justice Strategy (Department of Justice, 2021).

Pending trial, the court can, in the interests of the child, release a child on bail subject to a range of conditions (Children Act 2001, section 90), including requirements regarding training or education, association with peers and other restrictions on movement. In 2016, a pilot Bail Supervision Scheme was introduced involving a model of multi-systemic therapy that provides intensive support to the caregivers of children at high risk of bail refusal. An evaluation of the pilot in 2019 found that the scheme was associated with marked improvement in adherence to bail conditions, with the young people enrolled on the scheme showing a reduction in reoffending almost twice that of the control group (Naughton et al, 2019). The evaluation also suggested a link between the scheme and a reduced chance of custodial sanction being imposed subsequently (Naughton et al, 2019). The Scheme, which may be linked to a reduced number of children in detention on remand (see Chapter 4), is being extended nationally.

Disaggregated sentencing data are not available in Ireland and the latest data from the Courts Service indicate approximately 4,000 orders made by the Children Court in 2019, the vast majority of which concerned offences relating to drugs, assault and public order (Courts Service, 2020, p 85). Of these, there were approximately 2,000 substantive orders (the others being struck out and so on), nearly 50% (966) of which were Probation Orders, with 196 detention orders made. The poor quality of the recording and reporting of data makes it impossible to establish whether the orders set out in the Children Act are being made and/or accurately recorded (Kilkelly, 2014), but the picture appears stable in any event. There is also no means of identifying how many children are charged with or convicted of indictable offences such as murder, manslaughter or rape, as data relating to those convicted outside the Children Court are not aggregated by age. Anecdotally, the numbers of children being charged with or convicted of these most serious offences appear to have increased significantly in recent years (Oberstown 2020, p 8).

As a measure of last resort, the Children Act 2001, as amended, makes provision for the detention of children under 18 years in Oberstown Children Detention Campus on either remand or detention orders. Oberstown is a specialized facility, which falls under the responsibility of the (now) Department of Children, Equality, Disability, Integration and Youth. Under section 143, the court cannot make a detention order unless it is satisfied that detention is 'the only suitable way of dealing with the child'. This goes some way to meeting the recommendation of the Committee on the Rights of the Child (the CRC Committee) that children should not be deprived of liberty 'unless there are genuine public safety or public health concerns', although there is no provision in the law, as the Committee recommends, for 'an age limit below which children may not legally be deprived of their liberty, such as 16 years of age' (CRC Committee, 2019a, p 15). The court may also defer a detention order and place the child under the supervision of a probation officer, if this is a suitable way of dealing with the matter and it would otherwise be in the interests of justice (section 144).

Although detention as a last resort is explicitly recognized as a principle in section 96, there is no requirement in national law to ensure it lasts 'the shortest appropriate period of time', as Article 37(b) of the CRC requires. The only legislative requirement is that the length of detention should not be longer than a period imposed on an adult for the same offence (section 149). It is the principal object of detention under the Act to provide 'appropriate educational, training and other programmes and facilities' for children referred by a court (section 158) in order 'to promote their reintegration into society and prepare them to take their place in the community as persons who observe the law and are capable of making a positive and productive contribution to society'. This emphasis on reintegration is in line with international standards, although the Act makes no provision for the child's right to aftercare, which means that arrangements are often dependent on available community supports (Forde, 2014).

Important developments in youth justice
Youth justice in the Department of Children

Although passed by the Oireachtas (Parliament) in 2001, the Children Act was commenced in a gradual and ad hoc manner. By 2006, however, concerns about the pace and effectiveness of its implementation had led to a substantial review of progress. Commissioned by the Department of Justice, the Youth Justice Review undertook stakeholder consultation and reviewed international practice with a view to making recommendations on the legal and structural changes required for the more effective delivery of youth justice services (Department of Justice, Equality and Law Reform, 2006). The most important theme to emerge from the Review was that the Children Act 2001 provides 'a sound legal basis for a modern youth justice system and what is now required is for it to be fully implemented and supported by the necessary resources for that implementation' (Department of Justice, Equality and Law Reform, 2006, p 7). Additional themes concerned the need to emphasize prevention and early intervention, raise the age of criminal responsibility, coordinate services, promote existing interagency cooperation and ensure detention is a last resort through the resourcing of community-based sanctions. The Review considered submissions from community and other groups and took account of international best practice in youth justice, noting the emphasis in the international children's rights standards and other jurisdictions such as New Zealand and Canada on prevention, diversion, specialized delivery and a clear national strategy with a whole-government approach (Department of Justice, Equality and Law Reform, 2006, pp 25–6). The report's most significant recommendation was the establishment of a unified Youth Justice Service, with a remit to develop youth justice policy linked to broader child-related strategy and to oversee implementation of the Children Act, especially with regard to diversion, restorative justice and community-based sanctions. Very significantly, the Review recommended that the Youth Justice Service, set up in the Department of Justice, but which became an executive office in the Department of Children in 2012, take responsibility for the detention of all children under 18 years of age, including 16- and 17-year-olds who at that point were detained in prison. In this regard, the service was charged with the introduction of an education-focused model of detention for all children under 18 years (Department of Justice, Equality and Law Reform, 2006, p 41), ultimately giving rise to a series of measures, outlined in Chapter 4, that brought about that goal.

Youth justice as part of the National Children's Strategy

For many years, Ireland's approach to policy-making and responsibility for children was characterized by fragmentation and low political priority. However, the ratification of the CRC in 1992 and Ireland's subsequent appearances before the CRC Committee gave rise to heightened concern and awareness about the rights of children, leading to the implementation of a number of measures, recommended by the committee, which helped to shape the Irish policy and political landscape from a children's rights perspective. Three developments were particularly significant in this regard. First, in 2000 the government adopted the National Children's Strategy following a wide-ranging consultation process with children and the adults who work with and for them (National Children's Office, 2000). A whole-child perspective underpinned the Strategy, which committed to three goals, namely that children will have a voice in matters that affect them, that their lives will be better understood, and that they will receive quality supports and services. Second, a new approach to public policy and governance concerning children's matters led to the establishment of the first cabinet minister for children. This process first began in 2005 when the National Children's Office evolved into the Office of the Minister for Children, accompanied by a 'super-ministry' with dedicated funding and co-responsibility across key government departments (Kilkelly, 2006, p 17). In 2008, this became the Office of the Minister for Children and Youth Affairs (OMCYA) with a remit to harmonize policy issues that impact children in areas including youth justice, children and young people's participation and other initiatives for children (Office of the Minister for Children and Youth Affairs, 2010, p 3). Significantly, although the Irish Youth Justice Service (IYJS) was originally situated in the Department of Justice, OMCYA's cross-cutting remit meant that the IYJS fitted naturally within its scope and so it moved there in 2007 in line with the government's commitment that youth justice should be viewed as an area of children's policy. Further reform – spearheaded by the publication of the report of the Commission to Inquire into Child Abuse (2009), the Ryan Report in 2009 – led to the establishment of a full government Department for Children and Youth Affairs (DCYA) and the decision to keep the IYJS in the Department of Children was a reminder of the need for youth justice to stay connected to wider children's policy. This approach was consolidated in the adoption in 2014 of Better Outcomes Brighter Futures, the National Policy Framework for Children and Young People 2014–2020, which incorporated the Youth Justice Action Plan 2014–2018 (DCYA, 2014), set out later in this chapter. A review of the implementation of the Action Plan, designed to inform the drafting of the next youth justice strategy, confirmed the importance of ensuring that youth justice shares its administrative home with other areas of children's policy and services (Kilkelly and Forde, 2021). While the formation of the new government in 2020 saw the remit of the Department of Children expanded, however, this development also saw the transfer of responsibility for youth justice, including Garda diversion and the Bail Supervision Scheme, back to the Department of Justice, with the consequent disbandment of the IYJS. It is not yet clear whether a dedicated unit within the Department of Justice will be given responsibility for policy development and the coordination of services in this area. It is significant, nonetheless, that despite these developments, responsibility for child detention has remained with the Department of Children, Equality, Disability, Integration and Youth, in an important reminder of government's commitment to a child-centred approach to detention.

National youth justice policy

Following its establishment in 2007 on the recommendation of the Youth Justice Review (Department of Justice, Equality and Law Reform, 2006, pp 8–9), the IYJS developed Ireland's first National Youth Justice Strategy in consultation with key stakeholders, including children, to provide for the implementation of the Children Act 2001, as amended (IYJS, 2008a). The Strategy reflected the recommendations of the Youth Justice Review in its focus on diversion, the promotion of restorative justice and the enforcement of community sanctions, with detention as a last resort. It was based on the approach of the Children Act 2001, as amended, 'mindful of a child-centred approach to service delivery and outcomes, with the best interests of the child being paramount' (IYJS, 2008a, p 6). The Strategy committed to the implementation of the Act 'with reference to the rights of the child, addressing their needs and holding them accountable for their actions, while developing their futures in society' (IYJS, 2008a, p 6), and it had five high-level goals addressing leadership, diversion, the promotion of community sanctions, the strengthening of data-informed policies and providing a safe and secure environment for detained children to assist their early reintegration into the community. Each goal was accompanied by a set of actions designed to set the focus of youth justice agencies for the three years from 2008 to 2010 (IYJS, 2008a). The Strategy prioritized community-based diversion and other measures and, while acknowledging the long-term vision to extend the children detention schools to all children aged under 18, committed to undertaking the groundwork to prepare for this eventuality. It emphasized standardizing policies and practices across the schools and planning for the development of new facilities while committing to improved provision for healthcare, education, governance and staffing (IYJS, 2008a, p 18).

The National Youth Justice Oversight Group reported good progress in the implementation of the Strategy and, in 2012, it reported to government that the 'net effect of this combined effort has been to develop a more co-ordinated strategic approach, make better use of existing resources, create positive working relationships amongst stakeholders and deliver better outcomes for young people in trouble with the law and for the community in general' (IYJS, 2013a, p 3). The Youth Justice Action Plan 2014–2018 built on the earlier Strategy and 'underpin[ned] the principles and policies of diversion and the proportionate interventions envisaged by the Children Act 2001' (IYJS, 2013a, p 2). Focused on children in conflict with the law, the action plan sought to complement the Children and Young People's Policy Framework, Better Outcomes Brighter Futures (DCYA, 2014), thereby ensuring that youth justice remained connected to national children's policy. Like its predecessor, the Action Plan set five high-level goals:

- building public confidence in dealing with young people in trouble;
- developing the evidence base to support more effective policies and services;
- strengthening targeted interventions to reduce offending and divert young people from crime;
- promoting the increase of community sanctions, including restorative justice; and
- providing a safe, secure environment and necessary support for children in detention to assist their reintegration into the community. (IYJS, 2013a, p iv)

The Action Plan noted that responsibility for youth justice was now shared between the Minister for Justice (with responsibility for youth crime policy) and the Minister for Children (with responsibility for detention). With respect to detention, considered in more detail in Chapter 4, the Action Plan was clear that the aim was to reduce the necessity for detention, while committing to the establishment of a specialized national detention facility for all children under 18 years who were to be provided with safe and secure accommodation and receive appropriate care, education and opportunities to enable successful reintegration into the community on release.

A study of the implementation of the Action Plan concluded that there had been substantial progress made in the achievement of its goals, although some areas were more difficult to assess than others (Kilkelly and Forde, 2021). Following a process of consultation and review, the new Youth Justice Strategy 2021–27 (Department of Justice, 2021) builds on previous progress towards an evidence and rights-based youth justice system. It embraces a comprehensive multi-agency response to children in conflict with the law, while continuing the connection to national children's policy. The Strategy commits to a collaborative research and evidence-based approach to youth justice, with the voice of the child underpinning service design and delivery. In line with international standards, professional training is highlighted as a key priority, with a focus on engaging with young people and addressing complex issues of mental health and trauma. It addresses children out of school and supports strengthening provision for vocational education and apprenticeships. Particular reference is made to the need to continue to develop aftercare supports and services for those leaving detention, and commitments are made to expand the Bail Supervision Scheme and enhance the delivery of community-based interventions (p 28). A commitment is made to further embed the Children's Rights Policy Framework into operations in Oberstown Children Detention Campus and consideration is also to be given to those transferring to prison while making special provision for young adults (between 18 and 24 years) in detention (p 27). While its goals are ambitious, its development through a strongly consultative process provides further evidence of the continuing progression of Irish youth justice in line with international children's rights standards.

Conclusion

This chapter aimed to set out the law and policy framework for youth justice in Ireland, exploring its historical development and the extent to which it has developed in line with international children's rights standards. A number of conclusions emerge. The first is that, by any standard, the picture is of a stable youth justice landscape that has gradually evolved over time, in line with progressive influences including Ireland's international obligations. Indeed, the CRC, which was ratified by Ireland in 1992, has been influential through the periodic review of Ireland's implementation record by the CRC Committee. While these influences are discussed further in Chapter 8, it is important to note here that Ireland has a track record of responding favourably to its international children's rights obligations and this is especially true in the area of youth justice where the observations of the CRC Committee have influenced both the development and the implementation of the Children Act 2001. The second conclusion is that building on a solid legislative base, Ireland's policy-makers have been attentive to international best practice in the development of national strategy. For instance, when the Youth Justice Review was undertaken in 2005, Ireland chose to look to progressive jurisdictions and international standards, rather than the more punitive approaches that had taken root elsewhere (Muncie, 2008). This has continued with the adoption of a largely progressive new Youth Justice Strategy in 2021. The third conclusion is the connection that has prevailed between youth justice and the wider children's policy agenda. Reinforced through the location of the Irish Youth Justice Service in the Department of Children, in its various forms, this connection has ensured that youth justice is viewed through a children's (rights) lens. Although the Irish Youth Justice Service has since been disbanded, it is evident from the new youth justice strategy that notwithstanding this development, no change to the progressive direction of youth justice, in line with international children's rights standards, is currently contemplated. The decision to retain responsibility for child detention in the Department of Children (albeit with an expanded remit) is reflective of this approach.

4

Introducing Child Detention
in Ireland

Introduction

Having traced the development of Irish youth justice law and policy in Chapter 3, this chapter focuses more specifically on child detention, providing an historical and then a more contemporary point of reference for the reforms outlined in the rest of the book. Ireland has a long tradition of over-reliance on institutional care and, throughout the 20th century, children in industrial and reformatory schools suffered harsh and often abusive conditions (O'Sullivan and O'Donnell, 2012). Although the separation of children from adult prisoners took place as early as 1906 (Osborough, 1975), it was not until 1985 that proposals were made in the Whitaker Report (Commission of Inquiry into the Penal System, 1985) for a more enlightened model of detention for children, in small residential settings, with qualified and skilled staff (Sargent, 2016). In effect, however, rights-based reform of child detention took decades to achieve and required the adoption of a range of legal and administrative measures, including legislative reform, clear national policy and significant capital investment. The first part of this chapter sets out the role that these measures played in enabling the reform of child detention in Ireland. The second part introduces the current legal framework and governance arrangements for Oberstown Children Detention Campus, the national child detention facility in Ireland, while it also introduces the particular circumstances of the children who are detained there. In these respects, it provides important context for the deeper analysis that takes place in the chapters that follow.

The reform of child detention in Ireland

Contemporary reform of child detention in Ireland began with the introduction of the Children Act 2001, which introduced a new category of 'children detention schools', under the remit of the Department of Education, which detained girls and boys under 16 years of age in conflict with the law. Taken together, Trinity House School (1983), Oberstown Boys' School (1991) and Oberstown Girls' School (1991), all in Lusk, County Dublin, and Finglas Child and Adolescent Centre, nearer Dublin, could accommodate approximately 77 children (IYJS, 2008a). St Joseph's Clonmel (a former industrial school) could accommodate a further 40 children. The schools provided residential care, education and assessment services and they had varying levels of security (Kilkelly, 2006). For many years, children over 16 years of age had been detained in St Patrick's Institution, part of the prison system, and although the 2001 Act originally reflected this arrangement, consensus soon began to emerge in favour of a new, single model of detention for all children under 18 years of age, especially as the criticism of national and international bodies intensified about conditions in St Patrick's Institution (CPT, 2003a, 2015a; CRC Committee, 2006; OCO, 2011; Inspector of Prisons, 2013).

The Youth Justice Review

As explained in Chapter 3, concerns about the implementation of the Children Act 2001 prompted a review of youth justice services in 2005 that, for the purposes of this chapter, made two important recommendations that were central to the reform of child detention in Ireland (Department of Justice, Equality and Law Reform, 2006). First, the Review recommended that responsibility for Children Detention Schools should be transferred from the Department of Education to the new Irish Youth Justice Service (IYJS) under the Department of Justice (ultimately moving to the new Department of Children and Youth Affairs when that was established) (Department of Justice, Equality and Law Reform, 2006, p 40). Second, the Review recommended that the IYJS should take responsibility for all children in detention in a measure designed to ensure that the 'education-focused model' would become the standard for all children under 18 years of age (Department of Justice, Equality and Law Reform, 2006, p 41). Although ostensibly administrative in nature, these recommendations represented a milestone in the reform of child detention, setting the clear expectation that all children under 18 years of age, regardless of the gravity of the offence or their circumstances, would experience child-centred care. As this and subsequent chapters show, all measures necessary to implement a child-centred detention model – both the establishment of the new national facility and the closure of St Patrick's Institution – flowed from this.

The Expert Group on Children Detention Schools

The details of the child-centred model were agreed by an inter-governmental Expert Group on Children Detention Schools, which was set up in April 2006 to consider how best to take forward the recommendation to introduce child-centred detention for all children. Reporting to the newly appointed Minister for Children, the Group provided important leadership and structure to the process of developing a new national approach to child detention, in line with international children's rights standards. It also supported the various steps necessary to enable responsibility for 16- and 17-year-olds to be transferred from prison to child detention (Expert Group on Children Detention Schools, 2006). The First Report of the Group made a series of recommendations that would guide the development of the schools in improving the quality of the accommodation. A subgroup set up to consider the regime and ethos of the new schools proposed a number of principles, in line with the Children Act and following consultation with staff and children. In particular, they recommended that in a detention school, children's 'care, education, welfare and development shall be provided [for] in a safe, secure and drug free environment to the highest standard using evidence based best practice' (Expert Group on Children Detention Schools, 2006, p 13). Crucially, the subgroup also recommended that in the new schools, 'children's rights shall be upheld in keeping with national and international obligations, recognizing the importance of childhood and the individuality of the child', adding that every child in this setting should have 'the right to be heard and to be involved in decisions which affect him or her' in line with Article 12 of the United Nations Convention on the Rights of the Child (CRC) (Expert Group on Children Detention Schools, 2006, p 13). These recommendations, which were endorsed by the Expert Group, represented an unequivocal commitment to an approach to child detention that was both child-centred and rights-based, two principles that can now be seen in practice 15 years later.

The Final Report of the Expert Group on Children Detention Schools (2007) concluded, following robust and comprehensive analysis, that the preferred option in the development of the new national facility was to develop the children detention schools on the Oberstown Campus in Lusk, County Dublin. The recommendation was informed by the economies of scale that were possible on a single site relating to the quality of care and services, the site's expansive capacity for future development should it be required, and that the development could appropriately balance security and care considerations in line with good practice. With regard to the building, the report noted that the 'design of the campus', which was of 'crucial importance', would have to be 'innovative to ensure retention of a child-care model' (Expert Group on Children Detention Schools, 2007, p 23) and it also noted the requirement to ensure compliance with national and international standards. In terms of scale, statistical modelling had projected a demand for 167 places, but the report recommended that this analysis be repeated annually until the final phase of construction. The Youth

Justice Review noted that in 2004, 192 children between 14 and 18 years of age had been sentenced to St Patrick's Institution that year, while a further 177 children had been sentenced to the children detention schools, albeit with a declining average population of close to 80 children (Department of Justice, Equality and Law Reform, 2006, pp 15–16). The facility was eventually built for 90 places, although demand has come nowhere near that capacity in recent years.

Design and investment

Following government approval of the recommendations of the Expert Group on Children Detention Schools in March 2008, the IYJS began a process of consultation with staff and children, and experts in children's rights and youth justice, to ensure that 'physical design aspects of the new development were given appropriate consideration, at an early stage and reflected principles in legislation and international standards, related to children's rights' (IYJS, 2009, p 2). A separate group was set up to consider how the design could be informed by national and international children's rights standards and the report of that group addressed the fit between the design specification and children's rights (IYJS, 2009). As part of this process, for instance, it was agreed that the children's rights standards would be brought to the attention of those seeking to tender to design and build the new facility.

Significant capital investment was an accepted part of the commitments being made to deliver child-centred detention. In 2000, the Minister for Education and Science, who had responsibility for the schools at the time, announced a £21 million (€26.6 million) development plan to include a major refurbishment of facilities at Trinity House, the replacement of facilities at Oberstown Boys' and Girls' Schools and the development of a new highly specialized unit at the Lusk campus (Kilkelly, 2006, p 199). Finglas Child and Adolescent Facility was closed around this time. This was followed by further capital investment announced in 2012 when in furtherance of the recommendations of the Youth Justice Review and the Expert Group on Children Detention Schools, the government committed to the amalgamation of the four Dublin-based schools – Trinity House School, the Oberstown Boys' and Girls' Schools and the Finglas Child and Adolescent Unit – and the closure of St Patrick's Institution by making a capital investment of approximately €50 million in the development of new 'dedicated child-specific facilities' (IYJS, 2013a, p 24).

Complex legislative reform

From a legal point of view, these developments would involve a series of complex and interconnected legislative measures, which happened in three different stages and involved the transfer of responsibility for detention from the Department of Education to the Department of Justice (on the establishment of the Youth Justice Service) and finally to the Department of Children. The Children Act 2001 (section 147) had originally distinguished between children below 16 years of age, who were detained in children detention schools, and children over 16 years of age, who were detained in St Patrick's Institution (designated a Children Detention Centre under the Act). Although the Children (Amendment) Act 2015 finally amended the 2001 Act to provide for the detention of all children under 18 years in the children detention schools, in practice this required the introduction and repeal of a complex set of transitional arrangements, at different stages. Separate to the transfer of responsibility between government departments for children of different ages, the 2015 Act also provided (in section 163A of the 2001 Act) for the amalgamation of the children detention schools into a single entity. These provisions, establishing Oberstown Children Detention Campus (Oberstown), came into effect on 1 June 2016. By 31 March 2017, all the relevant transition provisions had been repealed, meaning that from this date onwards, all children under 18 years who receive a detention or remand order are sent to Oberstown. With this, St Patrick's Institution was closed.

Two other changes to the Children Act 2001 were brought about as part of this process of legislative reform. First, when responsibility for the children detention schools transferred from the Department of Education, responsibility for education transferred to the local Vocational Education Committee (which became the Education and Training Board, or ETB, in 2013). This ensures that the education of children in detention is connected to the national curriculum and qualifications framework, and the standard of education is assessed against that provided in the community. The second substantive change was to replace the provision in the 2001 Act (section 185) for the appointment of a dedicated Inspector of Children Detention Schools, with provision for a 'person authorised' by the Minister for Children to undertake annual inspections. Additionally, the provision requires the person so authorized to have 'expertise and experience in relation to the inspection of children's residential accommodation'. This is important as, as outlined in Chapter 2, the child-centred focus of inspection can only be assured where the inspection body itself has the appropriate expertise in children's rights.

Child detention in national policy

In line with the recommendations of the Youth Justice Review, the IYJS had responsibility for developing and coordinating implementation of Ireland's first national policy on youth justice. Both the National Youth

Justice Strategy 2008–2010 and the Youth Justice Action Plan 2014–2018 contained clear and precise commitments regarding the reform of detention. The first Strategy, for instance, identified the provision of a safe and secure environment for detained children to assist their early reintegration into the community, listing actions to promote and support the development of staff in the children detention schools, develop programmes focused on children's offending behaviour and standardize policies and procedures across the schools in line with international children's rights standards (IYJS, 2008a, pp 33–6). Indeed, it contained an explicit commitment to meeting the 'highest international standards' as part of its goal to provide safe and secure accommodation for all children detained by the courts (IYJS, 2008a, p 36).

Interestingly, however, the context for youth detention continued to evolve and by the time the Youth Justice Action Plan 2014–2018 was developed, the IYJS noted that since the last Strategy:

> the number of children detained by the Courts annually on criminal conviction has consistently dropped; the operational costs of detention have reduced by over 30%; the capital costs and space required in the new national detention facilities being built at Oberstown are approximately 50% of what was estimated in 2008; and youth crime has decreased. (IYJS, 2013a, p 2)

Amidst this changing context, it was important that reform of detention remained a dedicated national goal in the Youth Justice Action Plan 2014–2018, which committed to providing a 'safe, secure environment and necessary support for detained young people to assist their re-integration into the community' (IYJS, 2013a, p 24). The Action Plan identified a series of outcomes under this heading, including that children in detention will receive appropriate care and opportunities for rehabilitation, and improved access to educational opportunities to support their chances of remaining outside the criminal justice system on release. More generally, the action plan committed to ending the practice of sending young people to St Patrick's Institution and to establishing centralized facilities and integrated policies and procedures in the children detention schools with the delivery of all services to take place at a single location, to eliminate duplication and maximize opportunities for economies of scale (IYJS, 2013a, p 24). Objectives included the provision of evidence-based care and development opportunities for children to enable them to move away from offending on release, the completion of integrated services across the children detention schools, and the completion of the new building facilities at Oberstown by 2015 (IYJS, 2013a, p 27). A review of the implementation of the Action Plan reported significant progress in meeting these objectives, although it noted that continued commitment, including with ongoing resourcing and support, would be required to ensure the consolidation of this progress (Kilkelly and Forde, 2021, p 33).

The new Youth Justice Strategy 2021–2027 (Department of Justice, 2021) repeats the strong commitment to children's rights principles, including recognition of the right of every child to participate effectively in decision-making in the justice system and a commitment to ensure that policies, programmes and systems are informed by the voice of children with experience of system contact (p 11). With regard to detention, the commitment to ensuring detention is a last resort is repeated and the Strategy identifies a number of priority areas relevant to the continued development of child detention in line with international children's rights standards. These include commitments to continue to build on Oberstown's Children's Rights Policy Framework to improve outcomes for children in detention, to plan the future needs for child detention and to continue to align government policy on child detention with the national children's policy framework (2021, p 27). There is specific focus too on ensuring that progress achieved in Oberstown continues when a young person transitions to prison, and a commitment to improve timely and effective supports available to ensure children's successful return to their community on release (p 28).

The strategy indicates the extent to which national policy is beginning to stretch in ambition beyond the reform of child detention that is already under way, towards the expansion of services into the community in terms of aftercare for children leaving detention and extending childhood protections into emerging adulthood for children who will transition to prison. Expanding the children's rights approach in these two important ways, while also looking ahead in light of the decreasing numbers of children in detention, is important to ensure that progress continues, in line with international children's rights standards (Department of Justice, 2021). More generally, it is clear that national policy has played a vital role in charting the path of child-centred and rights-based reform of child detention. By consistently setting goals that align with children's rights standards, national policy has supported the continuously progressive reform of child detention, in terms of both pace and direction. It is important that this process continues.

The profile of children in Oberstown

As Ireland's national facility, Oberstown Children Detention Campus (Oberstown) has responsibility for the care of all children under 18 years of age, regardless of the offence with which they have been charged or convicted or whether their detention is ordered by the Children Court

Figure 4.1: Number of children in Oberstown on remand and detention orders, 2016–20

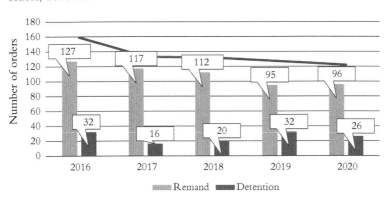

or the Circuit or Central Criminal Courts. Although its physical capacity is greater, the Campus is currently certified by the Minister for Children (under sections 195–6 of the Children Act 2001) to accommodate 46 children (40 boys and six girls), having been reduced in 2021 during the COVID-19 pandemic.

The number of children in Oberstown on detention and remand orders has fallen, year on year, as set out in Figure 4.1. In 2016, when 17-year-olds continued to be detained in St Patrick's Institution, 159 children were admitted to Oberstown during the course of the year. In 2020, notwithstanding that, by then, Oberstown accommodated all children on remand and detention orders up to 18 years of age, this number fell to 122.

The daily figures present another perspective on the falling numbers of children in detention. In 2016, for instance, the average daily population was 42, whereas even with the increased responsibility for all children up to age 18, this fell in 2020 to 36 (www.oberstown.com).

Again despite the increased responsibility for children up to age 18, the average age of a child in Oberstown continues to be 16 years. As Figure 4.2 demonstrates, however, Oberstown continues to receive children on detention and remand orders from all ages from 13 to 17.

Although only children under 18 years of age can receive a detention or remand order to Oberstown, there is some flexibility with regard to persons who turn 18 in detention. In particular, a young person who reaches their 18th birthday in detention but who has less than six months to serve or who is involved in education or training may remain in Oberstown for up to six months. This mechanism (section 155, as amended) can be used to prevent an 18-year-old being transferred to prison if certain conditions are met, and as such it minimizes or delays exposure to the prison environment

Figure 4.2: Age profile of children in detention in Oberstown, 2016–20

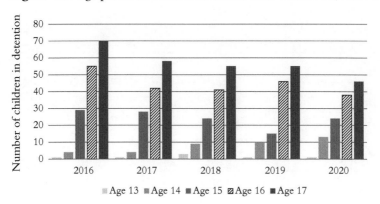

where possible. This meets the requirements set down by the Committee on the Rights of the Child (the CRC Committee), which has recommended that it should be possible for a young person to remain in a specialized facility when they reach 18 years of age if that is in their best interests and not contrary to the interests of the other children (CRC Committee, 2019a, p 15).

Since 2017, Oberstown has published data on the characteristics of children in detention (www.oberstown.com). Based on a desk-based review of individual records, data were collated on a range of areas, including care, health, education, offending behaviour and background, as well as information on substance misuse, mental health and family circumstances. In 2019, of the 75 children included in the study (who spent time in Oberstown in quarter 1), there were 31 on remand orders and 44 on detention orders (Oberstown, 2019a). Of this cohort, 45% were 16 years of age or younger. The age of these children on admission was as follows: four were aged 14, 13 were aged 15, 17 were aged 16, 33 were aged 17 and eight were aged 18. Just three were girls.

According to the data, 20 children came from the Dublin area, with the next biggest cohorts coming from Cork (ten), Limerick (9), Louth (7) and Meath (5) (Oberstown, 2019a). Of these children, 28 faced charges of theft, while other headline offences included road traffic offences (13 children) such as dangerous driving, drunk driving, driving without tax/insurance and false registration. Twenty children had offences relating to assaults. Criminal damage charges were linked to six children and three children faced firearms and offensive weapons charges. For 40% of the children, it was their first time serving a detention order (having previously been on remand on one or more occasions) (Oberstown, 2019a). In addition, the report noted that:

- 71% were considered to have substance misuse problems;
- 57% were not engaged in education prior to detention;
- 43% demonstrated challenging behaviour;
- 41% were either in care before detention or had significant involvement with Tusla, the Child and Family Agency;
- 41% had mental health needs and 25% had been prescribed medication;
- 31% had suffered the loss of a parent through death, imprisonment or no long-term contact;
- 23% had a diagnosed learning disability;
- 23% were considered to be at risk of abuse or neglect;
- 19% were members of the Traveller community (Ireland's ethnic minority); and
- 8% had a physical health concern.

The data demonstrate the complex needs and adverse circumstances and backgrounds of many of the children in detention in Oberstown and largely mirror the profiles of children in detention elsewhere (Nowak, 2019). The fact that nearly one fifth of children were from the Traveller community echoes equivalent concerns about disproportionate minority contact in other jurisdictions (The Traveller Movement, 2016), as discussed in Chapter 2. There has been surprisingly little focus on the circumstances and experiences of Traveller children in detention in Ireland. A substantial study on Travellers in the Irish prison system was published by the Irish Penal Reform Trust in 2014 (Costello, 2014), but this did not include or address children. The publication by Oberstown of this data led to calls from advocacy organization Pavee Point for 'targeted and specific measures to minimise the risk of young Travellers coming into contact with the criminal justice system' (Fagan, 2020). Despite this, the Youth Justice Strategy 2021–2027 is silent on the disproportionate numbers of Traveller children in detention, although it identifies Travellers among those with 'disadvantage' who require state-funded services to meet their needs (Department of Justice, 2021, p 6). At the same time, the only explicit reference to Traveller children in the strategy occurs in the commitment to ensure that Garda Diversion Projects are inclusive of those from 'minority and hard-to-reach groups', including those from Traveller and other minority ethnic communities (Department of Justice, 2021, p 26), although they may of course also enjoy the benefits of other areas of the Strategy's focus – such as early intervention, early school leaving and the renewed focus on youth services and development – even if they are not explicitly mentioned.

The Oberstown data also highlight the prevalence of children with experience of state care in detention in Ireland, highlighting that the phenomenon of 'crossover' children, between the child protection system and the justice system (Baidawi and Sheehan, 2020), is present in Ireland.

This issue has been the focus of national advocacy (Carr and Mayock, 2019) and of national policy insofar as the Youth Justice Strategy highlights children in state care as needing particular support (Department of Justice, 2021). Although the strategy names Tusla, the Child and Family Agency as a partner in the action to improve supports to help children to transition back to their community from detention, it does not include any measures to avoid care-involved children entering detention in the first instance. Importantly, however, the Strategy commits to 'research' on and 'pilot initiatives' for 'those who may be disproportionately represented in the youth justice system', including children with state care experience and those from minority ethnic backgrounds (Department of Justice, 2021, p 18). The special circumstances of girls are not mentioned at any point in the Strategy, however, in an effective illustration of this minority group being 'overlooked' (Goodfellow, 2017).

Oberstown's legal framework

The Director as quasi-parent

A range of provisions in the Children Act 2001 illustrate the national commitment to child-centred detention with regard to the provision of the child's needs in relation to care, education, health, development and reintegration, in line with children's rights standards. The Act provides for the unique role of the Director of Oberstown Children Detention Campus, who has responsibility like a parent over the children in their care. Under section 180 of the Act, the Director has both 'immediate control and supervision' of the campus, as well as responsibility for the care of each individual child. In particular, the Director shall:

(a) have the like control over the child as if he or she were the child's parent or guardian; and
(b) do what is reasonable … in all the circumstances of the case for the purpose of safeguarding or promoting the child's education, health, development or welfare.

Under the Act, the Director also has authority with regard to matters of religious observance (section 199), medical treatment (section 200) and discipline (section 201) and, as set out in the next subsection, they can grant early release and permit absence or mobility trips as part of the management of the child's care and to fulfil the objective of successful reintegration. These are explained in the next subsection but together they illustrate how the legislative framework for detention underpins the child-centred model of care.

Providing for the child's needs and preparing for return to the community

It is the principal objective of Oberstown under section 158 of the Children Act 2001 to provide 'appropriate educational, training and other programmes and facilities' for children referred by a court, 'to promote their reintegration into society and prepare them to take their place in the community as persons who observe the law and are capable of making a positive and productive contribution to society'. This confirms the reflection in national law of the obligations to prepare the child for successful return to their community in line with the clear requirements of the CRC.

The Act also recognizes that successful return to their community is to be achieved by:

(a) having regard to their health, safety, welfare and interests, including their physical, psychological and emotional wellbeing;
(b) providing proper care, guidance and supervision for them;
(c) preserving and developing satisfactory relationships between them and their families;
(d) exercising proper moral and disciplinary influences on them; and
(e) recognising the personal, cultural and linguistic identity of each of them. (Section 158)

In this way, the legislation clearly provides for the child's basic rights of education, health and wellbeing with an emphasis on the 'whole child', in line with international children's rights standards. The emphasis in the Act on providing 'guidance' and 'supervision', and the reference to 'moral and disciplinary influences', reinforce the right of the child deprived of liberty to treatment in line with the needs of the child (Article 37, CRC) and the desirability of promoting the child's reintegration (Article 40(1), CRC). The approach in the 2001 Act also echoes the recognition in the CRC of the child's identity (Article 30, CRC), taking account of the importance to the child of their family relationships (Article 37(c), CRC).

The Children Act 2001 has a range of powers that can be used proactively to support a child's return to the community, in line with the emphasis in children's rights standards on reintegration and the importance of a child successfully returning home. In particular, the CRC Committee has recommended that, in order to minimize the use of detention, there should be 'regular opportunities to permit early release from custody … into the care of parents or other appropriate adults … with or without conditions' (CRC Committee, 2019a, p 14). In this regard, it is significant that the Director has authority to grant a child permitted absence for family or other reasons associated with the child's reintegration (under section 202 of the 2001 Act) and this can be used for recurring or one-off reasons associated with the purpose of seeking employment or work experience, for additional training or education, for participation in sport or recreation in the community, or for any other purpose conducive to the child's reintegration into the community. It is also open to the Director to sanction 'mobility trips' (an authorised absence, under section 204), to promote the child's personal and social development, to increase their awareness and appreciation of matters of culture, education and recreation, and in order to access a programme of treatment or counselling. Third, the Director shall have (under section 205) a programme of temporary leave in place for each child, as appropriate, taking into account the child's needs and particular circumstances (section 206). And finally, the Director may place a child in the community under the supervision of the Probation Service (under section 207), taking account of the child's needs, behaviour and circumstances. Taken together, these provisions provide the Director with a range of measures that may be used to support the child's care, incentivize positive behaviour and facilitate their return to their community on release, fulfilling the child's rights under the CRC with regard to the provision of basic needs and preparation for leaving. These powers have also played an important part in Oberstown's management of the COVID-19 pandemic, where children for whom this was an appropriate and suitable option were permitted to leave detention early, many of whom were supported to successfully complete their sentence in the community (Oberstown, 2021, p 13).

The distinctiveness of child detention

The courts have also reinforced that Irish law makes provision for a distinctively child-centred model of care in a number of major decisions, including the High Court decision of *SF v Director of Oberstown* [2017] IEHC 829 and the Court of Appeal decision in *M v Director of Oberstown* [2020] IECA 249, both discussed further in Chapter 7. In both cases, the courts relied significantly on the legislative provision that the Act makes for the child-centred approach to detention, and the quasi-parental authority of the Director. In these cases and the other cases on remission outlined in this subsection, these elements were instrumental to the court's approach.

The one exception to this was *Byrne v Director of Oberstown* [2013] IEHC 562 in which the High Court upheld the claim of a child detained in Oberstown that he was entitled to 25% automatic remission on his sentence given that he would have had that entitlement were he detained in St Patrick's Institution (to which the Prisons Act 2007 applied). The case was heard prior to the closure of St Patrick's when children were either detained there or in the children detention schools in Oberstown depending on their age. The key question that arose therefore was whether Oberstown was sufficiently distinct from St Patrick's Institution as 'a place of detention' to justify the difference in treatment (*Byrne v Director of Oberstown* [2013]).

Considering the matter, Mr Justice Hogan observed the 'enlightened' regime in Oberstown where the applicant child had received a full, multi-professional specialist assessment, enjoyed good contact with family and was being cared for by dedicated staff in a humane and caring environment (para 13). Nonetheless, serving his sentence in Oberstown he was denied automatic remission, meaning that he would be released on 26 February 2014, instead of 26 November 2013. According to the High Court, 'such sharply different treatment in terms of custodial release dates' (para 36) impacted significantly on the child's constitutional right of personal liberty, constituting a difference in treatment that could only be objectively justified if it could be shown that detention at Oberstown was 'essentially different and served fundamentally different purposes in terms of criminal justice policy than detention regimes operating elsewhere within the juvenile justice regime' (para 37). According to Hogan J, while accepting Oberstown's fully 'laudable goals, aims and inspirations' and accepting further that the applicant would 'probably personally benefit from an extended stay in such a controlled environment', the language and structure of the 2001 Act 'negatives any argument that Oberstown is essentially different in this respect from other detention centres' (para 37). As a result, the court held, the difference in treatment complained of on such a fundamental basis as the right to liberty was 'impermissibly wide and indiscriminate' and therefore unconstitutional (para 40).

Although there were complex transitional legislative provisions regarding detention in place at the time that arguably played a role here, the material issue in this case was the existence of a comparable place of detention that the boy in Oberstown could use to ground his entitlement to automatic remission. It was not a surprise then when, following the closure of St Patrick's, a claim to enhanced remission made by a child detained in Oberstown was rejected by the courts, in *B v Director of Oberstown* [2020] IESC 18. The *Byrne* case nonetheless had a lasting effect in extending to all children sentenced to Oberstown an automatic entitlement to a 25% reduction in their sentence. In addition to resulting in the applicant's immediate release from custody, the judgment resulted in the release of a further seven children, all of whom had served 75% of their sentence at the time (Bohan, 2013). Since that date, 25% remission has been applied on an ad hoc basis to the sentence of every child serving a detention order in Oberstown. In 2015, the Oireachtas (Parliament) enacted the Children (Amendment) Act 2015, which inter alia made provision for enhanced remission (provisions that were enacted but never commenced) on the understanding that the decision of the High Court in *Byrne* made this entitlement inevitable. This proposed the adoption of a regime to provide for the award, forfeiture and restoration of this remission but because there were concerns about its appropriateness to the Oberstown environment, its enactment was paused pending the outcome of a further legal challenge.

By the time the Supreme Court considered the case for enhanced remission, in *B v Director of Oberstown* [2020], the legal context had changed insofar as Oberstown had responsibility for the detention of all children under 18 years of age and St Patrick's Institution had closed. In its review of the legal framework for child detention, the court recalled the object and purpose of Oberstown under the Children Act 2001 and drew particular attention to the authority of the Director under the Act to grant permitted absence and temporary leave to young people as part of their care. The court noted the 'wide discretion' that authorized the Director under section 203 to permit a child to be absent for any purpose 'conducive to the reintegration of the child into the community' (para 13).

On the facts, the applicant, who was serving a detention order in Oberstown, challenged his inability to apply for enhanced remission on the basis that the relevant legislative framework, referenced earlier, had been enacted but not commenced. He also argued that his inability to avail of enhanced remission placed him in a disadvantaged position vis-à-vis an adult prisoner. In rejecting his claim, the High Court (*B v Director of Oberstown* [2018] IEHC 601) observed that the Children Act placed a duty on Oberstown to adopt a 'tailored approach to the individual needs of a child in detention with a view to securing a sustained rehabilitation' (para 37). It was the view of Ms Justice Reynolds, therefore, that the opportunity to avail of an enhanced remission regime could potentially conflict with a situation where 'a planned and coordinated release' was envisaged, such approaches being 'clearly more appropriate for children' (para 37). The distinctiveness of the child-centred approach to detention set out in the Children Act therefore trumped the applicant's entitlement to enhanced remission.

The Supreme Court reached the same conclusion but for slightly different reasons. First, Ms Justice O'Malley for the court drew attention to the differences in development and maturity between children and adults and noted that, as a result, incentives to engage in positive behaviour differed significantly between them, with long-term objectives working better for adults than for children, for whom short-term goals are more appropriate (*B v Director of Oberstown* [2020], paras 71–2). The Court observed that no evidence had been put forward by the applicant to make the case that the regime in place in Oberstown placed the applicant at a disadvantage vis-à-vis a person in an adult prison. At the same time, the Court did not consider that such a case could not be made and, in this respect, O'Malley J rejected the view of the High Court that enhanced remission would necessarily conflict with the statutory process currently in place. This, she averred, was a matter of policy that could be made to work if that was what was deemed appropriate. In conclusion, the Supreme Court held that enhanced remission was at odds with the child-centred model of detention, a commitment set out by the legislature in the Children Act 2001. In response, the government must now clarify its policy position on the matter. While the case against enhanced remission is clear from the Supreme Court's judgment, there is now an argument to be made that in fact automatic remission, equally, has no place in a child-centred approach to detention, where individualized child-focused placement planning, rather than prison-type sentence management, is the intended legislative approach.

Governance of detention

The international standards are silent on the governance of detention although they do highlight the importance of accountability. Under section 164 of the Children Act 2001, a Board of Management was established with responsibility for the oversight and governance of Oberstown Children Detention Campus. Appointed by the Minister for Children, the Board has 12 members and an independent chairperson who have a collective responsibility to ensure Oberstown fulfils its mandate in line with national law and policy, providing assurances to the minister in this regard. The Board holds the Director to account regarding the day-to-day care provided to children and has in place appropriate mechanisms of scrutiny and oversight to this end. The Act (section 167) requires that membership includes representation or nomination from relevant government departments (currently the Department of Education, the Department of Children and the Child and Family Agency, Tusla), two members of staff, two representatives of the local community and five independent persons selected through the state board appointment process who are required to have relevant knowledge or experience. Under section 165 of the 2001 Act, the Board has 'all such powers as are necessary or expedient for the exercise of (its) functions' and, under section 179, may, with the consent of the minister, make rules for the management of the school and the maintenance of discipline and good order and may set out the procedures and conditions applicable to mobility trips, temporary leave or community placements. This unique model of governance has two main advantages, which help to underscore the child-centred approach. First, through its membership it enables diverse external perspectives to be brought to bear on the management of detention, ensuring high standards are met with regard to the care provided. The Board is underpinned by a collaborative approach and enables Oberstown to leverage the necessary support and resourcing. A significant role is played by the board in the implementation of national policy, on which it has provided direction and clarity of purpose. This is epitomized by the adoption of the Oberstown Strategic Plan 2017–2020 and the Children's Rights Policy Framework 2020, both of which aim to advance implementation of the rights-based model of care. The second advantage of the model is that the Board adds both scrutiny and accountability to the operation of child detention. As the Court of Appeal observed in its 2020 decision on single separation, discussed in Chapter 7, this brings substantive value from a legal as well as a governance perspective.

Independent inspection of child detention

According to the CRC Committee (2019a, p 16), independent and qualified inspectors should be empowered to conduct regular and unannounced inspections of places of detention, during which they should place 'special emphasis' on holding confidential conversations with the children. Similarly, Rule 125 of the European Rules requires that detention facilities are 'inspected regularly' as to their compliance with national and international law and that the conditions and treatment of children in detention must be monitored by an independent body to which the children shall have confidential access, and whose findings shall be made public.

In line with these international standards, the Children Act 2001 (section 185) provides that the Minister for Children must authorize a person, with 'expertise and experience in relation to the inspection of children's residential accommodation', to inspect Oberstown Children Detention Campus, a role currently performed by the Health Information and Quality Authority (HIQA), an independent statutory body that monitors the safety and quality of health and social care systems in Ireland. Under the Act (section 186), as amended, an inspection must take place, at least every 12 months, paying particular attention to:

(a) the conditions in which the children are detained and the facilities available to them;
(b) their health, safety and wellbeing;
(c) policies and practice concerning the preservation and development of relationships between them and their families;
(d) policies and practice concerning their discipline, care and protection; and
(e) policies and practice in relation to the normal routine of the school.

Under section 186(3), the 'authorised person' may hear complaints by children who at any time were or who are detained in Oberstown, and for that purpose may interview them (privately) and staff concerned, and access records relating to the administration of the school and the child. In fulfilment of the international requirements, the report of the inspection must be submitted to the Minister for Children and published. The details of recent HIQA inspections of Oberstown are analysed in Chapter 5.

Conclusion

This chapter provided the backdrop to the reform of child detention in Ireland, tracing the legal and policy developments that established and supported the implementation of a child-centred approach to the detention of children under 18 years of age. As the analysis shows, the process was gradual and complex, requiring several stages of transition and reform designed to set up the national service in Oberstown Children Detention Campus and to close St Patrick's Institution. Throughout the process, law and policy repeatedly restated the commitment that child detention aligns with the international children's rights standards and various administrative and other measures were adopted to put these principles into practice. It is instructive that the strength of the legislative position in favour of a child-centred approach acted as a bulwark when legal challenges could have weakened this approach. And it is important too that the most recent national strategy reaffirms the commitment to a rights-based approach (Department of Justice, 2021).

The chapter also introduced Oberstown Children Detention Campus and the characteristics of children detained there. It explained the unique features of the child-centred model, reinforced through legislative provision, especially the Director's role and powers, and the governance arrangements. Having set out this foundation, the next chapters of the book will now delve deeper into the reform process. Chapter 5 begins by narrating the process of change through the lens of independent inspection. It is then followed by Chapters 6 through 9, which document in more detail how substantial reform was achieved to give the rights-based approach further effect.

5

Oberstown and the Process of Change

Introduction

Chapters 3 and 4 traced the development of Irish law and policy on youth justice and detention and introduced the law and governance arrangements with respect to the child-centred approach to detention in Ireland. The national goal of introducing this model for all children under 18 years of age, in line with international standards, was clear. In practical terms, this had two main elements. First, the three remaining children detention schools were to be merged, creating a specialist national facility providing child-centred care for all children on detention and remand orders, including those previously held in prison – Oberstown Children Detention Campus. Second, the construction of the new facility was designed to ensure that the child-care model took place in an appropriately designed, modern environment. This chapter documents how these two goals were achieved, through a process of change and development.

If the destination of national policy was clear, it did not come with a map as to the route. As Tilley and Jones (2013, p 93) note with regard to managing change in health and social care, '[w]hile the case for change may be strong, there is no blueprint or formula for making it work'. In the case of Oberstown, a series of interconnected measures were required to effect the necessary change. These included: the design and completion of the new building; the creation of a new model of care for child detention that is consistent with children's rights; and the development of a supportive environment for staff, through clarity of purpose and direction. This chapter explains how these goals were achieved, in line with international standards. In order to track the progress achieved, the annual reports of the Health Information and Quality Authority (HIQA) inspection process help to provide an objective assessment of the various developments and improvements. First, to provide important context, the scale of the challenge is described.

Introducing the challenge

As described in Chapter 4, Irish law and policy provides that all children under 18 years of age who are detained by the courts should receive care and education in a single, specialized setting. As the relevant legislation, funding and capital elements of the plan were put in place, a process of reform and change got under way in the children detention schools complex (Oberstown, 2017a), to merge the schools, create a unified service and complete the large building project where the new Oberstown Children Detention Campus (Oberstown) – as it was to be known – would be based. In line with national policy, it was agreed that, as soon as it was possible to do so, responsibility for the detention of children aged 16 and 17 years would transfer to Oberstown. This began in 2012, when 16-year-olds on remand and detention orders were first sent to Oberstown, and the process ended in 2017 when the final cohort – 17-year-olds serving detention orders – began to be sent to Oberstown (17-year-olds on remand orders were sent to Oberstown from March 2015) (Oberstown, 2018). Thus, alongside the process of merging the schools was the challenge of preparing the campus to take responsibility for 16- and 17-year-olds who were currently detained in St Patrick's Institution.

Meeting these goals necessitated a significant change process, with the expansion and development of campus services in every area and a significant overhaul of work practices. Industrial relations issues had to be addressed and a sense of common purpose instilled in a disparate workforce. Delivering a specialist, child-centred model in a new environment required the development of new systems, approaches and technologies, the development of existing staff, recruitment of new staff and the enhancement of management and governance systems appropriate to a modern, child-centred facility. When the appointed chairperson of the Board of Management of the campus, Joe Horan, appeared before the Oireachtas Committee on Children and Youth Affairs on 8 March 2012, he outlined that the priorities for the campus included: consistent achievement in meeting the requirements of HIQA (the inspectorate); developing efficient services within an integrated campus; improving the linkages between the schools, agencies and services in the community; and the development of specialist services for children in detention. In the context of transferring the older children to the Campus from the prison service, a matter in which there was keen interest from the Committee, Mr Horan highlighted the need for this to take place safely (Joint Committee on Health and Children, 2012).

In addition to bringing together disparate staff groups and creating a unified approach to children's care, the expansion of the Campus, in terms of population and age group, was a significant challenge that created uncertainty, anxiety and at times resistance from staff. While the learning from this process is explored in Chapter 10, it is important to note at this point that the disruptive and difficult nature of the reform process provided the backdrop to all the developments in Oberstown throughout this period. HIQA inspections had pointed to a range of areas where improvements were required but crucially, too, they had highlighted that the individual children detention schools lacked a clearly articulated statement of purpose, and leadership on the part of the schools' boards of management was weak (HIQA, 2009a, 2009b, 2009c). Among the many other reforms required, therefore, providing clarity of direction was critical to the amalgamation process. In an important development in 2012, a single Board of Management was appointed, which brought coherence, clarity and accountability to the management of the Campus over the relevant period (Oberstown, 2017a).

Against this backdrop, the following sections detail the three key areas of development and change: the construction of the new facility; the development of a single approach to child-centred care; and the process to address the concerns of staff. Reference is made throughout to the international standards, principally the UN Rules for the Protection of Juveniles Deprived of Their Liberty (the Havana Rules) and the European Rules for Juveniles Subject to Sanctions and Measures (the European Rules), with a view to measuring the extent to which these are currently met, along with the process of measuring progress through independent inspection.

Oberstown: the new building

Following government's commitment to building specialist facilities for the new unified approach to child detention, consultation and planning for the project got under way, taking account of national and international children's rights standards. Construction began in September 2013 and, throughout 2015, the first five units of new residential accommodation became operational, along with the central administration building, and the new educational facility (Oberstown, 2017a, p 18). The modern campus now consists of a new building – including six new residential units, a school with educational and recreational facilities, a health and visiting suite and an administrative building – alongside a number of separate, older residential units.

As explained in Chapter 4, specific consideration had been given to meeting the requirements of international children's rights standards in the design of the new facilities (IYJS, 2009). A study of the effectiveness of the design of Oberstown Campus, conducted by the Council of Europe Development Bank in 2019, found very high satisfaction with the design and layout of the new units, considered appropriate for the 'realisation of the stated care and reintegration objectives' (Council of Europe Development Bank, 2019, p 57).[1] In terms of accommodation, the six residential units each consist of ten individual bedrooms with integrated bathroom, shower and television facilities, in line with the European Rules (Rule 63). Bedrooms can be personalized by each child with posters and other personal items, small items can be stored in their rooms and storage for larger items is available outside each room (Havana Rule 35). In line with Havana Rule 32, the residential units are designed to 'approximate life in the community as closely as possible', with numbers 'small enough to enable individualised care', and are 'organised into small living units' (European Rule 53). In this way, only eight of the ten bedrooms in each unit are occupied from an operational perspective and each unit has a number of shared spaces, including a kitchen where food can be prepared and staff and children can eat together, and a common lounge where people can sit. Multi-purpose rooms can be used for private telephone calls with family or for individual or small-group recreation activities, and each residential unit has its own enclosed outdoor area where children can play games or exercise. In this way, the design had regard to the child's needs for 'privacy, sensory stimuli, opportunities for association with peers and participation in sports, physical exercise and leisure-time activities' in line with Havana Rule 32 (Council of Europe Development Bank, 2019, p 58). HIQA has also commended the adequate private and communal facilities in terms of both indoor and outdoor spaces (HIQA, 2018). Balancing privacy with security, each bedroom has a viewing panel, which can be used for unobtrusive monitoring for child protection purposes, and an alarm for emergencies, in line with the requirements of European Rule 64. Each unit has a 'protection room', although their use has become almost obsolete.

The international standards recommend small, regional facilities, located in places that are 'easy to access and [which] facilitate contact' with family (European Rule 53.5). Although this was considered as part of the consultation process (IYJS, 2009), greater weight was given to the fact that the economies of scale associated with a single national facility would support a highly specialized approach to child detention. Although concerns were expressed about the decision to have just one national centre in light of the distance between children and their families, it was agreed to ameliorate these difficulties by supporting families to visit and introducing video-link facilities to minimize travel to and from court (Council of Europe Development Bank, 2019, p 54).

The austere design of the Campus exterior, especially its high outer-perimeter fence and internal walls, appears at odds with the recommendations

---

[1]   This is a document internal to the Council of Europe Development Bank, whose permission to use it here is gratefully acknowledged. A summary is available.

of the European Rules that any facility should apply the 'least restrictive security and control arrangements necessary to protect juveniles from harming themselves, staff, others or the wider community' (European Rule 53.2). The high level of outer security was justified at the time of the design by the need to ensure the facility was secure in light of its purpose as the national facility for the detention of all children under 18 years of age. Instead, focus was placed on ensuring that internally – both structurally and in terms of approach – the 'atmosphere' and 'feel' of the facility reflect the children's rights approach (Council of Europe Development Bank, 2019, p 56). The fact that the residential units are considered 'bright', 'airy' and 'spacious' bears this out (Council of Europe Development Bank, 2019, p 58).

The European Rules recommend that children be separated according to gender and, in Oberstown, residential units are currently allocated to either boys or girls. The small number of girls on Campus – frequently no more than one at a time – means that this can be an isolating experience for them, although efforts are made to have joint activities as part of the leisure and education programme. It is well known that the small number of girls in detention makes it difficult to develop and deliver gender-specific programmes and supports (Zahn et al, 2009) and so consideration needs to be given to the long-term plans in this area.

Separate from the new residential facility, children on remand are currently accommodated in older residential units, the quality of which has been a cause of concern with regard to both the fabric of the building and the limited outdoor and recreational spaces (Council of Europe Development Bank, 2019, p 58). While this echoes concerns in other jurisdictions, set out in Chapter 2, at the time of writing preparations are under way to accommodate all children in the new residential units which will ameliorate the situation in Oberstown.

Oberstown: the new model of care

A key priority in the merger of the Children Detention Schools was to introduce a unified approach to the care of children in detention. Prior to their amalgamation, the three schools on the Oberstown Campus – Oberstown Boys' School, Oberstown Girls' School and Trinity House School – had existed for several years as independent entities, with separate identities and cultures, different management structures, staff and children who never met and policies and practices that had developed in line with their distinct purpose and approach. Different levels of security also applied to each school. Absconds, especially from Oberstown Boys' School, were not infrequent and children's experiences varied depending on the school to which their detention was ordered. In 2009, for instance, external inspections of the three schools by HIQA highlighted concerns with regard to safeguarding practices, placement planning and the use of restrictive practices, including single separation and physical interventions (HIQA, 2009a, 2009b, 2009c). Recommendations were made across all the schools with regard to improving approaches to meeting children's needs, staff supervision, management and board oversight and record keeping. Schools' progress in responding to these recommendations was mixed (HIQA, 2009d, 2009e, 2009f).

Care, Education, Health, Offending behaviour and Preparation for leaving

A priority, therefore, once the merger process began, was to develop a single model of care for the campus that would provide a framework to guide all stages of a young person's journey from their admission to release, ensuring their needs were met in a holistic, consistent and multi-disciplinary manner. In 2014, a process was undertaken to consider how best to translate the legislative requirements of the Children Act 2001 into a model of care that was accessible to staff and effective in meeting the needs of children in detention. The result was the CEHOP model, which has five components relating to children's Care, Education, Health, Offending behaviour and Preparation for leaving (Figure 5.1; Oberstown, 2018). The *care* aspect of the model was drawn from section 180(8) of the Act, under which the Director of the campus has 'like control over the child as if he or she were the child's parent or guardian' and must do what is reasonable to safeguard and promote the child's 'education, health, development or welfare'. The *education* component was derived from the requirement in section 158 of the Act to provide educational, training and other programmes, while the *health* component arose from the Director's responsibility, set out in section 200 of the Act, to ensure that the child receives the necessary medical treatment as required. The *offending behaviour* element was a recognition that children detained in Oberstown have been charged with or convicted of a criminal offence and that this behaviour must be addressed to avoid further offending. It also drew on the Irish Youth Justice Service Standards and Criteria for Detention Schools, Standard 10, which requires provision for 'individual offending behaviour programmes consistent with the young person's assessed needs' (IYJS, 2008b, p 22). The final component, *preparation for leaving*, reflects the references throughout the 2001 Act to the child's reintegration and successful return to the community on release or their transition to prison.

Implementation of CEHOP, a trademarked approach unique to Oberstown, involves an integrated way of working across the campus, with interagency working underpinned by policies, procedures and systems that enable the recording and sharing of information. Although delivered primarily by care staff (residential social care workers and night supervising officers), it is a multi-disciplinary process including teachers and healthcare and therapeutic staff, supported by a range of external agencies and services. Inclusive, structured and coordinated placement planning enables the delivery

Figure 5.1: Oberstown model of care (CEHOP)

Note: ® CEHOP and the CEHOP graphic are registered trademarks of Oberstown Children Detention Campus.

of CEHOP, with regular reviews to ensure the needs of the children are being met (Oberstown, 2020, p 12).

The similarity between CEHOP and the children's rights model, set out in Chapter 1, is immediately apparent. Care is child-centred, as the rights-based model requires, and it addresses the child's basic needs – to healthcare and education – while ensuring their rights are met with regard to preparing them to return to their community. Further details of how the rights-based model is met are set out in subsequent sections of this chapter and in the chapters that follow.

Relationship-based care

In parallel with the development of CEHOP, a process was undertaken to reinforce the importance of relationships in the provision of care to children in detention. Research commissioned by Oberstown identified that successfully engaging children in detention through relationship building is about purposeful activity on three levels. Level 1 involves relatively informal, yet constructive, face-to-face interactions between staff and young people, such as during mealtimes (Bamber et al, 2016a). Level 2 involves children and staff participating together in specific, planned and structured activities, such as sport or art. These activities both equip children with knowledge and skills while providing the opportunity for interactions that facilitate positive communication. Level 3 consists of participation in more specialized interventions, for example via therapeutic care or evidence-based programmes. Following the completion of the research, a programme of work was undertaken to put this learning into practice. Staff engaged in a process designed to promote the idea that 'relationship building is best seen as a craft which needs to be taught, modelled and cultivated as opposed to something which can be required through procedures or simply acquired by following a manual of instructions' (Bamber et al, 2016b, p 3). This helped to develop a shared understanding and improved practice among staff across the campus in the provision of consistent and quality care. More generally, it served to reinforce the valuable and impactful nature of the relationship between staff and the children, reinforcing the child-centred model of care at a time of great change and challenge.

The Children's Rights Policy Framework

Given the prevalence of diverse approaches to the care of children across the children detention schools, the adoption of a unified policy base was a priority early in the merger process. This took place in stages, as the single entity took shape, and it was led by a cross-section of staff to enable experiences to be shared and relationships to be developed across the Campus. This policy base was further revised and streamlined throughout 2016 and 2017 in line with legislation and international best practice, with new policies adopted in the following areas: single separation; care; health and wellbeing; safeguarding; dignity and privacy; anti-bullying; medication management; handcuffs; information management; and supervision (Oberstown, 2018). As part of the continuing evolution of the policy base, and to further embed the children's rights approach into practice, the Children's Rights Policy Framework was developed in 2020 as a new set of rules and policies to guide the treatment of children in line with children's rights standards (Oberstown, 2020, pp 33 and 50). Informed by the international children's rights instruments set out in Chapter 1, the framework consists of 12 'rules', adopted by the Board of Management with the consent of the Minister for Children under section 179 of the Children Act 2001, which set out a high-level statement in each area. For each rule there is an individual policy, which details how the Rule is to be implemented, and a set of procedures to support implementation. Taken together, the framework sets the standards by which the performance of the Campus will be measured and it contains commitments to children's rights in the following areas: care, education, health, offending behaviour, preparation for leaving, safeguarding, consultation, positive behaviour, restrictive practices, staff, management and governance, the physical environment and authority to suspend the Rules. The Framework sets out the rights to which children are entitled under each Rule and identifies the duties on staff and management to ensure those rights are protected in practice. Staff training aims to support consistent implementation of these policies and procedures, with oversight provided by the Board. A new complementary inspection framework, under development by HIQA, will ensure that the annual, external inspections take place against these rights-based standards. Consideration will also need to be given to ensuring that the child's participation in the inspection process is rights-based.

Oberstown: the new direction

It was evident from the outset that one of the key challenges to the successful implementation of national policy – both the merger of the schools and building Oberstown's capacity to take all children under 18 years of age from the courts – would be staff buy-in. In recognition, four full-day consultation sessions took place during October and November 2012, with a view to updating staff on developments and explaining the changes that would be necessary to develop an integrated service, alongside the capital project. More than 170 staff attended these sessions, representing 80% of serving staff across all three of the schools on the Oberstown Campus prior to amalgamation, highlighting significant interest in the project. While the process highlighted a desire for more information, consultation and input into decision-making around the changes planned, the report of the process also highlighted the complexity of what lay ahead. Staff expressed concern, for instance, about losing the good practice that existed, especially working in smaller units, and cautioned about the risks of building the new facilities alongside existing operations. Anxiety was evident with regard to accepting responsibility for 17-year-olds, with staff concerned about their ability to care safely for children who would be physically bigger and stronger than the children currently detained in Oberstown (IYJS, 2013b). The exercise also highlighted the many different views among staff about how best to approach the goals set out by national law and policy and highlighted their concerns about the implications of the change process for their terms and conditions of employment.

Around this time also, a review of the senior management structure was undertaken by the Public Appointments Service, with a view to recommending the optimal management structure for the integrated service (IYJS, 2012). The review made seven recommendations to support the revised structure and transition to integration, including the creation of a new identity for the integrated service, the completion of a training needs analysis and the introduction of a performance management and development system.

Against this backdrop, the process of change got properly under way with the appointment in late 2013 of a Campus Manager from which flowed the adoption of a range of measures to: increase and strengthen staffing; develop management capacity; and amalgamate, standardize and enhance the systems and practices necessary to ensure the safe, effective and efficient operation of the facility. As HIQA noted throughout this period, the change agenda had a very disruptive effect on the Campus at all levels and particularly serious challenges were experienced in 2016, including serious industrial relations issues and multiple threats to the safety and security of the campus. Even though a list of employee concerns had been settled under the state's industrial relations machinery in 2014, the ongoing change process proved problematic and, in 2016, further agreement with the trade unions was reached to commission a number of external reviews designed to engage independent expertise in resolving the matters under dispute. These reviews included an appraisal of security, health and safety, and behaviour management approaches. A separate review of Campus operations was commissioned by the Board of Management as a supportive process to promote better implementation of children's rights. Each review took a different approach and form, and between them they produced more than 307 recommendations. To ensure their analysis, tracking and implementation, the Minister for Children established a Review Implementation Group (RIG) in 2017. This Group had representation from the Oberstown Board of Management, staff, management, trade union, the Department of Children and Youth Affairs and an external expert in child development. The Group met 10 times throughout 2017 to undertake its analysis, presenting interim reports to the Minister and the Board, before completing its final report on schedule in December 2017 (RIG, 2017). Separate reports on the implementation of the recommendations of the reviews were submitted to the Minister in 2018 and 2019 (RIG, 2018, 2019), with the final report indicating that all recommendations had either been implemented or were under way.

As a process, the commissioning of independent reviews enabled external expertise to be leveraged so that matters of ongoing dispute between staff and management could be resolved. For instance, the security and health and safety reviews helpfully identified the various detailed measures to be taken to make the campus safer and more secure, building staff confidence in the new environment. The Behaviour Management Review, on the other hand, presented an evidence-based assessment of the most appropriate approach to be taken to the care of children with complex needs (Perkins and O'Rourke, 2018). Taking account of staff concerns, this report accepted the challenges of caring safely for children in crisis whose behaviour could be violent and unpredictable. Although it recommended that access to emergency services be facilitated in exceptional cases, it endorsed the Oberstown approach to managing behaviour through a process of:

- effective risk management;
- embedding CEHOP in practice;
- intervening early to avoid situations of crisis emerging;
- learning as incidents arose;
- improving communication; and
- working simultaneously to meet the needs of children and address the concerns of staff.

Taken together, combined with a separate report on the use of personal protective equipment, these reports largely settled the running tension, common to places of child detention, between 'care' and 'control', while supporting the Campus to move forward.

The reviews were mainly designed to address the concerns of staff through the industrial relations process. While they perhaps highlighted how the needs of staff overshadowed the rights of children during the change process, they were an important reminder that until the adults felt cared for, they would not be able to care appropriately for the children. As the recommendations of the different reviews were implemented and the environment was made increasingly safe, emphasis shifted gradually back to the provision of child-centred care. To give this entire process structure and focus, Oberstown adopted its first strategy.

The Oberstown Strategy 2017–20

As part of the change process, the Board of Management adopted an action plan in January 2017 to give direction and clarity to Oberstown during a time of crisis. This had five goals focusing on children, people, communication, standards and governance, and these headings were also used by the RIG to structure the 307 recommendations that arose from the numerous reviews of campus operations. The decision to use a single framework helped to bring structure and coherence to the potentially overwhelming set of priorities, actions and goals arising from the various reviews, consultations and other learning and listening processes at this time. While the RIG process enabled the implementation of the reviews' recommendations to be tracked and monitored, the adoption of the Strategy helped to lay out the future direction for the campus, internalizing the goals of national policy. As the RIG process continued during 2017, therefore, the campus engaged in consultation around its new Strategy, which was approved by the Board and then formally launched by the Minister for Children in December that year, shortly before she was presented with the final report of the RIG.

The Oberstown Strategy identified five goals, namely: 'providing the best possible care for young people, developing our people and our organization, implementing the policies, procedures and standards consistent with the best model of detention for young people, enhanced communications aligned to our values and mission, and delivering robust governance at all levels and driving effective accountability' (Oberstown, 2017e). In addition to guiding the day-to-day actions of management, and supporting the continuing development of the campus, an annual review of the Strategy's implementation helped to ensure that progress remained on track. This detailed annual review of progress under the strategy has been included in the Board's Annual Report, which is submitted to the Oireachtas (Parliament) under the Children Act 2001. These actions have served both to improve the transparency of Oberstown's operations by placing detailed information into the public domain, while delivering greater accountability to the public on behalf of the Minister for Children.

Measuring progress through independent inspection

An important way to measure the progress achieved in the implementation of national policy to create a unified, child-centred and ultimately rights-based model of detention for all children is to trace the developments through the inspection reports from HIQA. As outlined in Chapter 4, these take place annually and are either full or thematic in nature, announced or unannounced, and this section highlights the key findings of these inspections during the period of change.

In 2014, HIQA undertook its first announced full inspection of the Oberstown Campus, having previously inspected the schools individually. The inspection report thus constitutes a useful baseline for this analysis. There followed an unannounced follow-up inspection in 2015, an announced full inspection in 2017, an unannounced full inspection in 2018 and an announced inspection in both 2019 and 2020. No inspection took place in 2016, with the agreement of HIQA, as an independent review, commissioned by the Board of Management and later shared with HIQA, was under way at the time.

Although set to change in line with the Oberstown Children's Rights Policy Framework, during this period HIQA inspected in line with the National Standards and Criteria for the Children Detention Schools (IYJS, 2008b), which contain 10 standards as follows: purpose and function; care of children; child protection; children's rights; planning for young people; staffing and management; education; healthcare; premises, safety and security; and tackling offending behaviour. Under each standard, there are multiple criteria against which practice is reviewed before a judgement is reached on whether the overall standard has been met or not (the wording of these judgements has changed slightly over time). More recently, these have been grouped according to the themes of child-centred services (children's rights), safe and effective services (care of children; child protection; planning; premises, safety and security; and offending behaviour), health and development (healthcare; and education) and leadership governance and management (purpose and function; and staffing and management). An inspection, according to the inspectorate's methodology, typically involves consultation with children, staff and management, inspection of documentation and observation of practice, and takes place over several days involving multiple inspectors. The inspection reports are published, together with an action plan to address any matters of non-compliance.

Following its full announced inspection in late 2014, HIQA concluded that of the 10 standards, only one (education) had been met, six required improvement and three (care of children; healthcare; and staffing and management) were identified as a significant risk (HIQA, 2014). By any standards, this was a poor assessment of Oberstown's compliance with the national standards even if HIQA noted in its report that the campus was 'undergoing a process of major change' (HIQA, 2014, p 35). In terms of the impact of that change, the report noted that 'good leadership was displayed by the senior management team in progressing the physical and other changes within the service', although it went on to observe that 'the changes were having 'a serious impact on how the staff team functioned' (HIQA, 2014, p 35). While some improvements were noted in 'corporate governance', and 'the standardizing of policies and procedures' and 'action plans to mitigate against risks' were being worked on, the fact that 'limited quality assurance systems (were) in place' was 'of concern considering the context of significant change' (HIQA, 2014, p 35).

Although there were some positive elements in the report, with regard to the care of children, HIQA's grave conclusion was as follows:

> Children were not always safe, as best practice was not always implemented in the areas of managing behaviour and medication management. The Authority issued immediate action plans in relation to both of these areas of practice and received satisfactory action plans. Children were on occasions separated from their peers in locked rooms for long periods of time, and it was not always apparent that all other interventions had been tried. (HIQA, 2014, p 8)

HIQA's bleak overall assessment of the compliance with the National Standards prompted a commitment to significant improvements across the board. The nature of its findings led to a two-day, unannounced follow-up inspection in June 2015, designed to assess the implementation of actions taken as a result of the 2014 inspection. The service was also inspected with regard to Standard 6 concerning staffing and management. By the time of this inspection, the new residential units were in use, prompting HIQA to comment on the change process again, noting that the ongoing construction, staff recruitment and new policies and procedures were all under way (HIQA, 2015, p 5). Although inspectors reported 'some progress' in addressing the deficits in the previous inspection, it noted that improvements were required in 'key areas such as the use of the restrictive intervention of single separation, care planning, medication management and training' (HIQA, 2015, p 5). Significantly, it noted that children's needs were not always comprehensively assessed, with care plans that varied in quality and were not consistently reviewed. The practice of single separation, it observed, 'had not improved despite various interventions such as closer monitoring of the frequency and duration of these interventions' and 'as per the last inspection it was not consistently used as an intervention of last resort and for the shortest duration in line with procedures' (HIQA, 2015, p 6). The two principal judgements reached were that Standard 9 (premises, safety and security) continued to be 'a significant risk' while Standard 6 (staffing and management) continued to 'require improvement'. HIQA highlighted a range of areas for improvement, including gaps in training, policy implementation and recording. Positively, HIQA noted that 'good leadership' was provided by the campus manager, senior management team and the board in 'implementing a change management programme' (HIQA, 2015, p 6). Noting the complexity of the process, it concluded that, despite this, many challenges remained in building a campus-wide culture (HIQA, 2015, p 6).

HIQA undertook its next full announced inspection in March 2017, with a seven-person inspection team over four days. By this time, the legislation amalgamating the children detention schools had taken effect and the building was largely complete. In the interim, HIQA had adjusted its judgement framework so that standards were found to be 'compliant', 'substantially compliant', 'moderate non-compliant' or 'major non-compliant', with each judgement triggering action of a different level of priority. Against this framework, HIQA (2017) found two standards to be 'compliant' (education; statement of purpose), six standards were classified as 'moderate non-compliant' and two standards (healthcare; care of children) were classified as 'major non-compliant'. HIQA observed that the context continued to be one of 'major change', with a new Minister for Children and Youth Affairs, a new Board of Management, many new structures including governance arrangements, newly recruited staff and a new human resources department (HIQA, 2017, p 6). A new system of placement planning had been introduced, and a new electronic case management system to record and manage information was being developed. A training programme had been improved and a system of formal supervision had been introduced (HIQA, 2017, p 6).

During 2016, there was major disruption to the campus, which had led to very significant challenges to its continuing safe and secure operation. As HIQA noted:

> A major incident on the campus during 2016 resulted in a fire and extensive property damage. A number of reviews were commissioned in the latter half of 2016 and early 2017 as a result. The board was committed to the implementation of the recommendations of these reviews and an implementation oversight group had been established. (HIQA, 2017, p 6)

Despite the very difficult context, the inspection observed some positive elements. Children had access to advocacy services, they were given information about their rights, they were consulted and they were given choices. They were listened to and their complaints were taken seriously, although the complaints system was not robust. HIQA observed 'a positive atmosphere in the residential units and inspectors observed warm interaction between children and staff' (HIQA, 2017, p 7). They found that children received adequate emotional and psychological care, that their needs were assessed on admission and that there were improvements in care planning and the involvement of families. But the inspection also found 'some poor practice' in the management of challenging behaviour, with a number of instances of children spending 'prolonged periods of time in single separation', with a 'lack of robust management oversight' of these incidents a particular concern (HIQA, 2017, p 7). The inspection reported staff concern about the approach to behaviour management, noting that the serious incidents that had taken place in 2016 had led to the dissatisfaction of staff and calls for 'increased security and improved personal protective equipment (PPE) to cope with difficult situations that might arise in future' (HIQA, 2017, p 17).

In March 2018, an unannounced, full inspection of Oberstown took place involving seven inspectors over five days (HIQA, 2018). The result showed continued improvement in the standards assessed, with inspectors finding that of the 10 standards, three were 'compliant' (education; healthcare; and purpose and function), two were 'substantially compliant' (children's rights; and child protection) and five (care of children; planning; premises, safety and security; offending behaviour; and staffing and management) were deemed to be in the 'moderate non-compliant' category. For the first time, no standards were found to be in the 'major non-compliant' category. Reflecting this improved assessment, HIQA noted that Oberstown was enjoying a period of 'relative stability' following 'a succession of major changes within the campus over the previous years' (HIQA, 2018, p 6). It noted that the external reviews commissioned to support the development of the campus had been finalized and a group established to develop a comprehensive plan for the implementation of the recommendations. According to HIQA, 'of those recommendations directly relating to Oberstown there was evidence that many were implemented in full and work on the remainder was underway' (HIQA, 2018, p 6). The inspectors highlighted the adoption of the Oberstown Strategy in 2017 and noted a range of new service developments and appointments. They remarked on: 'significant improvements' in the area of healthcare; 'progress' in relation to premises, safety and security, children's rights and care of children; and 'improvements' with respect to the planning and review of children's care. A placement planning system, 'inclusive of all key stakeholders, external professionals and family members, as well as the child', was in place (HIQA, 2018, p 7). Although there were clear procedures in place for these, they were not always adhered to, however, and inspectors reported that 'external services were not consistently engaged in this [placement planning] system and this compromised planning for children's future after detention' (HIQA, 2018, p 7). While HIQA noted 'an improvement in the management of challenging behaviour and a reduction in the necessity for use of restrictive practices', it recorded 'deficits in the recording, monitoring and management oversight of restrictive practices, including single separation, physical intervention and the use of handcuffs' (HIQA, 2018, p 8). At the same time, it found improvements with respect to 'the management of risk' and 'evident focus at all levels of management on ensuring risk was effectively identified, assessed and managed' (HIQA, 2018, p 8). Support mechanisms available to staff had also increased since the previous inspection, but 'deficits were found in the provision of supervision and performance development for staff' (HIQA, 2018, p 9).

In 2019, an announced three-day inspection took place, focused in particular on the capacity and capability of the service and its quality and safety. HIQA found that of the eight standards assessed, five were 'compliant' (purpose and function; children's rights; child protection; education; and healthcare), one (offending behaviour) was 'substantially compliant' and two (staffing and management; and care of children) were 'moderate non-compliant' (HIQA, 2020). In a significant shift in emphasis, the inspection report opened for the first time with the views of young people the inspectors met during their inspection. According to HIQA: 'Young people told inspectors that they felt safe in Oberstown. They said that the staff and unit managers treated them fairly and they were well looked after. ... All young people who spoke with inspectors spoke highly of the staff team' (HIQA, 2020, p 6).

On restrictive practices, considered further in Chapter 7, young people reported that 'when issues arose or incidents occurred for them, staff provided them with the support to try to avoid periods of single separation or restraint' (HIQA, 2020, p 6). They welcomed getting 'three or four chances or prompts to take some time away' and told inspectors that staff talked to them about anger management and helped them to see how their behaviour could be different (HIQA, 2020, p 6). They also told inspectors that 'they had been provided with opportunities during their time in Oberstown that they had not experienced previously in their lives, and they felt that they would benefit from these opportunities after their release' from detention (HIQA, 2020, p 6). Their complaints related mainly to the remand units, which they said were 'run down', and they expressed concern about having fewer opportunities for engaging in activities when on remand where they had more time to think, which they found difficult (HIQA, 2020, p 7).

The report noted substantial improvements in the governance and management of Oberstown with clear lines of accountability, although supervision remained 'ineffective' (HIQA, 2020, p 11). While inspectors observed a 'marked improvement' in the recording of restrictive practices (HIQA, 2020, p 12), they highlighted that greater improvement was required with regard to ensuring that all forms of restrictive practices (such as walking a young person to their room) were recorded as such (HIQA, 2020, p 18). In terms of culture, the report noted 'a raised consciousness in staff to ensure the rights of young people who experienced restrictive procedures were promoted' (HIQA, 2020, p 17), and observed a commitment to learning and reviewing incidents, accidents and assaults and to improve the safety and quality of the service as a result (HIQA, 2020, p 13). Separately, HIQA reported 'a concerted effort ... to continuously improve the quality and delivery of available offending behaviour programmes to young people' (HIQA, 2020, p 13).

The most recent HIQA inspection took place in December 2020, during the COVID-19 global pandemic. This was an announced thematic inspection, which focused on children's rights (including complaints and advocacy), care planning and staffing and management issues. For the first time, HIQA found no areas of non-compliance, judging that Oberstown was 'compliant' in the area of children's rights and 'substantially compliant' in both care planning and staffing (HIQA, 2021). Inspectors were complimentary of the advocacy service, which promotes the participation of children in decision-making in Oberstown, and the effectiveness of the complaint mechanism. At the same time, HIQA noted the need for further improvements with regard to documenting staff supervision and placement planning (HIQA, 2021).

The maturing approach to inspection

This summary of inspection reports – from 2014 to 2020 – tells the story of an organization that has gone through significant change, with impact at every level. Despite substantial and positive progress across all material areas, full compliance with the standards needs to be embedded more fully in the care planning process to ensure that the rights of every child are routinely upheld, regardless of any variables. Despite ambition to make continued progress, it is nonetheless remarkable to note that the change achieved to date has taken place alongside a major building project, an amalgamation of policies and practices across three separate entities and the expansion of the campus to take responsibility for 16- and 17-year-olds from the prison estate.

Compliance with international children's rights standards is explored in more detail in the next chapter, but two concluding remarks need to be made here. The first is to note that there is, implicit in the inspection reports, an increasing maturity in the analysis of practice being undertaken in the inspection process. As Oberstown is the only facility of its kind in Ireland, it has taken time for the inspectors to build experience and understanding of the service and the context in which the inspection framework applies. Having undertaken five inspections of the new facility, the inspectors are now more familiar with the service, its policies and systems and have built up a level of understanding and appreciation of the issues and their context, year on year. The second and perhaps related point is that with this maturity – and indeed the improvements in the care provided to the children in detention – there is an apparent shift taking place as HIQA's expectations increase in line with this improved performance. As an obvious example, with every inspection, HIQA has called for reductions in the use of single separation. Despite the fact that the incidence and duration of single separation fell almost 80% between 2014 and 2020, the inspection reports continue to push for even greater reductions in the practice. Moreover, as an example of the maturity of the analysis, the 2019 inspection report drew attention to practices at the periphery of formal interventions, urging management to extend recording to the full continuum of the restrictive practice. In doing so, the inspectors are promoting an understanding of the coercive effect of such practices, which may not technically or typically be considered part of the intervention. Although Oberstown might complain that the inspection goalposts are being moved, it is also arguable that the HIQA inspection process has itself evolved to influence ongoing progressive improvements in the way detained children experience their rights. This is no more evident than in the elevated status, with every report, of the views and experiences of the children themselves. In line with children's rights standards, HIQA must also be encouraged to put children at the centre of their inspection methodology.

Conclusion

The previous chapters articulated national policy, highlighting the key goals to be achieved in the development of a specialist, child-centred detention centre for children under 18 years of age. This chapter sought to identify the key stages of that process, from an internal point of view, highlighting the areas in which reform was achieved. It is difficult, through retrospective analysis, to do justice to the challenges experienced in bringing about the necessary change documented here. This chapter sought to articulate, from different sources, the scale and complexity of the process involved in the delivery of key national policy goals in the establishment of a child-centred model of detention. The next chapters delve deeper again into the extent to which this change has produced detention that is consistent with children's rights standards.

6

Implementing Children's Rights in Detention

Introduction

Chapter 5 outlined the various stages of the reform process designed to create a unified and specialist model of detention for children. Building on this analysis, this chapter considers the extent to which the rights-based model of detention is currently implemented in Oberstown. It examines the measures taken to implement an approach that is child-centred and fulfils the rights of the child to provision, protection, participation, preparation and partnership in a model to advance the rights of children in detention.

Child-centred care

At the heart of an approach designed to advance children's rights in detention is the requirement to take account of the needs of the child – Article 37 of the United Nations Convention on the Rights of the Child (CRC) – and to ensure that the 'conditions and circumstances' ensure respect for their rights (Havana Rule 12). The international standards require 'individual assessments' of need and 'a multi-disciplinary approach' (CRC Committee, 2019a, p 18).

International standards recommend that on admission to detention, the child should be interviewed and a comprehensive assessment of their health, psychological, educational and social needs undertaken so that the child's type and level of care, including security, can be identified. A plan of educational and training programmes should be developed in accordance with the child's individual characteristics, taking account of the child's views (European Rule 62.6). Information about the child's identity, their legal guardians, the reasons for the commitment and the date and time of admission should be recorded (European Rule 62), along with details of the child's personal property, information about the child's history including any education or welfare needs, and with regard to the child's protection, 'any visible injuries or allegations of prior ill-treatment' and any information about the risk of self-harm or other health conditions that are relevant to the child's physical and mental wellbeing (European Rule 62).

In line with these standards, Oberstown is committed to decision-making that is informed by the child's best interests. To enable this approach, every child's current and emerging needs are assessed on arrival and an individual plan is put in place to fulfil those needs. This multi-disciplinary process, called the 'Oberstown Journey Through Care', is undertaken by care staff with the involvement of clinical services and it takes the form of an initial Placement Planning Meeting (PPM), which takes place within 72 hours of the child's arrival, and a second PPM, which takes place within 14 days. This process has two purposes. First, it enables specific care measures to be put in place to meet the identified needs of the child in line with a placement plan that ensures those needs are met while the child is in detention. Second, this represents the start of the process to build relationships between the staff and the child, promoting a positive and collaborative relationship on which the Oberstown model of care is based (Bamber et al, 2016b). More recently, the process has also begun to use the 'Outcome Stars' assessment tool, which is a suite of collaborative, person-centred, evidence-based assessment tools for measuring and supporting change when working with young people (https://www.outcomesstar.org.uk/). The introduction of the 'Justice Star' is currently being rolled out following a successful pilot in two residential units in 2020 (Oberstown, 2021).

Individual plans delivered through partnership

In line with the child-centred approach, the international standards recommend that an 'individual plan' is drawn up for each child so that they can, from the outset of their detention, 'make the best use of their time … to develop skills and competences that enable them to reintegrate into society' (European Rule 79.2). The plan should work towards the child's release, make provision for appropriate post-release measures (European Rule 79.3) and be updated regularly with the participation of the child, relevant outside agencies and as far as possible the child's parents or guardians (European Rule 79.4). In line with the *partnership* theme of the rights-based model, international standards advocate an interdisciplinary and multi-agency approach, integrated with 'wider social initiatives' for children, to ensure a holistic approach to continuity of care (European Rule 15). 'Specialised services' such as probation, counselling or supervision are important, along with 'effective inter-agency coordination' (CRC Committee, 2019a, p 18).

As explained in Chapter 5, Oberstown developed its own bespoke model of care in 2014 to provide a framework for all stages of a child's journey from their admission to release, ensuring their needs are met in a holistic, consistent and multi-disciplinary manner. Known as **C**are, **E**ducation, **H**ealth, **O**ffending behaviour and **P**reparation for leaving (CEHOP), the framework is based on the legislative requirement to provide children in detention with care, education, healthcare and measures to address their offending behaviour and promote their successful return to their community. Implementation of the CEHOP approach involves an integrated and coordinated way of working across all campus staff and services, underpinned by policies, procedures and systems that enable the recording and sharing of information. PPMs take place every five weeks to review the children's needs and the services and supports they require. A designated person chairs these meetings to ensure consistency in approach, engagement, attendance, recording and achieving agreed actions (Oberstown, 2020, p 12). Separately, multi-disciplinary meetings take place weekly. In line with the *preparation* theme, a key principle behind the CEHOP framework and the Journey Through Care process is that planning for a child's release begins on the day they arrive in Oberstown. This aims to maximize the time in detention to address the child's unmet needs and ensure all necessary measures are taken to ensure the child's successful return to the community. Reflecting the importance of partnership, involving external agencies in placement planning from the outset promotes continuity of care both during and after detention, while family participation in placement planning aims to ensure that the family is both involved and supported in the process.

Provision

All children are entitled to have their basic needs met and for children in detention, who have frequently faced particular disadvantage in this area, it is particularly important that they are provided with their rights to health, education and development (Nowak, 2019).

Health

The right to healthcare is a fundamental right of all children, who should enjoy the highest attainable standard of health under the CRC (Article 24). It is especially important for children deprived of liberty, who often have pre-existing health conditions, making the provision of healthcare in detention crucial (Nowak, 2019, p 117). To this end, children's rights standards require not only that every child is examined by a health professional on admission, they must also receive 'adequate physical and mental health care throughout his or her stay', with access to facilities and services that meet all the requirements of health (Havana Rule 31).

A significant development in Oberstown has been multi-disciplinary healthcare, along with the provision of modern, clinical facilities. The health and wellbeing suite, in the new building, is managed by a clinical nurse manager, who works with a general and a psychiatric nurse, as well as a social care worker in the provision of healthcare. The Havana Rules provide that healthcare should be provided, where possible, by community health services (Havana Rule 49) and be safeguarded according to 'recognised medical standards' in the community (European Rule 69.2). Record keeping is vital (European Rule 72.1) and drugs should be 'authorised and carried out by qualified medical personnel' (Havana Rule 55). In Oberstown, access to a general practitioner, dentist and physiotherapist is available on demand, with treatment provided on site through access to community services. Children with acute or special needs have access to community-based hospital services as required (Oberstown, 2020, p 10). A multi-professional team, known as the Assessment Consultation Therapy Service (ACTS), is located on site, consisting of a psychologist, a drugs counsellor and a speech and language therapist. ACTS is a national specialized clinical service, of the Child and Family Agency, Tusla, that provides multi-disciplinary clinical and therapeutic interventions to children with acute or specific needs ensuring that they receive appropriate care quickly in line with the international standards. As it is part of a national service, as a national service, children can link in with the ACTS team in their local area, on release. In addition, the National Forensic Mental Health Service provides psychiatric services to children in Oberstown, in an increasingly integrated and multi-disciplinary approach to meeting children's mental healthcare needs (Oberstown, 2020, p 12).

The international standards require that children in detention should receive preventive healthcare and education, with the prevention of suicide and self-harm a priority, particularly during 'initial detention, segregation and other recognized high-risk periods' and for those children who are 'particularly vulnerable' (European Rule 70.2). Oberstown staff are trained in the use of STORM (Skills Training on Risk Management), an evidence-based programme designed to improve the confidence, knowledge and skills of frontline staff in relation to self-harm and suicide prevention among staff and young people (https://stormskillstraining.com/). By 2019, 94% of frontline staff had been trained in the STORM approach (Oberstown, 2020, p 40). A range of health education programmes are also provided to children. These include: the REAL U programme (Relationships Explored and Life Uncovered), which aims to equip children with the skills, knowledge and confidence to develop healthy relationships and delay the onset of early sexual activity; and the Teen Parents Support Toolkit, which aims to support staff and young people during young pregnancy and parenthood (Oberstown, 2019b, p 22).

According to the European Rules, healthcare should be part of an integrated multi-disciplinary programme of care, with healthcare professionals working closely with teachers and other staff (European Rule 74) so that any illness or condition that may hinder a child's reintegration can be addressed (Havana Rule 52). In line with this guidance, healthcare in Oberstown is integrated into the CEHOP model as part of the multi-disciplinary approach to care. Healthcare and clinical staff attend the PPMs alongside care staff, teachers and others to ensure health is also taken into account in identifying and reviewing progress in meeting the goals set out in the child's individual placement plan (Oberstown, 2020, p 12).

Education

Education is a basic right for all children (Article 28, CRC) and children in detention are entitled to education suited to their needs and abilities and designed to prepare them for their return to society (Havana Rule 38). Education should include access to state examinations and vocational training, including in occupations likely to prepare them for future employment (CRC Committee, 2019a, p 15).

In terms of delivery, education should ideally be provided in community schools but regardless, it should be provided by 'qualified teachers through programmes integrated with the (national) education system' in order to ensure continuity after release (Havana Rule 38 and European Rule 78). Special attention should be given to children with particular needs or learning difficulties (Havana Rule 39), with no age limit (Havana Rule 40). Qualifications awarded in detention should not identify that they were acquired in detention (Havana Rule 41). Children should have access to suitable educational and recreational reading material, which they should be encouraged and enabled to access (Havana Rule 42).

Oberstown has a state-of-the-art school, separate from the residential facilities, so that children can replicate the community experience of walking to and from school every day. Classrooms and workshops are large and available for both academic and vocational training, with a small pupil:teacher ratio of 3:1 (CEB, 2019, p 59) and an intensive, focused learning experience. The Education and Training Board (ETB), which has responsibility for education and training outside of the formal school system on a national basis, is responsible for the management of the school. While this retains an important connection to the national curriculum and the mainstream education system, it has at times made it challenging to ensure effective oversight of education by the Oberstown Board of Management, which has responsibility for education under the Children Act 2001. In 2019, a Department of Education inspection highlighted particularly acute concerns about the length of the school day, the range and choice of subjects on offer and the effectiveness of education and lesson planning (Department of Education and Skills, 2019). In 2020, stronger school leadership, supported by the ETB, enabled significant reforms to take effect, addressing these concerns and promoting a more integrated approach with campus vocational and activity programmes. A proposed legislative amendment to appoint an ETB representative to the Oberstown Board of Management aims to improve the integration and coherence of the approach further. Separately, work is under way to agree national curriculum objectives for children in detention in order to ensure that the education they receive meets their needs both academically and vocationally, improving their life chances on their return to the community.

In Oberstown, all children attend school regardless of age and ability. They are supported to learn, undertake state examinations and pursue different vocational training opportunities in line with their individual education plans. From an academic perspective, outcomes are measured by participation in formal state examinations. For example, in June 2019, 13 young people undertook the Junior Certificate in subjects including English, maths, art, music, materials technology (metal), materials technology (wood), home economics and environmental and social studies. Nine students sat at least five subjects at this level and a further two sat the Leaving Certificate, with each student taking exams in three subjects (Oberstown, 2020, p 10). For other children, improved literacy and numeracy is the priority, with the ultimate objective for all children being to equip them for their successful return to the community.

Vocational training programmes were introduced to the campus in 2019 with a view to providing children with accredited and practical employment skills, in preparation for future work opportunities. These include SafePass, a mandatory health and safety awareness programme for those who want to work in the construction industry. The Coffee Education Programme, delivered with Java Republic, provides intensive and certified barista training to young people, equipping them with the knowledge and confidence to go through a potential trial in a café (Oberstown, 2020, p 19). Certified training to become a fitness instructor is also available on site, using a blended teaching approach facilitated by the Oberstown school and activities team and Image Fitness Training, which provides fitness courses across Ireland. All the young people who successfully qualify from this programme are guaranteed a job interview for a role as a fitness instructor once they leave detention (Oberstown 2020, pp 20–1). This is an area marked for further development in the years ahead (Oberstown, 2021).

Development

Programmes and activities available to children deprived of liberty should be designed to promote the child's development (European Rule 76.1), meet the child's individual needs in line with their 'age, gender, social and cultural background, stage of development and type of offence committed' and 'be consistent with proven professional standards based on research findings and best practices in the field' (European Rule 76.2). They should focus on 'education, personal and social development, vocational training, rehabilitation and preparation for release' and include education and vocational training, individual and group therapy, social skills, physical education and sport, leisure time, creative hobbies and restorative justice programmes (European Rule 77). Activities outside the institution, such as on day leave, should be part of this programme, which should also look to prepare children for release or after care (European Rule 77).

Children deprived of liberty must be 'guaranteed the benefit of meaningful activities and programmes ... to promote and sustain their health and self-respect, to foster their sense of responsibility and encourage those attitudes and skills that will assist them in developing their potential as members of society' (Havana Rule 12). Children should spend as many hours a day outside their sleeping accommodation as are necessary for an adequate level of social interaction and should be able to access 'meaningful activities on weekends and holidays' (European Rule 80). Daily exercise, recreation and leisure are important (Havana Rule 47).

Oberstown has a large gym, an indoor sports hall and two large pitches that facilitate a varied activities programme that complements the school curriculum. The activities programme, which is constantly evolving, creates a range of opportunities for children to get involved in recreational, educational and vocational activities, typically drawing on resources in the community to inspire and develop children's skills and interests. The activities programme is increasingly integrated with the education and other priorities of the Oberstown approach, by offering accredited programmes designed to meet children's needs, develop skills and provide recreational and learning opportunities. In recent years, Oberstown has supported children to achieve the President's Award ('Gaisce') at bronze, silver or gold level in each of the following four categories: community involvement; personal skill; physical recreation; and adventure journey (https://www.gaisce.ie/). This award can be tailored to children's interests and provide motivation for them to meet personal targets, improve skills and give something back to their community. In 2018, the President of Ireland, Michael D. Higgins, visited Oberstown to present children with their silver and bronze awards (Oberstown, 2019b, p 25) and, in 2020, a child in Oberstown achieved the first gold award (Oberstown, 2021).

The development of programmes and supports is an ongoing focus in Oberstown, with new initiatives coming onstream annually. Delivered in partnership with staff, the children themselves and external organizations and providers, mapping them onto the Outcomes Star assessment tool, within the placement planning framework, ensures Oberstown meets the needs of each individual child. While preference is given to evidence-based programmes in this regard, their effectiveness in Oberstown has not yet been evaluated. While the approach is to make individual interventions available in response to each child's needs – in keeping with child-centred care – no tailored programmes have yet been introduced to respond, for instance, to the particular needs of Traveller children, children with experience of state care or girls.

Family contact

International standards recognize that children in detention have the 'right to maintain contact with family through correspondence and visits save in exceptional circumstances' (Article 37, CRC). Arrangements must allow children to 'maintain and develop family relationships in as normal a manner as possible' (European Rule 84) and visits should be regular, frequent and confidential (European Rule 61). Communication between the child and their lawyer should be unrestricted and confidential at all times (CRC Committee, 2019a, p 16). Adequate communication between the child in detention and the 'outside world' is 'an integral part of the right to fair and humane treatment' and 'essential to the preparation of juveniles for their return to society' (European Rule 59). In addition to visits, children should be able to 'leave detention facilities' for home visits and other reasons and be able to 'keep themselves informed regularly of the news' by reading, having access to radio, television and film, and through the visits of the organizations in which the children have interest (Rule 62).

Oberstown's approach to family contact and visits is flexible and frequent (HIQA, 2018, p 32), led by the needs and circumstances of the child, as part of the child's individual placement plan. The visiting suite enables either screened visits (in specially designed rooms) or unscreened visits, depending on the level of risk involved. Practical arrangements are in place to support family visits, such as linking with public transport (HIQA, 2020, pp 31–2) and, overall, the number of family visits has increased significantly in recent years (CEB, 2019, p 61). Telephone calls are permitted in line with the child's individual placement plan, which, depending on the circumstances, will make provision for permitted absence with a view to maintaining positive relationships between the child and their family, promoting their successful return home. Communication – in person, on the telephone or via a video conference – between child and lawyer is confidential and unrestricted and staff also communicate regularly with family members to keep them up to date. At the same time, children without family or whose family relationships have broken down may not enjoy the support of these relationships and alternatives need to be found to ensure all children benefit from an equivalent level of support. Moreover, the COVID-19 pandemic created challenges for physical visits and, during various levels of public health restrictions throughout 2020 and 2021, visits took place over videoconferencing technology, such as Zoom (Lynch and Kilkelly, 2021). This had the benefit of enabling children to maintain contact with family and to see extended relatives, their homes and their pets, for instance. It also allowed family living further away to have greater contact than would usually be possible. Despite these advantages, however, the return of physical visits was very welcome and a hybrid model is now in place to retain the benefits of both approaches (Oberstown, 2021).

Participation

The right of the child to be heard (Article 12, CRC) is a fundamental right of all children and a model to advance children's rights in detention must enable children's participation in decision-making in matters that affect them. Further to the National Strategy on Children and Young People's Participation in Decision Making 2015–2020 (Department of Children, 2015), Oberstown adopted its own participation strategy in 2017. This strategy aims to ensure that children are 'appropriately consulted' about matters concerning them and are supported to participate in decision-making about their individual care, in their residential units and at campus level, through the Campus Council, where they can provide feedback and raise concerns with senior management about matters that affect them (Oberstown, 2020, p 16).

In 2018, Oberstown appointed a full-time advocacy officer, who has responsibility for promoting children's views to be heard in matters that affect them and embedding a children's rights approach into decision-making at all levels (Oberstown, 2019b, p 24). This role has enabled a step change in the promotion of children's voices in decision-making in all areas and has 'much improved the transparency and speed with which young people's concerns and or issues with regard to their care [are] managed' (HIQA, 2020, p 19). In addition to advancing children's rights in detention, the improved participation of children in decision-making has also supported Oberstown to improve its performance against the national standards, a feature particularly commended by HIQA in its 2020 inspection (HIQA, 2021). The important and innovative nature of this approach makes it worthy of analysis in some detail here.

Individual decision-making in Oberstown

In Oberstown, not only are children invited to attend PPMs (HIQA, 2018, p 13), they also receive enhanced support to contribute to the process given the formal and potentially intimidating nature of such meetings (HIQA, 2017, p 11). The system for reviewing and progressing placement plans involving children directly, is considered to work well and children's attendance at these meetings ensures they are actively involved in their own care, taking responsibility for meeting their own needs where possible (HIQA, 2020, p 16). Children report feeling 'very positive' about their involvement in their care planning, feeling 'involved' in this process and 'decisions made about them' (HIQA, 2021, p 7).

In November 2019, 35 children were consulted by the advocacy officer about their understanding of CEHOP and the placement planning process (Oberstown, 2020). The advocacy officer found that detailed understanding of CEHOP was 'low' among those consulted, with fewer than 10% knowing exactly what was involved. On the other hand, their understanding of placement planning was 'high', with 97% aware of the process and the timing of their PPMs. There was 'good' understanding that the PPM process is optional and more than 90% attended meetings regularly by choice. All consulted about attending PPMs were happy with the process and saw the meetings as 'central to their care on Campus' (Oberstown, 2020, p 18). This was reinforced in 2020 when, during the HIQA inspection, children were 'very positive about their involvement in planning for their care', saying they felt 'involved in this process and in decisions that were made about them' (HIQA, 2021, p 7). One child told inspectors that they 'looked forward to their Placement Planning Meeting, because it gave them a focus, some goals and a timeframe to achieve these goals' (HIQA, 2021, p 7).

More generally, children in Oberstown are constantly interacting with staff, especially their keyworkers, about decisions that affect their lives both in detention and with regard to their return home or onward placement. Informal interaction with staff is a critical part of the child-centred model, through which staff seek to support and challenge the children's attitudes and behaviour (Bamber et al, 2016b). This 'support and advocacy' is valued by the children themselves (HIQA, 2018, p 18). Staff engagement with the children enables their priorities in relation to their care to be explored through an assigned keyworker and unit staff (HIQA, 2020, p 16).

Unit decision-making in Oberstown

The commitment in the Participation Strategy is that children's views are heard during meetings with the unit manager, an approach that is being implemented in all the units by the sharing of best practice. For example, one residential unit operates a restorative model, proactively engaging with children with 'excellent communication and collaborative decision making', although in other units, meetings are inconsistent or unstructured (HIQA, 2018, p 14). A further recent initiative in the residential units has been the development of 'unit charters', setting out expectations, agreed between the children and staff, around their behaviour and relationships (Oberstown, 2020, p 16). This is an important, child-led approach to promoting positive relationships that ensures they have a right to a say about their life in the residential units.

Campus decision-making in Oberstown

In line with the Participation Strategy, a Campus Council was established in 2017, evolving from the School Council, as a campus-wide forum that enables children to have a say in decisions that affect them, hearing directly from key decision-makers on areas of importance, chosen by them, in a safe environment. Children are elected to the Council by their peers and their meetings are held regularly and recorded, with senior managers and others invited to attend on matters that concern them (HIQA, 2018, p 13). The council agrees the agenda prior to each meeting and members provide feedback to other children on campus, informing them of decisions made and the reasons for those decisions (Oberstown, 2020, p 16). In 2018, for instance, the council discussed a range of matters including: activities; mobility trips; the possibility of having a sports day, like regular schools; and a Christmas concert. The council surveyed young people about their 'tuck bags', changing the contents as a result to include more items that young people wanted (Oberstown, 2019b, p 23). The Campus Council also extends invitations to guests from the community who come and speak to them about topics of interest. In 2018, the council invited the Minister for Children to meet with them (HIQA, 2018, p 13) and in 2019, the council met with a representative from the President's Awards ('Gaisce') who explained the awards in order to support their participation (Oberstown, 2020, p 16). The Campus Council also organizes children to give back to the local community, through fundraising for charity, and other initiatives.

The Campus Council enables formal consultation to take place with children on matters of wider interest and importance to the campus. In addition to the consultation about placement planning undertaken in 2019, children are regularly consulted and surveyed about their life and treatment on campus, including surveys about food options, generating ideas for decorating the visiting areas, a vote on television channels in the residential units and ideas for programme planning. Children were also involved in 2019 in the development of the Oberstown Children's Rights Policy Framework, as part of the strategic planning process, and they acted as the advisory group for the Global Study on Children Deprived of Liberty (Oberstown, 2020, p 18). Significantly, in 2021, children were involved in the process to recruit the new Oberstown Director. Working collaboratively with a large group of their peers to identify what traits they considered important in a new Director, two representatives then participated in a formal interview of the final two candidates for the role, posing questions and scoring their responses in a formal and weighted part of the interview process.

Overall, the participation of children in decision-making in Oberstown has been developing year on year to the point that there are now 'several systems in place to ensure the children's voices were heard and that their concerns or complaints were valued' (HIQA, 2021, p 10). In 2020, a Board of Management Young People Committee was established to meet regularly with young people so that children are heard directly by members of the board on matters of importance to them (HIQA, 2021, p 11). This builds on the direct engagement between the Director and young people (HIQA, 2017, p 11), which has helped to reinforce the importance to all staff of hearing children's views. While important in its own right, the increased participation of children in decision-making, and the extent to which their views are sought and taken into account, also represent a continuous cultural shift towards the embedding of the child at the heart of decision-making in detention, meaning that it is a central component of the rights-based approach to child-centred care.

Information and complaints

A fundamental element of rights-based detention is that children have a right to information about their rights (Article 42, CRC). They should be provided with a copy of the rules of the institution and details of their rights and obligations should be 'explained in a language and manner that the juvenile understands' (European Rule 62.3). Understanding and knowledge of human rights must be promoted among children themselves, through the school curriculum and in other ways (CRC Committee, 2003, p 13).

An effective complaint mechanism is essential to rigorous monitoring and oversight and according to the Committee on the Rights of the Child (the CRC Committee) (2019a, p 16), every child should have the right to make requests or complaints to the authorities, without censorship, and be informed of the response without delay. The CRC Committee is clear that 'children need to know their rights and to know about and have easy access to request and complaints mechanisms' (2019a, p 16). This is reinforced by the European Rules, which provide in addition that complaint procedures must be 'simple and effective' (European Rule 122.1). Mediation and restorative conflict resolution must be given priority as a means of resolving complaints or meeting requests and if a request is denied or a complaint rejected, reasons must be provided, along with the right to appeal to an independent authority (European Rules 122.2 and 122.3). The Havana Rules recommend that an independent office (for example, an ombudsman) should be able to receive and investigate complaints by children deprived of liberty (Havana Rules 75 and 77).

Although information was previously provided to children verbally on admission (HIQA, 2017, p 10), this led to inconsistent practice and children's understanding (HIQA, 2018, p 12). Oberstown now has a young person's handbook, developed in consultation with young people, which provides them with the information they need on life in detention and how they can raise a concern or make a complaint. Information about their rights is also 'prominently displayed on noticeboards throughout' (HIQA, 2021, p 10). The advocacy officer meets every child following admission and provides them with a copy of the booklet, which explains campus programmes, the CEHOP model of care and the role of the clinical team (ACTS) and other staff. They are also provided with information on how they can access information about them that is kept on file, how to access Empowering People in Care (EPIC) – the Campus visiting advocacy service – and the Ombudsman for Children, and how to make a complaint (Oberstown, 2020, p 16). Reports indicate that both EPIC and the Ombudsman for Children's Office (OCO) have engaged actively with children who are supported to meet with them and raise matters of concern (HIQA, 2018, p 16).

For some time, concerns were expressed that the Oberstown complaints process in place was 'not robust' (HIQA, 2017, p 11) although it was known to and used by young people who, for instance, made 74 complaints in the 12 months prior to one inspection (HIQA, 2017, p 11). Matters that were the subject of complaint around this time included their treatment by staff and, in serious cases, this resulted in disciplinary action being taken against the staff in question (HIQA, 2017, p 12). However, children did not have faith in the complaints process (HIQA, 2017, p 12) and problems were experienced in prioritizing complaints over child protection concerns, with no analysis conducted of the complaints received (HIQA, 2017, p 13). By 2018, although the complaints process was 'widely used', it was still not considered 'sufficiently robust to provide assurances that all complaints were responded to and managed effectively' and the records failed to show satisfactory follow-up and closing out of the issues (HIQA, 2018, p 14). A survey of children, carried out by the advocacy officer in March 2019, found that 87.5% of them knew what to do if they wanted to make a complaint. Of those who had made a recent complaint, however, there were mixed views as to whether the process was fair. This situation has continued to improve with the sustained attention to the process by the advocacy officer who now has responsibility for the management of complaints. For instance, HIQA found in 2019 that children were reported to be 'well aware of their right to complain' and felt issues they raised, with regard to the management of incidents, for instance, were listened to (HIQA, 2020, p 7). In December 2020, this had shifted to a level of satisfaction that complaints raised had been addressed (HIQA, 2021, pp 6–7). In addition, a review of the records found that the outcomes of the complaints were clearly recorded, with an indication of whether the children were satisfied or not with the outcomes. There was also evidence that the children's complaints were taken seriously and addressed promptly and that audits had been completed when patterns emerged (HIQA, 2021, p 11). These improvements resulted in this area of campus operations being judged 'compliant' with the relevant standard for the first time and this was augmented further in 2021 with these matters being brought directly to the board of management on a monthly basis.

The Ombudsman for Children's Office (OCO) offers an independent, external complaints mechanism, and its monthly outreach visits to Oberstown, established in 2017, ensure that this service is accessible to children in detention (OCO, 2018, p 34). The Ombudsman's 2019 annual report indicated that 6% of complaints came from the justice sector (it is not clear whether all came from detention) and the case study provided indicates that the OCO can secure information for children about their future that might not otherwise be available (OCO, 2020a, p 63). Important measures are in place to ensure that the service is brought to the attention of children on their admission to detention and children are alerted when the OCO visits the campus, when they can meet with them privately to discuss concerns not addressed through internal channels. This increased visibility meant that 40 children engaged with the OCO in 2018, a service that is now, according to the Ombudsman for Children, firmly embedded in Oberstown (OCO, 2019, p 32). A variety of issues are raised by children, including: time away from the campus (including home visits), behaviour management issues and education. In general, these concerns are brought to the attention of the management and/or school principal and are quickly and informally resolved (OCO, 2018, p 34).

Preparation

The CRC (Article 40(1)) places a strong focus on the need to ensure that time in detention is spent preparing a child for successful return to their community. Standards require that children in detention are:

> guaranteed a variety of meaningful activities and interventions according to an individual overall plan that aims at progression through less restrictive regimes and preparation for release and reintegration into society. These activities and interventions shall foster their physical and mental health, self-respect and sense of responsibility and develop attitudes and skills that will prevent them from re-offending. (European Rule 50.1)

The European Rules require provision for 'the possibility of early release' (European Rule 49.2), so that children are assisted in 'making the transition to life in the community' via special interventions, including 'partial or conditional release combined with effective social support' as part of a child's individual plan (European Rule 100). In line with the partnership theme, this requires relevant agencies and services to work together, from the beginning of the detention period, to enable children to re-establish themselves in the community on release by assisting their return to their family, finding accommodation for them, enabling their access to continuing education or training, finding employment for them, referring them to social care and healthcare agencies and providing financial assistance (European Rule 102.1). Such community-based services shall be supported to access children prior to their release and be obliged to provide 'effective and timely pre-release assistance' (European Rules 102.2 and 102.3).

In addition to the range of educational and developmental programmes available in Oberstown, children's preparation rights are also addressed through their participation in individual and group offending behaviour programmes, as part of a multi-disciplinary, developmentally appropriate approach to their placement. Placement Planning Meetings review progress in the implementation of key milestones relating to the 'offending behaviour' pillar of CEHOP, and also consider what measures are required to facilitate the child's successful return home or transfer to prison. As explained in Chapter 4, this may involve making proposals to the Director for permitted absence to return home or engage in education or training, or a mobility trip to support transition to independent living. The involvement of external agencies may also facilitate the child's transfer from detention to the community or indeed to prison should their sentence continue beyond the age of 18 (or 18 years and six months in certain circumstances) (section 155 of the Children Act 2001) (Oberstown, 2018, p 18). In the latter situation, a prison representative attends the PPM to help support the child's transition to prison and a Pathways programme was piloted in 2018 as a means of assisting children in their preparation for leaving Oberstown. Following a positive evaluation in 2019, sessions to familiarize staff with the Pathways material were undertaken and the programme was introduced as a keyworking framework for all young people (Oberstown, 2020, p 15).

The Youth Justice Strategy 2021–2027 commits to building on existing procedures and practices to promote 'continuity of work done in Oberstown' for those who transition to prison (Department of Justice, 2021, p 27), although further work needs to take place to ensure the developmentally appropriate treatment of young people over 18 years in the prison system (Costello, 2015). The appointment of a Probation Officer to Oberstown in 2018 enhanced the approach to offending behaviour (Oberstown, 2019b), with the delivery of offending behaviour programmes in partnership with the Probation Service (Oberstown, 2020).

Oberstown offers a range of developmental and therapeutic activities that seek to serve multiple purposes depending on the needs and circumstances of the individual child. Programmes meet the child's health and wellbeing needs while addressing the factors associated with their offending behaviour. They provide children with an opportunity to learn practical skills that will support their return to the community and reduce the likelihood of reoffending, while group and individual programmes aim to develop skills such as victim empathy, dealing with impulsive behaviours and reducing misuse of drugs and alcohol (Oberstown, 2020, pp 12–14). For instance, the Victim Empathy Programme 'What Have I Done?' is designed to promote empathy in children who have hurt others through their actions and it challenges them to face the harm they have caused and consider what they can do to help put things right (Oberstown, 2020, p 15).

Programmes also support positive behaviour development. For instance, the Decider Life Skills Programme, based on cognitive behavioural therapy, is an approach that uses skills that are effective, fun, memorable and easy to use to develop effective coping skills and build resilience. The emphasis is on helping young people to deal with impulsive behaviours. This programme was delivered 12 times throughout 2019 to both children on remand and those on detention orders and on 10 occasions it was delivered as a group-work intervention, with two programmes delivered in a one-to-one setting based on the children's needs. In total, 35 children undertook the Programme in 2019 (Oberstown, 2020, p 15).

In addition to relationship education and parenting skills, programmes teach children life-saving first aid, including managing a stab wound or drug overdose through the Street Doctors programme (Oberstown, 2019b, p 22). A significant number of these programmes are delivered by external organizations who partner with Oberstown in an approach that strengthens the connection between Oberstown and the community to mutual benefit (Oberstown, 2019b, pp 26–7). For instance, the Crinan Drug Relapse Prevention Programme is delivered by a community organization as a group-work intervention that aims to teach participants how to examine the triggers for and the consequences of their drug/alcohol use (Oberstown, 2020, p 15). Young people are supported to develop strategies that help them effectively manage and overcome any stressors or triggers in their environment that may cause a relapse (Oberstown, 2020, p 15). Similarly, the Anti-Violence Restorative Practice Training programme (ART) is based on restorative practice, delivered in collaboration with the Tallaght West Childhood Development Initiative on a residential unit basis (Oberstown, 2020, p 15). The programme enables participants to deal with potentially violent situations in new and creative ways. Workshops use the shared experiences of participants, interactive exercises, games and role-plays to examine the ways in which the participants respond to situations where injustice, prejudice, frustration and anger can lead to aggressive behaviour and violence. The aim of the programme is to start building cooperation, community, self-esteem and trust in the group, and to introduce skills in conflict resolution, communication and anger management (Oberstown, 2020, p 15).

Work on offending behaviour has been improving in recent years and, according to HIQA in 2019, this was a result of a 'concerted effort' to 'continuously improve the quality and delivery of available offending behaviour programmes' (HIQA, 2020, p 13). HIQA noted that a review of the programmes had been undertaken by the young person's programme manager in 2019, identifying a significant increase in the participation of children in such programmes, finding their delivery 'successful and worthwhile' (HIQA, 2020, p 13). An outstanding recommendation of that review is the need to identify a 'tool for the effective assessment of young people's progress' while in detention (HIQA, 2020, p 13) and this ties with the proposed inclusion in the Youth Justice Strategy of a commitment to develop a methodology for measuring outcomes for children in detention (Department of Justice, 2021). The Outcome Stars approach adds clear value here (Oberstown, 2021).

An important part of the preparation theme of rights relates to the importance of ensuring a strong connection is maintained with the 'outside world' in order to facilitate children's return to their community. In this regard, an extensive range of activity takes place in Oberstown connecting the child with the 'outside world'. A number of organizations are involved in the delivery of the activity and other programmes, including those that provide mentoring, advocacy and therapeutic and restorative interventions (Oberstown, 2019b, pp 26–7). For instance, Street Law is a programme delivered by trainee solicitors designed to provide young people with an understanding of the law as it applies to their lives and better equip them in their dealings with, and understanding of, the legal system to help them develop critical thinking and communication skills (Oberstown, 2020, p 23). Individual visitors – from the world of sport and the arts for instance – also undertake structured engagement and ad hoc visits to the campus, acting as important role models for young people seeking to move away from offending behaviour.

Conclusion

This chapter sought to evaluate the extent to which the key elements of the children's rights model of detention were being fulfilled in Oberstown as part of its child-centred approach. The chapter considered the international standards that support this approach, with an emphasis on the key rights themes of provision, participation and preparation. As the analysis shows, these elements of the children's rights model are already evident in the Oberstown approach insofar as services are now in place to provide for children's rights in key areas of health, education and development. The child-centred approach is evident too from the individualized assessment of need and the multi-disciplinary placement planning process. It is with regard to fulfilment of the child's participation rights, however, that the transformative effects of the rights-based approach are coming into view. As children become more visible in decision-making at all levels, a cultural shift towards the rights-based approach has begun to occur. Similarly, the value of fulfilling partnership rights is also beginning to emerge. As the Oberstown experience shows, collaboration, interagency working and the coordination of services, supports and programmes, within and outside of detention, however challenging to achieve, have the potential to truly unlock a rights-based approach to the care of children in detention.

7

Children's Rights to Protection from Harm

Introduction

Chapter 6 considered the extent to which Oberstown Children Detention Campus has implemented the rights-based model of detention. While noting the progress made in the advancement of children's rights to child-centred care, provision of need and preparation for leaving, the chapter concluded by noting the potentially transformative effects of fulfilling children's rights under the themes of participation and partnership.

This chapter notes that protection rights are fundamental to children's rights in detention in two ways. First, they relate to children's need for protection with respect to trauma or injury experienced prior to coming to Oberstown. Second, they concern children's right to protection from harm while in detention, including measures taken to protect themselves or others from injury. In exploring this important and challenging area, this chapter pays particular attention to restrictive practices such as separation and restraint, which have, as Chapter 2 noted, continued to threaten children's protection rights around the world. In this context, this chapter identifies the measures taken to improve children's rights to protection in Oberstown, highlighting some of the steps that have helped the transition towards a more rights-compliant approach.

Safeguarding

Every child in detention has a right to be protected from harm and ill-treatment – under Article 19 of the United Nations Convention on the Rights of the Child (CRC) – and in light of the fact that children can be 'highly vulnerable', especially during the initial period of detention (European Rule 109), states are required to take measures to 'protect their physical and mental integrity and foster their well-being' (European Rule 52.1). Particular care must be taken of children who have experienced physical, mental or sexual abuse (European Rule 52.2) and measures must be in place to identify, report and follow up instances of maltreatment (Articles 19 and 39, CRC).

Oberstown complies with the national legislative safeguarding framework, based on the Children First Act 2015, and has an established system in place for the reporting, referral and follow-up of instances of harm and ill-treatment. A range of measures are in place to 'safeguard children and protect them from abuse' and safeguarding training is efficient and regular (HIQA, 2018, p 28). A full-time social worker performs the role of 'designated liaison person' to whom all referrals are made for onward reporting to the national authority – Tusla, the Child and Family Agency. This relates to both incidents of harm or ill-treatment that take place in Oberstown and those that have taken place prior to arrival. For instance, children who have injuries on admission as a result of alleged police ill-treatment will be supported to make the appropriate complaint to the policing ombudsman (the Garda Síochána Ombudsman Commission) as well as have those concerns reported to Tusla. Concerns have been expressed at the pace of Tusla's response to child protection concerns made with respect to children in Oberstown, compared with children in the community (HIQA, 2020, p 28). Separately, the absence of a Tusla nominee from the Board of Management for long periods has not helped address these matters (HIQA, 2018, p 30). Safeguarding practice has continued to improve in Oberstown, with improvements in technical systems bringing about increasing transparency. According to HIQA in 2019, 'although there were examples of practice which fell outside campus policy and were being addressed, the opportunities for unsafe practice to go unidentified and unmanaged were few' (HIQA, 2020, p 19).

A child who feels unsafe in detention has an individual crisis plan to support their placement, and work is under way to advance a more integrated approach in this area. All children are met on admission by the designated liaison person, who explains their role and the supports provided; this information is also set out in the Young Person's Booklet. An internal survey of children was undertaken by the advocacy officer in March 2019 when 97.5% of those surveyed reported feeling safe on their first night in detention. Asked how safe they felt in Oberstown, 85% said that they felt 'very safe', a further 10% said they felt safe sometimes while 5% said they felt unsafe sometimes. All children (100%) responded that they had never felt bullied or threatened by another child, whereas 10% reported feeling bullied or threatened by a staff member. Children reported a range of people when asked who they would turn to for help, including: unit staff (62.5%), family (27.5%), a senior manager (22.5%) or an advocate (17.5%). However, 25% said they would not tell anyone.[1]

Restrictive practices

The right of the child to protection from harm and respect for dignity also applies to the use of restrictive practices such as separation or restraint, which can present risks to children's safety and wellbeing. The timing and nature of searches can also impact on children's rights to protection from harm and whether children feel safe, as can the use of handcuffs.

Searches

According to international standards, detailed procedures must be in place to govern searches of 'juveniles, staff, visitors and premises', and the law should set out when and in what form a search is permissible (European Rule 89.1). Staff should be trained to carry out searches effectively and with respect for personal dignity and possessions (European Rule 89.4). The child's privacy must be respected 'as far as possible' and the search should be carried out by staff of the same gender, with 'intimate' examinations conducted by a medical practitioner and only justified in exceptional circumstances (European Rule 89.2).

Oberstown conducts a personal search of every child on admission, in a manner that respects the children's right to dignity, privacy and wellbeing. Outside of this, personal searches are only approved for use as a measure of last resort where there is reasonable cause to believe that a person (a visitor or child) may have on them an item likely to pose a danger to the safety, health or wellbeing of themselves or of others on campus. Intimate searches are not conducted, and general searches are not routinely used in Oberstown. Where they occur, they are recorded on the individual's case file, although these data have yet to be collated at a Campus level for the purpose of external scrutiny.

Physical intervention

In light of the risks posed to children's safety, international standards require physical intervention to be used only 'as a last resort' (European Rule 90), 'when the child poses an imminent threat of injury to himself or herself or others' (CRC Committee, 2019a, p 16). Physical intervention should

---

[1]   With thanks to Oberstown Children Detention Campus for permission to use this data.

never be used as punishment or to secure compliance, and it should never involve 'deliberate infliction of pain' (CRC Committee, 2019a, p 16). It should be used 'under close, direct and continuous control of a medical and/ or psychological professional' and the 'amount of force' used shall be 'the minimum necessary' and 'applied for the shortest time necessary' (European Rule 90). Detailed procedures should govern its use and provide for the recording and review of such practices (European Rule 90.4). Staff should be trained 'on the applicable standards' and a violation of these standards should be 'punished appropriately' (CRC Committee, 2019a, p 16).

Managing behaviour can be challenging in a secure environment where children can sometimes display unpredictable, inappropriate or aggressive behaviour in light of their complex needs and circumstances. In Oberstown, residential social care staff are trained and supported to anticipate and respond to this behaviour in line with the principles, practice and use of the Management of Actual and Potential Aggression (MAPA) methodology and strategies. Although staff originally expressed concern about the suitability of MAPA for older children, in anticipation of taking responsibility for 17-year-olds from prison (HIQA, 2017), this matter was resolved when a review of behaviour management in 2017 endorsed it as an 'appropriate approach' in light of its 'emphasis on working with well established relationships developed with the young people' (O'Rourke and Perkins, 2018, p 10).

The recording and review of physical interventions, while improving, has been a concern (HIQA, 2018, 2019). By 2020, however, the number of physical interventions had reduced substantially, with enhanced and timely intervention and de-escalation techniques helping to improve practice in this area (Oberstown, 2021). A number of actions, explored further in this chapter, helped to bring this about, including the introduction of a clear policy on the use of restrictive practices, the communication of management expectations about the type of intervention permitted to manage aggressive or inappropriate behaviour and the scrutiny given to such practices at board level (HIQA, 2020, p 9). Also important to improve practice has been the commitment to a process of continuous learning, epitomized by the introduction of systematic reviews of all physical interventions in an After Incident Review (AIR) process (HIQA, 2020, p 13). AIRs are part of the Incident Management Response process and they enable lessons to be captured and reflections to take place on what worked or did not work well, when incidents, events or near misses occurred. While part of a risk management approach, the practice also supports team development, problem-solving and communication throughout the organization. As is increasingly understood, violent or aggressive behaviour from a child can be symptomatic of a range of issues and their access to therapeutic supports, through campus clinical services, is vital to ensure their needs are met in a preventive and proactive

Figure 7.1: Number of physical interventions in Oberstown, 2016–20

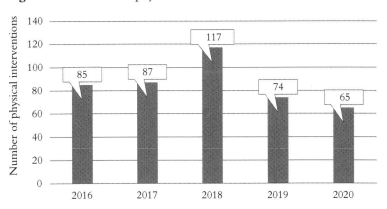

manner. Trauma-informed practice is being introduced in order to further enhance this approach (Zettler, 2021).

Figure 7.1 sets out the number of physical interventions – including but not limited to a full physical restraint – undertaken in Oberstown between 2016 and 2020. The spike in restraints in 2018 was succeeded by a significant fall in 2019, a trend that continued in 2020, indicating that the various measures being taken are continuing to lead to a fall in the number of physical interventions, with fewer injuries to staff when they do occur, as explored in Chapter 8. Note that the daily population also fell during this period from 42 to 36. It is likely that a whole range of measures have contributed to the fall in the number of physical interventions – from improved practice to enhanced monitoring and accountability – but while these improvements are welcome, the risks associated with any physical intervention make it essential that their use is reduced even further and subjected to continuous scrutiny.

In addition to the number of interventions, how children experience them is also important. According to the Health Information and Quality Authority (HIQA), children have reported that 'where they were involved in a physical restraint, they still felt well looked after' and they have told inspectors in this context that staff talked to them about anger management and helped them to see how their behaviour could be different (HIQA, 2020, p 6). The commitment to involve children in the AIR process, with the support of the advocacy officer, has the potential to improve their agency in this process further, ensuring greater compliance with the rights-based approach.

Handcuffs

International standards permit the use of handcuffs only when 'less intensive forms of the use of force have failed' and if 'essential as a precaution against violent behaviour or escape during a transfer' (European Rule 91.1). The use of handcuffs in Oberstown is considered an exceptional measure, only justified following a risk assessment. Although, in 2019, inspectors had to be provided with assurances regarding the maintenance of the handcuff log (HIQA, 2020), by 2020, their use on campus had been all but eliminated through improvements to behaviour management and the establishment of approval and oversight processes. They may be used, where justified by a risk assessment, as part of the security measures associated with children's visits to court, hospital or transfer to prison where the balance may tip in favour of minimizing the risk of a child absconding. In such instances, it is important that the children understand the reasons behind their use.

Separation and isolation

International standards provide that solitary confinement 'should not be used for a child' and 'any separation of the child from others should be for the shortest possible time and used only as a measure of last resort for the protection of the child or others' (CRC Committee, 2019a, p 16). Where it is necessary to hold a child separately, this should be done 'in the presence' or 'under the close supervision of a suitably trained staff member', and the 'reasons and duration' should be recorded (CRC Committee, 2019a, p 16). The European Rules provide that 'isolation' 'in a calming down cell as a means of temporary restraint' must be 'exceptional', 'only for a few hours' and not for more than 24 hours. A medical practitioner should be informed of such isolation and given 'immediate access' to the child (European Rule 91.4). If separation is used 'for security or safety reasons, this shall be decided by the competent authority on the basis of clear procedures laid down in national law, specifying the nature of the separation, its maximum duration and the grounds on which it may be imposed' (European Rule 93). Such separation shall be subject to 'regular review' and any aspect of it may be the subject of a complaint by the child (European Rule 93).

Single separation – or separating a child from their peers – is a contested practice in child detention and the analogy with the process of solitary confinement has resulted in severe criticism and censure of Oberstown in inspections, by external bodies and indeed in litigation. Although Oberstown policy and indeed the National Policy on Single Separation use (Department of Children and Youth Affairs, 2016) are clear that single separation is an exceptional measure to be limited to circumstances where the child's behaviour poses a risk to themselves or others, the frequency and length of the practice have been a long-standing cultural problem in Oberstown. However, the use of separation has reduced dramatically in recent years in terms of both its frequency and its duration. Figure 7.2 maps the decreasing use of single separations from more than 3,000 incidents in 2016 to fewer

Figure 7.2: Number of single separations in Oberstown, 2016–20

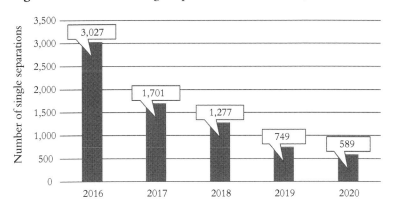

than 600 in 2020; again, note the decline in Oberstown's population during this time.

Several measures were taken to bring this about. Policy and expectations about the use of separation were reinforced with staff, with particular emphasis on the approval, monitoring and recording of the practice, and staff practice was also improved through a heightened level of management oversight (Oberstown, 2019b, p 35) and regular scrutiny by the Board of Management (HIQA, 2020). The regular publication of data on the use of the practice helped to improve transparency, and discussion with Oberstown's external stakeholders and the media helped to improve the wider understanding of the linkages between single separation, the management of behaviour and wider systemic reforms. Legal challenges to the practice, discussed in the next section, also helped to refine the policy, especially with regard to improving the procedural safeguards.

Children's experience of separation also continues to improve. In 2019, for instance, children told inspectors that they saw a period of separation as 'an opportunity to "calm down" when something was bothering them' (HIQA, 2020, p 6). They also explained that staff helped them to complete 'problem solving exercises' so they could 'learn from situations and avoid repeating them' (HIQA, 2020, p 6). Even during periods of separation, they reported being able to maintain contact with their families by 'phone and visits'. In 2020, children who spoke to the inspectors said they 'understood why they were separated and felt this was fair', although they said that at times, they were bored (HIQA, 2021, p 7).

A question that continues to arise, in light of the permissive nature of international standards on the use of separation, concerns the acceptable level of the practice in child detention. A shift in the approach to one that focuses on where the practice is *not* used, in terms of individual children or in particular residential units, as opposed to where it is used, may help to disrupt the use of the practice further. Incentives for both staff and children also need to be explored as a means of decreasing reliance on the practice for staff and improving systems of self-regulation and control for children.

The role of litigation

As with other jurisdictions, litigation has played an important role in the use of single separation in recent years, with improvements to policy and practice arising from a series of cases taken against Oberstown. The case of *SF v Director of Oberstown* [2017] IEHC 829 arose out of the events of 29 August 2016 when, during industrial action, eight children, including the four applicants in this case, broke out of their rooms, took over a residential unit and caused serious damage, including the lighting of a fire, which burned one unit to the ground. The event was a major incident that required emergency services to attend the scene and when the situation was brought under control, the four applicants were separated and detained in conditions that became the subject of litigation. The applicants argued that their treatment was unconstitutional insofar as they were separated from their peers and deprived of access to running water, normal bedding, communication with their families, any form of entertainment and exercise. They alleged violations of their rights with regard to the duration of the separation, the totality of the deprivations imposed and the absence of procedural safeguards regarding the continuation of the separation.

Before addressing the merits of the claim, the High Court dealt with an interesting question about the authority of the Director of Oberstown to impose a period of single separation on a child under the Oberstown policy. The applicants argued that the policy limited the Director's authority, but the court concluded instead that the policy merely provided guidance for the Director whose authority was actually drawn from section 180 of the Children Act 2001. In particular, Ms Justice Ní Raifeartaigh held that the Director of Oberstown has the authority 'to separate a detainee from his peers where this is necessary for the maintenance of order and to prevent damage to property or injury to persons' (para 111). In her view (para 111), this power is rooted in section 180(1) of the Children Act 2001, which gives the Director overall responsibility for the Campus, requiring him to have 'overall regard to the safety of all the young persons and staff in the institution, and the physical integrity of the premises'. Although the Director has considerable latitude in dealing with children in line with the quasi-parental nature of the role, the court held that this did not allow action 'to dip below a certain minimum constitutional level when one is dealing with the specific issue of solitary confinement' (para 114). It may be imposed, the court said, 'in circumstances, which render it, and for so long as it is, strictly necessary, and no longer' (para 116).

Procedural safeguards were implicitly important in such an instance and the High Court said that 'a more formal decision-making and review system would assist in keeping the appropriate objectives [that is, a risk-assessed individual approach to behaviour management, not punishment] to the forefront at all times' (para 120). On the merits of this case, however, the Court concluded that the constitutional rights of the applicants had been breached insofar as there were:

> no procedural safeguards relating to the imposition of separation and associated deprivations, in particular, the formal written recording of decisions and reasons regarding the imposition and continuation of the regime; and the failure to provide the applicants with some form of opportunity to make representations in relation to the deprivations, such as, for example, through an independent advocate as envisaged by Oberstown's own policy. (Para 131)

On the substantive issues, the judge found a limited breach of the constitutional rights of the children concerned. On the length of separation, the judge concluded (para 122) 'with some reservation' that a period of three weeks could not definitely be said to breach a constitutional norm. On the facts, she considered it not to be disproportionate, due in particular to the severity of the threat posed by the children, which could not be said to have been exaggerated (para 123). Similarly, regarding the totality of the measures imposed, the judge considered that although they were severe at the outset, this could not have been said to be disproportionate in the circumstances. Although the pace at which these restrictions were relaxed could be criticized, to do so, the judge said, would involve the court stepping into the realm of the executive. Concern was expressed about the absence of education, given its importance, but the judge rejected that there was any intention to debase or humiliate the young people. Crucially, she considered it important on the evidence that they 'knew that they could have an impact on the conditions of their detention by modifying their behaviour' (para 127) and it was similarly significant that despite the potential for harm, there was no evidence that they had in fact suffered harm as a result of the circumstances of their separation (para 128).

However, two specific aspects of the regime did cause the court concern and, on this basis, a limited breach of the children's constitutional rights was found. These were the complete absence of any form of exercise – the judge was not convinced given the size of the campus that this could not have been organized safely – and the restrictions on contact with family, which were found to be similarly disproportionate (paras 129–30).

The judgment in the *SF* case was the first of its kind to scrutinize the implementation of the Oberstown policy on single separation and the judge took great care in striking a balance between the actions taken by management and the rights of the children concerned. While it was perhaps a surprise that the court did not find the length of the separation and the totality of its conditions to be disproportionate, implicit in the judgment was an appreciation of the uniquely grave situation that management faced at the time and the very exceptional nature of both the risk and all the circumstances. It is implicit in the judgment that the latitude that the Director enjoyed as a result of the crisis would not be available should a similar matter arise again. Learning from the judgment (as from the circumstances of the case) was crucial and it was to this end that the Board of Management commissioned a review of the judgment so that lessons could be learnt, Oberstown policy revised and practice improved. The Board's steps in this regard were commended by the Court of Appeal when it considered a further challenge to the practice of single separation in 2020.

M v Director of Oberstown [2020] IECA 249 presented an altogether different set of circumstances. The case was an appeal from an unsuccessful judicial review, which had been rejected by Mr Justice Simons in the High Court (*MG v Director of Oberstown Children Detention Centre & ors* [2019] IEHC 275) relating to measures of separation applied between 18 and 24 September 2018. The separation of the applicant had been applied following his involvement in an eight-hour stand-off with staff, which involved threatening behaviour of a sexualized nature. According to the High Court, the separation measures imposed were limited. The applicant was permitted to reside in his bedroom, he had access to the multi-purpose room in his residential unit and to education materials, he had telephone calls with his girlfriend, parents and solicitor, and he had physical activity, in some instances in the company of a peer (paras 12–13). According to Simons, J., the case did not exhibit any of the features that had caused concern in the *SF* case and the analogy with the case was rejected. With regard to the applicable safeguards, the judge distinguished this particular case from *SF*, finding that a 'minimum threshold of severity' must be achieved before an entitlement to the particular safeguards claimed by the applicant could be 'triggered' (para 25). Regardless, the court concluded that procedural safeguards set out in the Oberstown policy had been complied with by the Director (again in contrast to *SF*). Importantly, the court noted that since the Court's judgment in *SF*, many if not all the safeguards articulated in that judgment had been put on a formal footing in revised policy and procedures (paras 55–61).

The applicant in *M* had also alleged that his treatment was contrary to the constitutional guarantee of equality (set out in Article 40.1 of the Irish Constitution) on the grounds that he was denied the procedural protections to which an adult is entitled under Rule 62 of the Prison Rules. The court rejected this comparison for a number of reasons, including, most importantly, that a different legislative framework governs child and adult detention. In particular, the court noted that the Children Act 2001 defines the relationship between the child and the Director of Oberstown in different terms than that between a prisoner and prison governor, the former being a paternalistic relationship that justifies measures being taken in the interests of the health and safety of the child, without the necessity for the procedural safeguards provided by the Prison Rules 2007. Separately, the court held, given that the Children Act does not put the child in an inferior position (as was alleged by the applicant), no argument as to discrimination on the grounds of age could be sustained.

In September 2020, the Court of Appeal dismissed the applicant's appeal. Whelan, J. for the Court of Appeal, recalled the clear legislative intent underpinning the establishment of Oberstown Children Detention Campus, whose object is to provide education, training and other programmes, with an obligation to exercise 'proper moral and disciplinary influences' for the purposes of promoting the appellant's reintegration into society and preparing them to take their place in the community as a person who observes the law and is 'capable of making a positive and productive contribution to society' (para 75). Importantly, in its consideration of whether the threshold had been reached so as to require procedural safeguards to apply to the exercise of this discipline, the court held the following elements to be important: the nature and extent of the principal objectives of Oberstown, the comprehensive regime for oversight by the Board of Management and the position and status of the Director who acts in loco parentis under the legislation. The court cited the Oberstown values, highlighted how the separation policy was guided by the principles of the child's best interests and cited the international children's rights standards as its source. Significantly, the court noted (at para 85) that:

> A guiding principle in evaluating any legislative regime concerning children must be Article 42A.1 of the Constitution ('the children's rights amendment') … [which] provides: – 'The State recognises and affirms the natural and imprescriptible rights of all children and shall, as far as practicable, by its laws protect and vindicate those rights.'

This, the court said, 'orients the priorities of those in charge of the detention of a child towards the rights and welfare of the child in question' (para 85).

The court reiterated the reluctance, articulated by Ms Justice Ní Raifeartaigh in *SF*, to interfere in the 'day to day running and operation' of a detention centre unless clear and cogent reasons for doing so are demonstrated (para 88). Notwithstanding the 'margin of appreciation' afforded to the Director, however, the court held that 'there are constitutional limits and safeguards on the treatment of young people in detention' (para 89). Significantly, the court reiterated the view of O'Malley, J. in *B v Director of Oberstown* that 'the educational focus of the school, and the quasi-parental role and power of the director, did not mean that a young person in Oberstown had fewer constitutional safeguards in relation to such measures than an adult in prison' (para 90). At the same time, the court concluded that it was clear that in all the circumstances, 'what occurred is not fairly characterised as a punishment, but rather circumstance-, conduct- and age-appropriate supervision which was on any fair analysis of the undisputed facts, objectively warranted, proportionate and reasonable in the context of the quasi-parental relationship that subsisted' (para 92).

Contrary to what was alleged by the applicant, therefore, the court held that (para 94):

> The measures taken by the Director were warranted in the appellant's own interests and bear no relationship to the materially different response adopted in S.F. which rightly warranted judicial criticism. Indeed it is significant that the single separation procedure operated by the Director represented a significant modification brought about directly as a result of the Director, in conjunction with the Board, considering and taking into account the decision of Ní Raifeartaigh J. in that case. The Single Separation Policy as applied in the case of the appellant has not been shown to have breached any relevant constitutional safeguard.

It is relevant in this case that the allegation by *M* that he had been subject to an ad hoc punishment regime was not borne out by the evidence, an interesting point given the prohibition on separation as punishment in the international standards. Moreover, the applicant's characterization of the Director's response to his behaviour failed, the court said, to have regard to 'the nuanced, child-oriented remit of the Children Acts 2001 to 2015 and in particular the objectives identified in s.158 of the 2001 Act' (para 116). According to the Court of Appeal, the process adopted was 'proportionate, appropriate and involved direct personal engagement aimed at addressing serious negative behavioural issues and incentivizing personal improvements' (para 116).

The court made a number of important points that highlighted its understanding of the distinctiveness of the Oberstown approach. First, the fact that the Children Act provides that no court shall commit a child to prison 'underscores the wholly distinct nature of the children detention regime from a prison regime in all material respects' (para 117). Second, on the facts, the court fully endorsed the approach of the Director in his approach to the applicant's single separation, finding that rather than punishment, segregation was necessary in the interests of the welfare of the appellant and having due regard to the appellant's own best interests, including his psychological and emotional wellbeing. It represented no more than a reasonable and proportionate exercise of appropriate supervision over the appellant in circumstances where his behaviour represented a risk to his mental and moral development and his welfare and undermined the process of his reintegration into society upon his release. (Para 118)

While endorsing the Director's approach, the court clearly considered his course of action one he was not just permitted, but in fact mandated, to take. As the court explained (para 120), it is 'in the interests of the welfare of all detainees – as well as of the appellant – that threatening behaviour does not go unchecked'. Indeed, the court held that:

The requirements of security and stability in the day to day environment is a necessary prerequisite for the delivery of the principal objectives of Oberstown as specified in s. 158 of the 2001 Act. The segregation operated was tailored to the circumstances of the appellant including that it took place in his own room, an environment with which he was clearly familiar, and was for a limited duration. It was on balance indicative of a minimum, necessary measure warranted to ensure the safety of the appellant himself, other inmates and staff and was, in all the circumstances, proportionate. (Para 120)

In a particularly nuanced assessment of single separation, therefore, the court rejected that enhanced procedural safeguards should be mandatory. According to the court, triggering the panoply of safeguards contended (especially in a case of this nature) would be 'disproportionate, unrealistic and would significantly undermine the capacity of the Director to discharge his statutory functions and obligations with due regard to s. 180(8) and achieve the primary objectives specified in s. 158 of the 2001 Act' (para 124). It would, the court held, be:

significantly counterproductive insofar as it would escalate relatively routine issues as might be encountered, particularly amongst teenagers and young persons, into a formalised process and hinder quick, targeted responses calculated to address the immediate state of affairs identified as posing a risk to the detainee, peers, staff or property. (Para 124)

The court continued that '[i]n the context of young persons in detention it would significantly undermine the capacity of Oberstown's Board and its Director to provide guidance and to exercise proper moral influences on the young person in question and risks impeding the promotion of their reintegration into society following the detention period' (para 124).

In short, what the court clearly recognizes here is that the Director has a responsibility to balance 'a series of competing interests', including:

> the welfare of the appellant himself as a young person who was clearly engaging in wholly inappropriate behaviour which warranted being checked; the safety, health and welfare of staff at the centre who were entitled to work in an environment where they are not subjected to sexual harassment and threats; and, the impact on other inmates of such behaviour and the importance of ensuring that such conduct was not endorsed or acquiesced in or treated as normative given the objectives of the detention centre and the statutory regime under which it operated. (Para 125)

The Court concluded (para 126) that the measures taken by the Director in respect of the young person were 'welfare oriented, reasonable and proportionate in all the circumstances and in light of the risks that were unfolding'. Crucially, it said, the Director 'at all times acted in loco parentis', which it regarded as 'an important prism through which his actions and the measures taken in the circumstances must be viewed with due regard to the statutory remit and the express provisions of s. 180 of the 2001 Act' (para 126).

The court noted that the Director 'maintained at all material times appropriate and comprehensive oversight of the process' (para 121). In recognition of his discretion, however, it noted equally that he in turn was subject to oversight by the Board of Management 'in the discharge of his duties of care and control' (para 121).

It is significant that the court found that the mission statement of Oberstown 'wholly accords with its statutory remit' set out in section 158 of the Act (para 122) while noting also from the terms of the Single Separation Policy that it had been 'carefully developed with due regard to the relevant jurisprudence and legislation and it readily acknowledges that "separation from their peers has the potential to negatively impact young people"' (para 123). As the Court noted, there are 'fundamentally different challenges and objectives arising in a child detention centre such as render comparisons with the rules and regimes in adult prisons of the kind being raised in this case wholly misplaced' (para 130).

Discipline in a safe and secure environment

These judgments illustrate the courts' keen awareness of the approach required to maintain discipline and order in a child-centred manner in the detention of children with complex needs. As the courts noted, the twin requirements of 'care' and 'control' require at times a delicate and dynamic response when children's behaviour oversteps safe boundaries. The courts clearly identified the role that separation can play in this process once particular requirements are met. Relevant too are the other legislative and other measures that provide for good discipline in a safe and secure environment.

The European Rules require that 'good order' is maintained in detention by 'creating a safe and secure environment in which the dignity and physical integrity of the juveniles are respected and their primary developmental goals are met' (European Rule 88.1). They provide that 'particular attention shall be paid to protecting vulnerable juveniles and to preventing victimisation' (European Rule 88.2) and require a 'dynamic approach to safety and security which builds on positive relationships with juveniles in the institutions' (European Rule 88.3). They provide that children should be 'encouraged to commit themselves individually and collectively to the maintenance of good order in the institution' (European Rule 88.4).

Under the Havana Rules (Havana Rule 25), children should be supported to:

> understand the regulations governing the internal organization of the facility, the goals and methodology of the care provided, the disciplinary requirements and procedures, other authorized methods of seeking information and of making complaints and all such other matters as are necessary to enable them to understand fully their rights and obligations during detention.

Disciplinary procedures shall be 'mechanisms of last resort', with priority given to 'restorative conflict resolution and educational interaction with the aim of norm validation ... over formal disciplinary hearings and punishments (European Rule 94.1). In particular, disciplinary matters should be limited to 'conduct likely to constitute a threat to good order, safety or security' (European Rule 94.2); and national law should make provision for a disciplinary process to deal with such arrangements to ensure all the safeguards associated with fair procedures and due process apply (European Rules 94.3 and 94.4). Any disciplinary punishments used must have 'educational impact' (European Rule 95).

Cruel, inhuman or degrading treatment or punishment should be prohibited (Article 37, CRC) and any disciplinary measure in breach of this standard must be 'strictly forbidden' including 'corporal punishment, placement in a dark cell, solitary confinement or any other punishment that may compromise the physical or mental health or well-being of the child concerned' (CRC Committee, 2019a, p 16). Children should never be deprived of their basic rights, including family contact, food, water, bedding, education or exercise, as a disciplinary measure, and their treatment must always be 'consistent with upholding the inherent dignity of the child and the fundamental objectives of institutional care' (CRC Committee, 2019a, p 16).

The Oberstown Children's Rights Policy Framework (2020) provides that children shall be 'supported to understand and demonstrate norms of good behaviour that ensure long-term positive outcomes' (www.oberstown.com). The approach is based on developing positive and mutually respectful relationships between staff and children, so that children are supported to understand and support the norms of good behaviour. Emphasis is placed on an individualized approach that respects the children's rights, designed to ensure a proper balance is maintained between the individual child's needs and rights and those of other children, staff and the security of the campus as a whole. In Oberstown, this process is a dynamic one where the relationship between staff and the child is used to promote good behaviour and influence positive outcomes (Bamber et al, 2016b). This clearly works best when relationships are positive and, in this regard, it is notable that in 2020, HIQA inspectors reported observing staff and children 'chatting and enjoying each other's company' while their management of complex situations was described as 'responsive and respectful', with interactions observed as 'caring, warm and supportive' (HIQA, 2021, p 6).

Staff are trained to develop children's positive behaviour and to engage continuously with them, identifying and addressing concerns as they arise. The introduction of 'Outcome Stars', an assessment tool that measures and supports progress and change by young people, has given further structure to the promotion of good behaviour. In 2019, six-unit managers and 12 residential care workers were trained and the process is now being rolled out throughout the campus (Oberstown, 2020, p 38).

HIQA has noted 'improvement in the management of challenging behaviour' (HIQA, 2018, p 8), with children reporting positively on the way in which behaviour is managed in Oberstown, year on year (HIQA, 2020, 2021). In general, relationships between staff and children are a very positive feature of inspection reports. For instance, in 2018, inspectors observed staff being 'warm, empathic and child-centred in their interaction with children on the units', while also appearing 'firm in their ability to establish safe and consistent boundaries' with them (HIQA, 2018, p 17). In 2019, children reported that they liked the problem-solving approach from staff (HIQA, 2020, p 6) and, in 2020, they told the inspectors that they found the rules 'fair' (HIQA, 2021, p 6).

Conclusion

This chapter sought to examine the extent to which the child's right to protection from harm is implemented in Oberstown with regard to both safeguarding practices designed to refer and report injury and abuse and measures to prevent harm occurring, especially during physical or other interventions as part of the approach to managing challenging behaviour. These are complex issues that require a variety of approaches and measures that can indeed be effective in reducing these practices, as the Oberstown data show. Litigation on single separation has also played an important part in bringing about a change in the way behaviour is managed in Oberstown, improving transparency and oversight, approval and recording practices as well as bringing about greater engagement with children to help them understand and regulate their behaviour. The rigour of external inspection and regular monitoring by the media have also played their role, as outlined in Chapter 9.

Together with Chapter 6, this chapter completes the analysis of the extent to which children's rights are enjoyed in practice in Oberstown in line with the rights-based model of child detention. Chapter 8 now goes on to address the key measures taken to support the implementation of the child-centred approach. In particular, it considers the role that staff support and communication have played in advancing the rights of children in detention.

8

Staff Wellbeing and
Communication

Introduction

Chapters 6 and 7 have explored the extent to which the model to advance children's rights has been implemented in Oberstown Children Detention Campus, addressing the requirements of child-centred care, and children's rights of provision, protection, participation, preparation and partnership. In addition to recognizing the children's rights that are important to children deprived of liberty, the international children's rights standards also identify the different measures that must be taken to achieve implementation of those rights. As Chapter 1 explained, two areas that are key in this respect are staffing and communication. As the standards illustrate, the recruitment, training and performance of staff are essential to ensuring that children's rights are protected in detention. The suitability of staff for working with children and the inter-disciplinary mix of staff are both important. The standards also recognize the importance of research and communication, including the importance of regular review and evaluation. More generally, the standards recognize the importance of ensuring that children who come into conflict with the law are understood through public engagement and awareness-raising activity.

This chapter will assess the extent to which the children's rights standards in these areas have been met in Oberstown as a means of further illuminating the application of the children's rights model to the practice of detention. It begins by addressing the range of issues relevant to staffing, including recruitment, learning and development, communication and staff safety. The second section considers the importance of awareness, research and evaluation, before the chapter concludes with a discussion of communication.

Staffing

The United Nations Convention on the Rights of the Child (CRC) notes the importance to the implementation of children's rights of staff in facilities and services that care for children being suited and well equipped for the protection of children's rights. In particular, Article 3(3) requires that 'institutions, services and facilities responsible for the care or protection of children shall conform with the standards established by competent authorities, particularly in the areas of safety, health, in the number and suitability of their staff, as well as their competent supervision'. International standards make general recommendations and ones specific to detention regarding the recruitment, training and supervision of staff, and these issues are explored in the sections that follow. An issue perhaps not explicitly addressed in the international standards, however, is the importance of staff wellbeing and support. While the European Rules recognize that staff working for children in conflict with the law 'perform an important public service' (European Rule 18), they stop short of acknowledging that caring for children in crisis can be demanding, emotionally and physically, for staff. At the same time, the Rules recognize that 'recruitment, special training and conditions of work' must ensure that staff are able to provide the appropriate standard of care to meet 'the distinctive needs of juveniles' and provide 'positive role models for them' (European Rule 18). It can arguably be inferred from this that special measures are required to ensure staff are not just recruited and trained to care for children in conflict with the law, they must also be proactively supported to do this work.

Oberstown recognized early on the important link between 'health and well-being, staff engagement and organisational performance' and following the appointment of a full-time organizational psychologist, it has, in recent years, implemented a comprehensive health and wellbeing strategy in parallel with a learning and development programme for staff (Oberstown, 2020, p 38). The Working Well framework, with four pillars, was launched in January 2019, addressing the different elements of staff health and wellbeing and their relationship to workplace health and safety (Oberstown, 2020, p 38). In addition to multiple elements that promote health and wellness and positive mental health, Working Well features an in-house, onsite peer-to-peer support service for all employees, with staff trained in critical-incident stress management, ensuring that they are in a position to support colleagues after an incident. Important external validation was achieved when Oberstown secured accreditation from IBEC, Ireland's largest business representative group, following an audit of practice in the area in 2019, and it won the wellbeing initiative of the year at the annual IBEC KeepWell awards in 2020, since being listed as among the top 100 companies in Ireland in this regard (www.ibec.ie). A core strength of the Oberstown Health and Wellbeing

Strategy is that it is integral to the care provided to children in Oberstown, that staff need to look after their own wellbeing in order to deliver the best possible care to children (Oberstown 2021, pp 50–2).

Recruitment

The Committee on the Rights of the Child (the CRC Committee) has highlighted the importance of ensuring that facilities for children deprived of their liberty are 'staffed by appropriately trained personnel' (CRC Committee, 2019a, p 15). As the European Rules recognize, to ensure detention facilities are 'suitably and adequately staffed' requires 'special recruitment and selection procedures' that take into consideration the 'qualities of character and the professional qualifications necessary to work with juveniles and their families' (European Rule 128.1). The Havana Rules echo this need to get staffing decisions right if children's rights are to be protected in detention, recommending 'careful selection and recruitment of every grade and type of personnel' given that the 'proper management of detention facilities depends on their integrity, humanity, ability and professional capacity to deal with juveniles, as well as personal suitability for the work' (Havana Rule 82). Staff must be sufficient in number, suitably remunerated and qualified, and include a range of specialists to meet the needs of the children in their care (European Rules 132–4). According to the Havana Rules, staff should include 'educators, vocational instructors, counsellors, social workers, psychiatrists and psychologists', supported by the 'remedial, educational, moral, spiritual, and other resources and forms of assistance' that are available in the community (Havana Rule 82).

Chapter 4 explained that the early establishment of the children detention schools introduced the concept of such facilities being staffed by social care workers. As a result, when the child-centred model of detention was set out in the Children Act 2001, and the commitment was made in national policy to extend this approach to all children under the age of 18, it became the accepted position that care would be provided to children in such settings by residential social care workers. Although, historically, staff working as residential social care workers in the detention schools did not require a social care qualification, relying instead on in-house training (formal and informal) to develop knowledge and skills, with the establishment of the new facility, agreement was reached that newly recruited residential social care workers would be required to have a level 7 qualification on the National Qualifications Framework. This was designed to further professionalize the workforce in advance of registration under the Health and Social Care Professionals Act 2005. A similar approach applied to the recruitment of night supervising officers, who provide care to children at night-time, who are now also required to be appropriately qualified. Once these positions were reached, recruitment began, for the first time in a decade, and several rolling campaigns have since taken place to increase the staffing capacity of the Campus. In December 2013, for instance, the number of staff employed on the Campus was 198 and recruitment undertaken since then has enabled improvement and expansion of the campus, enabling 'the appropriate mix of skills and experience' (HIQA, 2017, p 45). During 2014 and 2015, staff numbers rose to 256 and 272 respectively (Oberstown, 2017a, p 13) and, in addition to care staff, the campus now employs healthcare staff, programme and activities teams, a social worker, an occupational psychologist, managers at different levels and a range of ancillary staff to manage and deliver maintenance, catering, household, security, health and safety and security services. As the Campus has matured and expanded, new roles have been created to align with the needs of the service, including a care office manager, a health and safety officer, an advocacy officer, a care worker medical team, site managers and a young person's programme manager (Oberstown, 2019b, p 39). Oberstown has also appointed a training officer, a communications officer and a head of risk, creating opportunities for staff development and internal movement within the Campus as well as external appointments that bring fresh perspectives and additional expertise (Oberstown, 2021, pp 46–7).

To oversee this recruitment, Oberstown established a human resources (HR) department and appointed its first HR manager in 2015, expanding this role to the more strategically focused chief people officer position in 2020. This development has been key to ensuring that Oberstown has direct responsibility for the recruitment, onboarding and training of staff (HIQA, 2017, p 45), while measures have been taken to ensure consistency and fairness in recruitment and promotion in line with standard national policies (Oberstown, 2019b, p 40). A comprehensive induction process is in place for all new staff, with a buddy system to help new staff settle into the environment (HIQA, 2017, p 46), and the various measures outlined in this chapter are helping Oberstown to become an employer of choice in the children's sector. This also ensures the strategic development of the people function, beyond efficient, transactional HR matters, into broader staff learning, development and wellbeing (Oberstown 2021, p 47).

Learning and development

States have an obligation to provide 'capacity building and training' for all those involved in the implementation of children's rights and who work with and for children (CRC Committee, 2003, p 12). Training should 'emphasise the status of the child as a holder of human rights' and 'increase knowledge and understanding of the Convention [CRC]' (CRC Committee, 2003, p 13) and it should be evaluated periodically as to its effectiveness, reviewing the extent to which it has contributed to 'developing attitudes and practice which actively promote enjoyment by children of their rights' (CRC Committee, 2003, p 13).

'Continuous and systematic training of professionals in the child justice system' is crucial to the implementation of children's rights (CRC Committee, 2019a, p 8) and this training should be multi-disciplinary in character (CRC Committee, 2019a, p 18). Professionals should work in interdisciplinary teams, and be 'well informed about the physical, psychological, mental and social development of children and adolescents, as well as about the special needs of the most marginalized children' (CRC Committee, 2019a, p 8). Training should include 'established and emerging information from a variety of fields' relating to the causes of crime, children's social and psychological development, disparities that may amount to discrimination against certain marginalized groups, the culture and the trends in the world of young people and the dynamics of group activities (CRC Committee, 2019a, p 19). Training shall also focus on ethics and values, standards on children's rights, child development and working with children, proven methods of intervention and good practice, including making interventions in a respectful and positive manner (European Rule 129.3).

In Oberstown, various gap analyses and reviews have recommended enhanced and expanded training across all areas of care and this has taken place in line with the evolving needs of the campus and the workforce. The Health Information and Quality Authority (HIQA) raised the lack of mandatory training, in areas such as health and safety, child protection and crisis prevention, as a concern during its full inspection in 2014, requiring this to be immediately actioned (HIQA, 2014, p 9). While improvements were observed in 2015, there were still key areas of training that were outstanding and training was not being delivered within the timeframe required (HIQA, 2015, p 6). Importantly, by 2017, training records showed that 95% of staff were trained in a recognized approach to behaviour management and a 'Train the Trainers' methodology had been followed to roll out staff training (HIQA, 2017, p 18).

Some of this training is systematic and continuous, with refresher training undertaken in areas such as the Management of Actual and Potential Aggression (MAPA), Children First (Safeguarding) and risk assessment (HIQA, 2018, pp 52–3). Ongoing support has also been provided in the operation of the new case management system (HIQA, 2020, p 13), while bespoke training has been delivered in areas such as the Critical Incident Stress Management (CISM) Service that was launched as a certificate programme in Oberstown in 2016. CISM refers to a package of techniques and tools that assist staff to address stress that may arise following a critical incident, including policy, procedure, workshops and a peer support team. The role of the peer supporter is to provide a confidential, accessible and highly responsive 'psychological first aid' service to fellow staff who are experiencing emotional distress arising from a critical incident at work (Oberstown, 2018, p 21). The peer support team now comprises more than 40 staff members, from different roles across campus, who have successfully completed the qualification (Oberstown, 2018, p 21).

In 2019, those in leadership roles at different levels completed a bespoke programme to develop the skills and competencies required to ensure the campus meets best practice in providing care for children in detention. Twenty managers became the first to complete the programme in October 2019, taking modules on personal awareness, practical management, coaching, motivating others and team development (Oberstown, 2020, p 37). Other workplace training supports include: STORM (Skills Training on Risk Management), referenced in Chapter 7, which was delivered to care teams and peer support workers during 2019; restorative practice, which had 97% participation from frontline staff in 2019; and refresher training provided to 35 peer support workers. In total during 2019, as an example, 334 training courses were delivered, including MAPA, CISM, Manual Handling, First Aid, Fire Awareness Training involving evacuations and drills, the **C**are, **E**ducation, **H**ealth, **O**ffending behaviour and **P**reparation (CEHOP) framework and Children First – Safeguarding (Oberstown, 2020, p 38). Internal training is reinforced with external, accredited education in order to ensure that standards are maintained and learning is continuously up to date. The roll out of the new Children's Rights Policy Framework has also required an extensive training programme, designed to embed the rights-based approach into practice.

Management and communication

According to the Havana Rules (Havana Rule 86), the 'director of a facility' should be 'adequately qualified', with 'administrative ability and suitable training and experience', highlighting the importance of ensuring that such organizations are led by professionals with the appropriate skills, knowledge and experience. The Havana Rules (Havana Rule 84) recommend that organizational management and structure should 'facilitate communications between different categories of staff' so as to 'enhance cooperation between the various services engaged in the care of juveniles, as well as between staff and the administration, with a view to ensuring that staff directly in contact with juveniles are able to function in conditions favourable to the efficient fulfilment of their duties'.

Communication has been a challenge in Oberstown throughout the change process and HIQA inspection reports regularly reported staff dissatisfaction with the frequency and quantity of information received, at the same time noting that there were 'good formal communication mechanisms in place', 'listening exercises' were taking place and the Board of Management was providing staff updates from its meetings (HIQA, 2015, p 22). HIQA noted 'improved communication systems' in 2017, with effective systems in place at different levels (HIQA, 2017, p 41).

In Oberstown, as part of the Strategic Plan 2017–2020, a Communications and Engagement Strategy was adopted in 2017 to put in place 'effective, modern communication systems ... to create a more accessible and proactive communications culture' (Oberstown, 2017b, p 5). Internally, the strategy committed to: promoting awareness and understanding of the role of individual staff in providing the best possible care of young people; ensuring that all information shared is accurate and of a consistent quality; involving all internal stakeholders in campus development; and implementing two-way communication and an ongoing system of feedback (Oberstown, 2017b, p 7). The Strategy also identified the key channels to be used to improve staff communication at all levels including through regular unit, staff and manager meetings, and holding Town Hall sessions to communicate with large groups of staff. More recently, Oberstown has enhanced internal staff communications, taking measures to enable the exchange of workplace information in a timely and direct manner, promoting a positive and open culture and rolling out Workvivo, an online networking tool, newsletters and bulletins to this end (Oberstown, 2020, p 42). Strong communication systems have been especially critical during COVID-19 (Oberstown, 2021, p 14).

Staff responsibilities

The Havana Rules set out the specific functions and duties that should fall to staff in detention facilities (Havana Rule 86), including specific duties to respect, protect and fulfil the dignity and rights of the child, operating with professionalism and confidentiality, and reporting any breaches or potential breaches of the rules. Staff should be 'continually encouraged to fulfil their duties and obligations in a humane, committed, professional, fair and efficient manner, to conduct themselves at all times in such a way as to deserve and gain the respect of the juveniles, and to provide juveniles with a positive role model and perspective' (Havana Rule 83). In the performance of their duties, staff should respect and protect the human dignity and fundamental human rights of all children, ensuring the full protection of their health and wellbeing and seeking to minimize any differences between life inside and outside the detention facility that tend to lessen respect for the dignity of juveniles as human beings (European Rule 87).

With the establishment of its own HR department, Oberstown developed an employee handbook, providing clarity to staff on their terms and conditions, opportunities for leave and procedures for raising workplace concerns. During 2019, a HR Policy Review Project was undertaken, whereby 48 employee policies and six data protection policies were reviewed and updated in line with legislation. The review involved consultation and feedback from colleagues, managers, department heads and union representatives (Oberstown, 2020, p 38). As noted in Chapter 5, the Children's Rights Policy Framework sets out the duties on both staff and the Director with regard to the fulfilment of children's rights, in addition to clearly stating the rights to which every child is entitled. Based on the international children's rights standards, each policy – and Rule/Policy 10 on Staffing and Governance – articulates the detailed responsibilities of staff with regard to their treatment of children and the fulfilment of their roles, while also articulating the duty of management to ensure that staff are provided with the necessary support and development to undertake these responsibilities fully. As this rolls out across the campus, the framework will provide the basis for all staff learning and development, their supervision and their accountability.

Supervision and performance review

The European Rules require that the 'professional competence of staff' is 'regularly reinforced and developed through further in-service training, supervision and performance reviews and appraisals' (European Rule 129.2). Ensuring accountability is in place where children are deprived of liberty is vitally important to protect their rights. As the international standards indicate, this needs to happen at the level of individual employees, who interact with children on a day-to-day basis, as well as at management and board levels. Creating a culture of accountability is a gradual process and progress in this area has, at times, seemed slow to develop in Oberstown. HIQA, for example, has routinely highlighted the importance of improving the quality and consistency of the supervision of care staff. By the time of its 2019 inspection, HIQA noted that there were 'clear and effective lines of accountability throughout the Campus and managers and staff were clear about who held them to account' (HIQA, 2020, p 11). In addition, 'responsibility for improving practice where opportunities to do so arose, was at the forefront for managers who met with inspectors … there were good examples of improvements to practice, and a noticeable enthusiasm for more' (HIQA, 2020, p 10).

Notwithstanding clarity around accountability, HIQA has routinely criticized the inadequacy of supervision in Oberstown, the process used within social care to monitor and reflect on practice, and to identify areas that need development. In 2014, for instance, HIQA found that 'good quality supervision was not regularly provided to staff' (HIQA, 2014, p 9) and, in 2018, both the practice and the records indicated inconsistent supervision and 'no evidence of a formal performance management system' (HIQA, 2018, p 52). In 2019, HIQA found that 'the system in place to hold staff and managers to account through the provision of staff supervision remained ineffective, in that supervision was not delivered consistently across the Campus' (HIQA, 2020, p 11). A step change was evident in HIQA's 2020 inspection, however, which concluded that 'supervision was taking place across the service and all grades', with evidence to show that 'individual performance or issues related to team dynamics were addressed within the supervision process' (HIQA, 2021, p 9). Group supervision was found to be utilized by managers as 'an effective way to promote group cohesion and joint decision making across teams' (HIQA, 2021, p 9). In all likelihood, the leadership training provided to managers in 2019 has begun to pay dividends, although there is still work to be done to embed a robust system of performance review and development into daily practice.

In partnership with accountability is the priority given to Oberstown as a learning environment. As HIQA noted in 2019, opportunities are in place to enable 'learning from incidents, accidents and assaults and to improve the safety and quality of the service', including the daily review of incidents by different teams across the Campus from health and safety, child protection, care and medical perspectives (HIQA, 2020, p 13). An After Incident Review (AIR) mechanism facilitates individual and organizational learning based on what worked well and what could be improved after each event (Oberstown, 2020, p 38). A critical incident management system ensures risks are responded to in line with their level of severity and as a marker of external validation, the Oberstown health and safety team won the overall award from the State Claims Agency in the National Incident Management System Incident Investigation category in 2018 (Oberstown, 2019b, p 29). Taken together, mechanisms and approaches for responding to and learning from incidents and other events have been found, by HIQA, to bring about changes to policy and procedures while also regularly informing staff training needs and priorities (HIQA, 2020, p 13). While there will nonetheless be times when the circumstances of an incident or event require a disciplinary process rather than a learning approach, the adoption of a constructive, team-based approach to learning has been important in ensuring staff buy-in to the rights-based approach.

Safety of staff

Detention can at times be an unsafe environment, as the behaviour of children in crisis poses a risk to their safety and that of people around them and staff at times struggle to intervene or respond safely. In order to address staff concerns about the safety of the work environment, management commissioned a review of health and safety on the campus in 2016, as outlined in Chapter 5. The recommendations of this review were implemented throughout 2017 and 2018. A number of permanent posts were created in the areas of risk management and health and safety and an investigations officer was appointed to investigate all incidents, accidents and injuries to address reports to the Health and Safety Authority and the State Claims Agency, the relevant statutory bodies (Oberstown, 2018, p 21). A head of risk was appointed in 2021 to further embed and mainstream risk management across the entire organization.

At this time, a daily incident, accident and assaults meeting was established to provide an overview of all such incidents and near misses on campus, with this information recorded on a weekly basis, enabling it to be tracked, the causes identified and addressed, and learning applied throughout the campus. This approach was scaled back when it was no longer required. As a result of these and other measures – including enhanced health and safety training and the development of dynamic risk assessment tools – the lowest number of Health and Safety Authority (HSA) reportable injuries to date was achieved in 2019, a reduction of 41% on 2018, as mapped in Figure 8.1. This also impacted on the number of staff work days lost due to injuries, falling to 19 in 2019, down 48% from the previous years (Oberstown, 2020, p 41).

Figure 8.1 sets out the number of incidents, years on year, from 2016 to 2020, highlighting the number of staff work days lost due to injuries. An example of this is in 2020 when 87 incidents occurred, and 20 incidents resulted in one or more lost days of staff working due to an injury sustained. Sixty incidents occurred where staff reported an injury but did not require to take time off due to the injury.

Figure 8.1: Comparison of staff lost-day and no-lost-day injuries in Oberstown, 2016–20

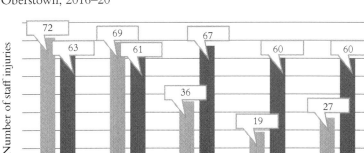

Staff views

Staff surveys are one way to take the temperature of the workforce in an organization and, to this end, Oberstown undertook a staff survey in 2017, repeating it again in 2020 to enable comparable results (Oberstown, 2021, p 49). Apart from increased engagement – 104 staff completed the survey in 2020, up from 62 in 2017 –substantial improvements were evident across the survey data, indicating greater confidence among the workforce in their own roles and abilities, those of management and in the direction of the organization. For instance, in terms of the staff view of their work, 77% of respondents in 2020 believed that Oberstown was at the 'forefront of good practice', compared with 28% in 2017. Similarly, in 2020, 73% responded that Oberstown did the 'right things in the fulfilment of its mission', up from 28% in 2017. An equivalent number reported having the skills necessary to do their job in both surveys, while 59% either agreed or strongly agreed that they had the opportunity to learn new skills, compared with just under 40% in 2017. When asked if they would recommend Oberstown as a place to work, 77% said that they would, a significant increase from 30% in 2017. A slight increase was evident in the numbers of those who were positive about feedback from their manager, up from 58% to 64%, and a majority (54%) said they get the right training when they ask, up from 20% in 2017, although 25% still disagreed. In 2020, almost two thirds considered that they were fairly rewarded for the work that they did, up substantially from one third in 2017, and a roughly similar percentage across the two surveys agreed that their supervisor was aware of their skills (64% in 2020 and 61% in 2017). The survey indicated a significant increase in the numbers who felt encouraged to bring forward innovative ideas to work practices – 57% agreed in 2020, up more than 20% on 2017. In an important shift of actual or perceived accountability, nearly half (47%) strongly disagreed that staff underperformance was not tolerated in 2020, compared with just 21% in 2017. On communication, nearly half (46%) said they received timely communication about changes that affect their area, an increase from 25% in 2017, large proportions understood the priorities in their area (90%) and outside their area (66%), while 78% agreed in 2020 that they had a clear picture of the overall priorities of Oberstown, up from 49% in 2017. Confidence that the results of the survey would be acted upon rose to 46% in 2020, while in 2017 the converse was true with 53% giving a negative response, illustrating a clear improvement in the confidence that staff have in the leadership of the organization.

As explained in Chapter 5, a process of consultation, undertaken in 2012, had established a baseline of Oberstown staff concerns in light of the plans to unify and expand the service in a new purpose-built facility (IYJS, 2013b). The themes that emerged from this process included:

- the importance of communication and consultation;
- concerns about health and safety;
- behaviour management approaches, especially with regard to older offenders; and
- various risks and concerns relating to plans to amalgamate the workforce.

As the analysis in this chapter shows, these concerns persisted throughout the change process and have been systematically addressed over the last number of years. In addition, as already outlined, Oberstown has developed an award-winning and popular model of staff health and wellbeing, indicating that alongside improvements to the care provided to children in detention, those developments that support the care of staff are vitally important. Although further work is necessary to bed down good practice, especially in the areas of learning and development, staff supervision and performance management, the progressive approaches under way in the recruitment and support of staff are having a positive effect such that the work environment is largely unrecognizable from 2016.

Awareness-raising, research and evaluation

The CRC has highlighted the importance to the implementation of the Convention of robust data collection, evaluation and research (CRC Committee, 2003, p 11). The recommendations of the Committee on the Rights of the Child (the CRC Committee) are relevant to detention too insofar as they highlight the value of disaggregated data and qualitative and quantitative studies of children's rights implementation that help to 'identify problems' and 'inform policy' (CRC Committee, 2003, pp 11–12). Measures that involve children directly in the evaluation and related discussions about how their rights are protected are particularly important (CRC Committee, 2003, p 12).

The CRC Committee recommends that states 'systematically collect disaggregated data' on a number of factors including 'the use and the average duration of pretrial detention' and the number of children deprived of liberty (CRC Committee, 2019a, p 19). The European Rules require that data are collected on the personal and social circumstances of juveniles and on the conditions in institutions where children may be held (European Rule 136.2).

The publication and dissemination of annual reports on the state of children's rights are commended as a means of generating parliamentary and public debate (CRC Committee, 2003, p 12). The European Rules recommend that the media and the public should be provided regularly with 'factual information' about conditions in child detention, as well as the work of staff done in such facilities, in order to encourage a better understanding of the issues (European Rule 139.2). Regular reports should be published on developments in child detention (European Rule 140) and the media and members of the public with a professional interest should be given access to institutions where children are detained, provided children's privacy is protected (European Rule 141).

The CRC requires awareness-raising with respect to children's rights under Article 42 of the CRC and the CRC Committee has recommended that education and other campaigns be undertaken, with media and other stakeholders, with a view to countering the negative publicity faced by children in conflict with the law in the media, given that this can give rise to 'discriminatory and negative stereotyping', leading to primarily punitive responses (CRC Committee, 2019a, p 18). Children should be involved in awareness-raising efforts where possible (CRC Committee, 2019a, p 18).

Data

The National Youth Justice Strategy 2008–2020 identified the 'deficit in accessible information in the youth justice system', committing to a high-level goal to 'strengthen and develop information and data sources in the youth justice system to support more effective policies and services' (IYJS, 2008a, p 19). Although this was primarily focused on the macro level, the strategy also undertook to work with stakeholders to establish what information can be shared in order to improve service delivery at the local level. Despite this commitment, little progress was made in improving the availability of high-quality data on the youth justice system under the strategy. The Youth Justice Action Plan 2014–2018, which itself contained some statistical analysis on youth crime for the first time committed as a high-level goal to 'strengthen and develop our evidence base to support more effective policies and services, having regard to the voice of young people' (IYJS, 2013a, p 15). Most of the actions arising from this goal focused on addressing gaps in national, macro and interagency data and only one specific commitment was included in relation to children deprived of liberty, a project to track children's journey into detention, which was not advanced. However, a renewed focus on data collection and research, including with young people, to inform policy development and service delivery is set out in the Youth Justice Strategy 2021–2027.

As part of the modernization of operations in Oberstown, significant investment was made in new information technology (IT) systems with regard to both staff and the care of children. The creation of a bespoke case management system began in 2017 with the digitization of record keeping with regard to children's care (Oberstown, 2018, p 20). This has continued to develop in line with improved record-keeping and information management as part of the commitment to ensuring that the relevant information is at the disposal of staff and managers at appropriate levels to support decision-making with regard to children's care (Oberstown, 2020, p 12). The positive impact of the case management system was noted by HIQA during its 2019 inspection, which noted that at an operational level, there were 'improved reporting arrangements in place ... supported by the introduction of an electronic case management system from which data and information could be stored and drawn' (HIQA, 2020, p 10). While the system was noted to be continuously developed and improved, HIQA noted that it had led to 'increased accessibility of information and data for relevant staff across the Campus and oversight of practice' (HIQA, 2020, p 10).

In addition to ensuring that staff have access to relevant data on children's care, the case management system has also enabled the generation and analysis of statistical data on the operation of the Campus. Technology has also enabled a range of other functions on the campus (Oberstown, 2021, p 44). The adoption of a Communications and External Engagement Strategy in 2017 advanced a commitment to place greater data about Oberstown in the public domain for the purposes of improving transparency about the service. The Strategy also committed to collating and analysing good-quality data to support the care provided to children. Since 2019, the website has contained data on occupancy, month by month, broken down by age, gender and remand/detention order status, and since 2018, monthly data have been published on the incidents of single separation, the reasons and the duration, along with monthly data on physical interventions and incidents of self-harm or attempted self-harm.

Research and public debate

In 2017, Oberstown began to publish a 'Point in Time' snapshot analysis of the characteristics of children on the campus, drawing attention to their backgrounds and indicators of their health, education and involvement with the care system. These were published monthly throughout 2017 at which point a decision was made to publish a more in-depth analysis of the characteristics of children on the campus during quarter 1 in 2017 (Oberstown, 2017c). This analysis was repeated in quarter 1 of both 2018 and 2019 and published both in the annual reports and on the Oberstown website. This rich data, set out in Chapter 4, provided clear statistical evidence of the complexity of need among children deprived of liberty in Oberstown and highlighted the significant adversity in their backgrounds. It also drew attention to the disproportionate representation of Traveller children in detention and to the small number of girls, features consistent with international data set out in Chapter 2. Featured on the website and in the annual reports, these profile reports gathered significant media attention, generating debate and awareness about the profile of young people in detention (Oberstown, 2020, pp 8–9). Disseminated widely, presented at stakeholder events and highlighted in media reports, the data have served to improve public awareness about the particular circumstances of children in detention, the acute and complex nature of their needs and the impacts that these circumstances have on their care in detention and on their treatment in the youth justice system more generally.

External engagement

As part of its Communications and External Engagement Strategy, in 2017 Oberstown began to host regular public events and stakeholder meetings designed to keep partner agencies, non-governmental organizations and related services up to date on developments and to stimulate dialogue on matters of concern. These events take place both in Oberstown, so stakeholders can visit the facilities, in city centre locations and, since the global COVID-19 pandemic, online, enabling wider audiences to attend. In addition to addressing concerns such as education, and mental health and substance misuse, events have taken place to launch the strategy, to publish the annual reports and to showcase the achievements of children in art, craftwork and other areas. In 2017, for instance, the Minister for Children was presented with a personal portrait when she addressed a public event designed to bring the work undertaken with children in detention into the wider public domain (Oberstown, 2018, p 24) and the President of Ireland received his portrait when he addressed children on Campus in 2018 to present them with the President's Awards (Gaisce) (Oberstown, 2019b, p 25). More recently, bespoke events have been developed to raise awareness among the judiciary and legal professionals of the particular challenges young people face in interacting with the legal system and this has been an important extension of Oberstown's advocacy work where concerns raised by young people have led to the campus engaging with stakeholders best placed to respond. In addition to stakeholder events, the campus has convened regular meetings with the local community to keep them updated on developments on campus and to discuss any issues or concerns they have in this regard. Longstanding events, especially at Christmas, are important to maintaining the relationship between the campus and its neighbours; they recognize the importance of community support for Oberstown and help to strengthen awareness among the wider public of the important work to advance the rights of children deprived of liberty.

Views of young people

In line with the international standards, the Youth Justice Action Plan 2014–2018 committed to 'actively seeking the views of young people involved in the youth justice system … with regard to youth crime, policy and practice' (IYJS, 2013a, p 17). This was reinforced by the National Strategy on the

Participation of Children in Decision-making, adapted for detention in the Oberstown Strategy for the Participation of Young People in Decision-making (Oberstown, 2017f). It is echoed too in the Youth Justice Strategy 2021–2027. As illustrated in Chapter 6, the appointment of an advocacy officer in Oberstown has helped to implement commitments to involve children in decision-making at individual, residential unit and campus levels. The role has led to increased input by children into matters that affect them in their daily lives in detention (HIQA, 2020). For instance, a survey of children's experiences was undertaken in 2016, and repeated in 2019, helping to understand and track improvements in children's enjoyment of their rights. Consultation has also enabled children's views to be fed into the available food options, decisions about how to spend the art budget and the choice of television channels (Oberstown, 2020, p 18). More substantive matters on which they have been consulted have included programme planning (establishing their wishes and preferences), the experience of videoconferencing during the COVID-19 pandemic, research on the experience of children on remand, and consultation on the development of a revised 'Children in Care and Children in Detention: Curriculum Guidance to Support Students Accessing the National Curriculum', being developed by the Department of Education through the National Council for Curriculum and Assessment. In 2021, children participated in a formal manner in the recruitment process for the Director in an especially innovative and important development. Consultation with children and taking their views into account in decision-making in all areas is now increasingly commonplace, including up to Board of Management level (Oberstown, 2021, p 19). Ensuring it takes place in line with the Lundy model of space, voice, audience and influence promotes its compliance with both national and international children's rights standards (Lundy, 2007). The commitment by the Board of Management to rights-based advocacy is designed to ensure that young people are central to Campus decision-making and external engagement, consistent with their rights.

Conclusion

While international children's rights standards are clear that staff who work with children deprived of liberty must be appropriately selected, trained and supervised to undertake this work, this chapter highlights that staff must also be adequately supported if they are to carry out this work effectively and safely. As we explain, it is the Oberstown experience that a focus on staff development and wellbeing pays dividends not only in terms of creating a healthy and safe workplace for staff, but also in having an important and direct impact on the quality of care that staff in turn provide to children. Here, it is certainly arguable that while the children's rights standards are useful at a high level, they pay insufficient regard to the relationship between staff care and the care of children in detention and the importance, more generally, of staff wellbeing.

The children's rights standards recognize the important role played by data in ensuring that the care of children in detention continues to improve amid heightened public awareness and understanding of the challenges faced by children in such circumstances. Advances in technology and record-keeping have enabled Oberstown to improve the use of comprehensive and timely data in decision-making, and the commitment to placing statistical and other data into the public domain has also been important in generating wider, public support for the children's rights approach. The voices of children have begun to be heard as part of this process, internally but now externally too. Gaps still remain, however. There is little robust evaluation of Oberstown programmes in terms of their effectiveness on the long-term life chances of children in detention and there is no national system to track children through the youth justice system. Without this more holistic approach to data collection and analysis across the system, policies will be insufficiently informed by the evidence of children's experiences and circumstances.

9

International and National Influences and Advocacy

Introduction

It has been observed that despite some weaknesses, international children's rights standards on youth justice are 'an effective benchmark against which law, policy and practice can be measured' (Kilkelly, 2008a, p 191). Of course, in the absence of effective enforcement mechanisms, implementation of standards depends on the advocacy, support and scrutiny of national and international bodies. Ireland has an active human rights community and children's sector with organizations that have actively influenced the reform of child detention in Ireland. As a state party to multiple United Nations and Council of Europe human rights treaties, Ireland is subject to the monitoring and scrutiny of these bodies, which have played a similarly important role in advocating reform. Given legitimate public concern, child detention has also been the subject of parliamentary scrutiny and media interest in Ireland, as elsewhere. All of this combined, in recent years, to place the reform of child detention under intense and regular scrutiny.

The aim of this chapter is to explore how these external influences helped to bring about the implementation of children's rights standards in Oberstown Children Detention Campus. It begins with an analysis of the monitoring of child detention by the Committee on the Rights of the Child (the CRC Committee), the European Committee for the Prevention of Torture and Inhuman or Degrading Treatment or Punishment (CPT) and the European Commissioner for Human Rights and the impact that their recommendations had on reforms. The chapter then moves to the national level where the impact of bodies such as the Children's Rights Alliance, the Irish Penal Reform Trust and statutory human rights bodies is outlined. Finally, the chapter highlights the role of the Oireachtas (Parliament) and media in providing a further layer of public scrutiny. Overall, the chapter aims to illustrate the important role played by these various bodies in promoting the reform of child detention through an approach that scrutinized and challenged in equal measure. The chapter ends with some reflections on the impact of the intense scrutiny of the period.

International influences

The Committee on the Rights of the Child

Ireland ratified the United Nations Convention on the Rights of the Child (CRC) in 1992, meaning that the development of the modern Irish youth justice system took place in parallel with implementation of the CRC during this period. As explained in Chapter 3, the new legislative framework for youth justice – first published as the Children Bill 1996 – took many of the CRC's provisions into account and generally pointed the way towards greater compliance with its obligations. The timing of Ireland's first appearance before the CRC Committee in 1998 allowed the committee to address the compatibility of the Children Bill with the CRC (Kilkelly, 1998) and through this and subsequent sessions, the committee's recommendations had a direct impact on Irish law and policy. For instance, recommendations to increase the age of criminal responsibility (CRC Committee, 1998, p 4), adopt a rights-based youth justice strategy (CRC Committee, 2006, p 14) and ensure detention is a measure of last resort, all prompted government action. The committee's recommendation that the mandate of the Ombudsman for Children be extended to all children in detention also found favour (CRC Committee, 2006, p 14).

In 2016, when the Committee considered Ireland's combined 3rd/4th Report on Convention implementation, it commended the repeal of legislation providing for children to be detained in prison (CRC Committee, 2016h, p 2), although it expressed concern that the practice had not yet ended (CRC Committee, 2016h, p 17). The Committee recommended that Ireland bring its juvenile justice system 'fully into line with the Convention and other relevant standards' and, in particular, urged the increase of the age of criminal responsibility to 14 years (CRC Committee, 2016h, p 17). The committee also noted that where detention is unavoidable, Ireland should ensure that detention is 'for the shortest possible period', children are not detained with adults and that 'detention conditions are compliant with international standards, including with regard to access to education and health services' (CRC Committee, 2016h, p 17). All these recommendations served to reinforce the direction of national policy to end the use of imprisonment for children and promote an approach to child detention with greater adherence to international standards.

Ireland now awaits the consideration by the committee of its 5th/6th Reports on implementation of the convention and in 2020 government received from the committee an indication of where it will focus its dialogue. In the List of Issues, the Committee sought more information on raising the age of criminal responsibility to 14 years, the new Youth Justice Strategy, the application of the youth justice system to children tried in the higher courts and the promotion of alternatives to detention (CRC Committee, 2020j, p 9). With respect to child detention, the Committee has asked about measures taken to 'ensure that detention, including custody and pretrial detention, is used as a last resort and for the shortest possible period of time, that children are not detained with adults and that detention conditions are compliant with international standards, including with regard to access to education and health-care services' (CRC Committee, 2020j, p 9). It has also sought information on the rehabilitation and reintegration services available for children leaving detention (CRC Committee, 2020j, p 9). Government will next provide this information to the committee, so that these matters can be discussed during its hearing with the state party delegation. It is important in this respect that the Committee will hear not just from Government and from NGOs on these issues, but also from children in Oberstown, as part of a consultation process undertaken by the Ombudsman for Children.

The European Committee for the Prevention of Torture and Inhuman or Degrading Treatment or Punishment

Ireland ratified the European Convention for the Prevention of Torture and Inhuman or Degrading Treatment or Punishment in 1998 and has, to date, had seven visits from the eponymous committee (known as the CPT) whose role it is to visit places of detention to scrutinize implementation of its standards. The CPT has been influential in the reform of child detention in Ireland. At the time of its visit to Ireland in 2002, for instance, government was giving consideration to building a new facility for 14- and 15-year-olds in St Patrick's Institution and the CPT took the opportunity to stress that children deprived of their liberty should be held in 'detention centres specifically designed for persons of their age, offering regimes tailored to their needs and staffed by persons trained in dealing with young persons; particular vigilance is required to ensure that the physical and mental well-being of detained children is adequately protected' (CPT, 2003a, p 39). The government's response confirmed to the Committee that the proposed unit would not in fact go ahead (CPT, 2003b, p 44). During that visit, the CPT also visited Trinity House School and reported reasonably favourably on the facilities and the treatment of the children there, with regard to relationships with staff, material conditions, education and contact with family. The Committee recommended the addition of a psychologist to the health team and welcomed proposals on the external inspections and complaints bodies and on the introduction of a new approach to behaviour management (CPT, 2003a, p 42).

It was 2014 before the CPT visited child detention facilities in Ireland again. By then, the process to amalgamate the detention schools was under way, along with measures to discontinue the detention of children in prison. The CPT noted the transition at the time of its visit and highlighted the importance of this process taking place in a smooth and planned manner, rather than with a rushed timetable that might create instability (CPT, 2015a, p 66). Although the facility was being planned for a capacity of 90 children, it cautioned against filling this capacity given that at the time of its visit, there were fewer than 50 children detained on remand and detention orders. The government, in its response, reiterated that its emphasis would be on diversion, with detention used only as a measure of last resort (CPT, 2015b, p 74).

Following its visit, the CPT reported positive experiences from its conversations with children and noted that there was a 'young person centred, and caring approach in place', although concerns were expressed in relation to their treatment at the time of arrest by the Garda Síochána (CPT, 2015a, p 66). Reports of the facilities and the regime, including education and healthcare, were detailed and generally positive, although recommendations were made to improve the 'austere' living conditions and extend the extent of vocational training available (CPT, 2015a, pp 67–8). The government's response was to highlight the transitionary nature of current arrangements, highlighting that it was the intention to refurbish bedrooms and expand vocational training in line with national policy (CPT, 2015b, p 77).

Following complaints by children that they had on several occasions been confined to their bedrooms until after midday due to alleged staff shortages, the CPT recommended alternative arrangements be made in such circumstances. Significantly, in its response, government advised that 'all managers and staff in the Children's Detention Schools have been directed that the practice of confining children to their rooms until after midday is to cease with immediate effect' (CPT, 2015a, p 68). The CPT noted the 'favourable staffing levels', which, 'combined with the fact that the majority of staff were care workers with practical experience, reflected the commendable emphasis the Children's Detention Schools placed on education and rehabilitation rather than on control and security' (CPT, 2015a, p 69). Staff concerns associated with taking on responsibility for 17-year-olds were reported by the CPT, which noted that although accepting the 16-year-olds had been smooth, the next phase would coincide with the process to amalgamate the Children Detention Schools, which would require additional staffing and measures to ensure the ethos was maintained. In light of staff absences, the CPT recommended that management take measures to understand the reasons behind the absences and, in particular, take steps to 'debrief staff after managing challenging behaviour and consult with staff on a regular basis, particularly during the transition period' (CPT, 2015a, p 69). The government noted in its response that a range of measures were being taken to ensure staff were adequately supported and counselled after incidents (CPT, 2015b, p 79). These were set out in Chapter 8.

Specific, additional observations and recommendations were made regarding the recording of injuries following admission, debriefing children and staff following incidents of physical restraint, and ceasing the use of handcuffs on the campus (CPT, 2015a, p 72). The CPT also examined records of single separation and highlighted complaints received from young people 'about what they perceived to be an excessive use of separation, which they did not think addressed their behavioural issues in a meaningful way' (CPT, 2015a, p 73). Commitments were made following the visit to provide further training for staff to improve recording and ensure separation only occurs in line with policy. The CPT urged that any room used for 'protection' should have natural light and sufficient ventilation, be used for the shortest period possible and any young person placed there should be provided with suitable clothing. The government responded by providing details of the range of measures being taken by management to address the issues raised, clearly reflecting the seriousness with which these matters were being taken (CPT, 2015b, pp 84–5).

Following concerns about children's access to the complaints procedures, the CPT was assured by government following its visit that a range of measures were being put in place to ensure staff were better equipped to support complaints by children and recording improved to enable trends to be assessed periodically (CPT, 2015a, p 75). The CPT was also advised that the support of Empowering Children in Care (EPIC) would be sought to provide an independent advocacy service to children in detention and that the Ombudsman for Children would also visit to provide information on complaints mechanisms to children.

The previous chapters have highlighted the extent to which the concerns raised by the CPT, especially during its visit to Ireland in 2014, have now been addressed. Importantly, the CPT had noted at the time of that visit that a significant process of change was under way, and it was careful to note with sensitivity the challenges that this presented. In particular, it cautioned in its report against applying a rushed timetable to the transition process, aware of the risk of instability (CPT, 2015a). Its balanced approach on this issue can justifiably be weighed against its call for direct and immediate action with regard to its concerns about the excessive use of single separation. The CPT's most recent visit to places of detention in Ireland took place in 2019 when its focus was on police stations, prison and those in psychiatric and social care facilities. While its decision not to visit Oberstown on this occasion no doubt reflects its limited resources, it is arguable that the information provided in advance of its visit provided reassurance as to the progress being made in meeting the convention's standards.

The Council of Europe Commissioner for Human Rights

The inaugural Council of Europe Commissioner for Human Rights (Commissioner HR), Thomas Hammarberg, visited Ireland in 2007 and considered youth justice and detention in detail in his report. In particular, he expressed concern about the 'rigid exception' to the age of criminal responsibility that 'makes it possible to charge a very young child with the most severe crimes in an ordinary criminal court not specially equipped to deal with children' (Commissioner for Human Rights, 2008, p 19). Among the range of concerns highlighted in his report was the risk to the child's right to privacy 'in a world of strong media attention for juvenile crimes' (Commissioner for Human Rights, 2008, p 20). During his visit, the commissioner visited Trinity House School and his report reflected the concerns of staff that because children were receiving shorter sentences (fewer than two years), this made it 'difficult to develop and implement a meaningful care plan providing for education and social integration' (Commissioner HR, 2008, p 22). He also reported the view of staff that 'it would be beneficial to have on-site family accommodation to enable visiting parents not living in the vicinity to stay overnight, a need that was also expressed by the children spoken to' (Commissioner HR, 2008, pp 20–1). The Commissioner welcomed that under the Children Act 2001, children can only be detained in the children detention school model of care, education and rehabilitation but expressed concern about the current interim provision whereby children continued to be imprisoned 'in [St Patrick's Institution] an out-dated facility together with adult prisoners up to the age of 21' (Commissioner HR, 2008, p 22). Noting the Minister for Children's announcement to invest in the Lusk campus, the commissioner urged the Irish authorities to 'live up to their commitment as expressed in the Children Act 2001 and discontinue the imprisonment of children, making the detention school model available whenever detention is deemed necessary' (Commissioner HR, 2008, p 22).

Commissioner Hammarberg visited Ireland again in 2011 when his visit focused on human rights under austerity. He did, however, consider matters relevant to youth justice and in particular commended the work of the Ombudsman for Children in relation to the rights of young people in St Patrick's Institution and reiterated his concern that while the remit of the Ombudsman covered children in detention schools, it did not extend to children in adult prisons. He reiterated his 2008 recommendation that this gap be closed, 'as a matter of urgency' (Commissioner HR, 2011, p 5). At the same time, the Commissioner commended the progress being made in the reform of youth justice and invited the authorities to align approaches further with international standards, including ensuring detention is a measure of last resort, with an emphasis on diversion and restorative justice (Commissioner HR, 2011, p 12). While he expressed appreciation about the decision to end the imprisonment of children in St Patrick's, his frustration at the failure to identify a timeframe for this was evident from his report. In particular, he called for the authorities to 'speed up' the process, by phasing out St Patrick's 'immediately by moving a pilot group to Lusk and integrate the experience made into the planning process for the enhancement of the detention schools' (Commissioner HR, 2011, p 15).

Mr Hammarberg's successor, Commissioner Nils Muižnieks, visited Ireland in 2012 and in a follow-up letter to the Minister for Justice he repeated the concerns of his predecessor about the pace of ending the use of St Patrick's Institution for child detention. Welcoming that measures had been taken to end the detention of 16-year-old boys there, he requested consideration be given to 'a speedier process, possibly by identifying those remaining young offenders who could already be transferred to a detention school' (Commissioner HR, 2012). The Minister's response confirmed that government investment would allow the childcare model of detention to be extended to all children under 18 years of age by mid-2014, while he also highlighted that the feasibility of accommodating 17-year-olds in the detention schools before that date was being 'actively considered' (Minister for Justice and Equality, 2012).

Two points are evident from this brief survey of international monitoring reports on Ireland's record of youth justice and detention. First, it is apparent from the nature of the conclusions drawn by the various bodies and their recommendations that they are well informed on the issues from an Irish perspective. Many of the points raised touch on the key concerns relating to the use of detention and the extent to which children enjoy their rights when deprived of their liberty. Whether briefed by civil society groups, national human rights institutions or children themselves, the monitoring bodies' observations are well-informed and relevant. The second observation from this analysis is the extent and nature of government engagement with the bodies and their various recommendations. An analysis of the government's responses to these bodies indicates fulsome, engaging responses to the concerns raised – the CPT is an excellent example – and in almost every instance, there is evidence that the advice had been or would be taken on board. It could also be noted that the fact that the bodies focused repeatedly on a small number of issues – the closure of St Patrick's is a good example – allowed for an accumulation of recommendations on this priority area from a range of bodies. The fact that those who visited the detention facilities took time to meet children and staff allowed them to present an authority that gives their recommendations weight. The resulting conclusion is that the influence of international human rights bodies on Irish youth justice and especially detention has been very significant. While government policy, for instance on the decision to develop the childcare model of detention for children, provided fertile ground for the recommendations made by United Nations and Council of Europe bodies, these recommendations nonetheless added important momentum to the reforms being progressed.

National advocacy

While international human rights bodies have played an important role in scrutinizing and monitoring respect for children's rights in youth detention in Ireland, a range of national bodies have also been influential in tracking and promoting the achievement of reform. Oversight provided by inspection bodies such as the Health Information and Quality Authority (HIQA) is examined in Chapter 5, and the role that litigation has played in promoting accountability for child detention is set out in Chapter 4 (regarding remission) and Chapter 7 (regarding single separation). This section explores the various contributions that the various national organizations have made in the promotion of children's rights in detention in Ireland. The learning from this process is set out in Chapter 10.

Civil society

Ireland's civil society is well resourced, informed and dynamic, and several organizations play a role in the promotion of children's rights both generally and in the area of youth detention. The Children's Rights Alliance (CRA) (https://www.childrensrights.ie/) is an umbrella organization, established in 1995, made up of more than 100 organizations that work for better implementation of the CRC. Although the CRA does not focus on youth justice and detention specifically, it sometimes comments on developments and events relevant to its remit. For example, it comments on the publication of HIQA inspection reports, when it has focused on the use of single separation (CRA, 2017a), while the organization has also strongly supported the decision to end the use of adult prison for children, recommending in 2015 that 'every effort is made to ensure that (Oberstown) embeds children's rights principles into all elements of its operation and regime' (CRA, 2015a).

The CRA's most important annual publication, since 2009, is its *Report Card*, which assesses government's delivery of its own commitments in the areas of education, health, material wellbeing, safeguarding and realizing rights. As a specific commitment to end the use of prison for children was included in the Programme for Government 2011–2016 (it had been contained in the 2008 programme too, without impact), its implementation was tracked in the CRA's *Report Card* publication for these years.

The government had a poor start in this respect, leading to the award of an 'F' grade in the 2012 *Report Card*, the lowest grade possible (CRA, 2013, p 57). This assessment was based primarily on the continuing use of St Patrick's Institution for the detention of children over 16 years of age, a situation that the CRA referred to as 'a glaring human rights violation in direct contravention of Article 37 of the Convention on the Rights of the Child' (CRA, 2013, p 57). The *Report Card* reflected the extensive national and international criticism in respect of St Patrick's Institution, while recommending that government commit the necessary capital funds to build the new national children detention facility required to put in place a child-centred approach for all children deprived of liberty.

The following year, however, the picture was very different, leading the CRA to award a 'B+' grade for child detention in its 2013 *Report Card* (CRA, 2014, pp 76–7). This was as a result of the allocation of significant capital expenditure to the new child detention facility and the progress made in the planning, design and approval of the new development. This was warmly welcomed by the CRA, which commented (at p 77) that:

> We now have a unique opportunity to build a world class facility and put in place a child centred, education-focused regime in the new facility, rooted within a children's rights framework. Critical to this is delivering a rights-based approach to youth justice and an understanding that, first and foremost, all those under 18 years are children.

The *Report Card* recommended consultation with stakeholders, including children, about the design of the facility to ensure it meets their needs, while it urged the completion of building works that would enable an end to the detention of children in St Patrick's Institution to be on schedule in 2014. At the same time, the CRA noted the serious concerns of inspection bodies and others about the treatment of young people currently in St Patrick's and recommended the adoption of urgent measures to reduce the high dependency on a protective regime of 23-hour lock-up (CRA, 2014, p 79).

Government retained its 'B+' grade in the 2014 *Report Card* where it was noted that sustained progress had been made both in the development of the new children detention facility and in the delivery of 'a programme of operational reforms' aimed at enhancing the effective management and capacity of services on the Oberstown campus in advance of, and to support, the expanded facilities (CRA, 2015b, p 115). According to the Irish Penal Reform Trust at the time, commenting on the closure of St Patrick's Institution, '[t]he decision by Government to close the prison is a strong statement that where institutions cannot meet basic human rights standards, radical action will be taken. In that respect, this decision is a powerful vindication that the Inspection system is working' (CRA, 2015b, p 94).

Despite this very welcome progress, however, concerns were expressed about a range of matters, resulting in recommendations to: ensure that legislative entitlement for aftercare extends to children leaving detention; review the use of detention on remand; and introduce a case tracking system to track the outcomes of those who leave detention to enable better planning for the future (CRA, 2015b, p 119).

By the following year, the government's performance was considered to have fallen to a 'B-', according to the CRA, on the basis that although progress was being made with the new detention facility, the legislation to underpin the facility was not yet enacted and some children continued to be detained in an adult prison (CRA, 2016, p 104). In addition to urging government to expedite the transfer of all children from prison to child detention, the CRA reiterated its recommendations to review the use of detention on remand and to ensure legislation provided for the child's right to aftercare on leaving detention (CRA, 2016, p 106).

In 2016, the final year of the *Report Card* on the 2011–2016 Programme for Government, the government's progress was graded at an improved 'B+' as a result of the enactment of the Children (Amendment) Act 2015 to provide for the establishment of a single detention facility to accommodate everyone under 18 years of age and the repeal of all legislation permitting the detention of children in adult prison (CRA, 2017b, pp 98–100). While the *Report Card* noted that the final provisions could not take effect until staffing in Oberstown reached the requisite levels to accommodate the 17-year-olds, it also noted with some satisfaction that, according to the Department of Children and Youth Affairs, it is 'now a matter of when, and not if, there will be a final end to the practice of detaining children in adult prison facilities' (CRA, 2017b, p 101). To facilitate this, the 2016 *Report Card* recommended that all necessary supports, including staffing, be provided to enable Oberstown to accept responsibility for 17-year-olds while recommending that the relevant legislation be enacted to end the detention of children in prison (CRA, 2017b, p 102).

The Irish Penal Reform Trust (IPRT) has engaged in rights-based advocacy around child detention since its establishment in 1994, seeking to 'work towards progressive change in youth justice policies and practice, as well as engaging with wider policy and practice issues relating to youth justice, such as the provision of alternatives to detention, diversion and early intervention programme' (https://www.iprt.ie/). Over the years, the IPRT has regularly hosted and attended events and seminars and made submissions to public consultations around law and policy in the area of youth justice and detention. It has issued regular press releases and contributed to public debate on a range of matters concerning the detention of children, specifically the detention of children in St Patrick's Institution, calling repeatedly for its closure, and the operation of Oberstown where it has commented on operational matters including industrial relations disputes and the use of restrictive practices as documented in inspection (HIQA) reports (www.iprt.ie).

The IPRT published a timely report in 2009 (Martynowicz and Ní Dhrisceoil, 2009) designed to 'influence the debate on the design and best practice policies in the new National Children Detention Facility at the Oberstown Campus in Lusk, whilst renewing a call for an immediate end to the detention of boys in adult prison' (IPRT, 2016). The report considered the application and implementation of international human rights standards to child detention in Ireland and made 63 recommendations regarding how these standards can be best achieved in the Irish context including on: admissions procedures; physical environment; healthcare; protecting children from harm; discipline; inspection and complaints systems; suitable and qualified personnel; rehabilitation; and social integration into the community. While frequently responding to national and international inspection reports on child detention, focusing specifically on the use of restrictive practices, the IPRT has also published briefing papers (such as the briefing paper on the detention of children in St Patrick's Institution, IPRT, 2012). It also published action-oriented research on the overlap between the care and justice systems, concerned that children in state care too often end up in detention, and it made 23 recommendations aimed at improving law and policy (Carr and Mayock, 2019). Its research on Travellers and the prison system put this issue under the spotlight, although it did not address Traveller children (Costello, 2014). The IPRT has also, from time to time, incorporated the treatment of children into its existing research and policy work including, for instance, a report on solitary confinement (Martynowicz and Moore, 2018). While focused mainly on the use of segregation in adult prisons, the report referred to single separation in child detention, noting the concerns of HIQA in this regard (Martynowicz and Moore, 2018, pp 38–9). The report recommended that the Minister for Children adopt 'statutory rules governing detention of children', which should include 'an absolute prohibition of the use of solitary confinement for children' (Martynowicz and Moore, 2018, p 47).

More recently, the IPRT has focused on the issue of emerging adults, advocating for the extension of the protection of the youth justice system to those aged between 18 and 24, and its submission to the consultation for the Youth Justice Strategy 2021–2027 recommended that support for transition into adulthood should be a priority area (IPRT, 2020). With respect to child detention, the IPRT recommended the development of 'innovative early release schemes' designed to ensure detention is a measure of last resort (IPRT, 2020, p 2). It also repeated its 2018 recommendation that solitary confinement of children be prohibited by law and that statutory regulation prescribes the use of single separation (IPRT, 2020, p 6). Recommendations from the CRA's *Report Cards* were repeated here also, with regard to making legislative provision for aftercare for children leaving detention and introducing a system to track the longitudinal needs and outcomes of children in conflict with the law. The submission also included a general recommendation to ensure that the voices of children are heard in the reform of youth justice policies, programmes and systems (IPRT, 2020, p 2). As noted earlier, many of these recommendations have ended up as commitments in the strategy in a clear endorsement of IPRT advocacy (Department of Justice, 2021).

The Ombudsman for Children

The Ombudsman for Children's Office (OCO) was set up in 2002 to promote the rights and welfare of children inter alia through awareness-raising, monitoring, research and law and policy work. Significantly, the OCO has a complaints remit and, under section 8 of the Ombudsman for Children Act 2002, is mandated to examine and investigate complaints from individual children or their representatives with respect to matters that may have adversely affected the child and where the action has been taken without proper authority, based on erroneous or incomplete information or is otherwise contrary to fair and sound administration. To facilitate access to the OCO by children deprived of liberty, the Ombudsman for Children conducts outreach visits to Oberstown Children Detention Campus to meet children who might otherwise find the office hard to reach (OCO, 2020a, p 63). The Ombudsman also plays an important role in advising the Oireachtas (Parliament) on legislative reform relating to children and it is influential also in the monitoring work of international bodies, especially the CRC Committee. For instance, in 2015, the Ombudsman's submission to the committee on the occasion of its examination of Ireland's consolidated 3rd and 4th report highlighted the need to end the detention of children in adult prisons and recommended a review of the use of detention on remand (OCO, 2015, p 47). More recently, the Ombudsman made a submission to the committee to inform its next periodic examination of Ireland (OCO, 2020b). This submission encouraged the committee to request government to outline the measures being taken to: 'address the needs of specific groups of children who are over-represented in the child justice system, including children in alternative care and Traveller children'; 'provide timely, appropriate and coordinated supports to children when they leave detention'; and 'measure and reduce the rate of recidivism among children' (OCO, 2020b, p 29).

The Ombudsman's work in St Patrick's Institution will stand out, however, as the OCO's most influential intervention in the implementation of children's rights standards in child detention in Ireland. In 2011, the Ombudsman published a report on St Patrick's Institution (OCO,

2011), which at the time accommodated 48 16- and 17-year-olds in an environment that had been the subject of repeated international criticism. The aim of the report was 'to encourage, support and secure change' in St Patrick's Institution and it did so by first, consulting directly with young people whose views and experiences were captured directly in the study and second, by seeking a response from prison management to the issues raised by the young people and the recommendations of the Ombudsman (OCO, 2011). The result was a powerful and compelling case for reform that made the important recommendation to close the institution impossible to ignore (Kilkelly and Logan, 2021). The report addressed a number of the children's concerns, including: a lack of accessible information on admission about the rules, regime and sentence management; a failure to separate them from adults; and poor living conditions, access to healthcare and education and contact with family. Access to effective complaints mechanisms and their protection from harm were also highlighted. Detailed recommendations made by the Ombudsman sought to improve children's treatment in St Patrick's. Ultimately, however, the direct and honest nature of the report, which presented the woefully inadequate experiences of the children detained there, in their own words, challenged others to speak out about the conditions of their detention. In particular, the publication of the Ombudsman's report was followed by the publication by the Inspector of Prisons of an unreservedly stark account of human rights breaches in St Patrick's. Here, the Inspector concluded that he was satisfied that 'the Irish Prison Service can no longer guarantee the safe and secure custody of young offenders detained in St. Patrick's Institution' (Inspector of Prisons, 2013, p 22). Accordingly, the report recommended that St Patrick's Institution should be closed 'forthwith' and the timeline for the transfer of 17-year-olds to Oberstown revisited with a view to bringing it forward (Inspector of Prisons, 2013, p 22). It was, of course, to be several more years before this action was completed, but the combined reports finally made this outcome a political priority.

Public and parliamentary scrutiny

International standards require that the media and the public shall be provided regularly with 'factual information' about the conditions in detention facilities (European Rule 139.1) through the publication of regular reports (European Rule 140) and permitting visits by those with a professional interest. Measures need to be taken to widen public understanding of the important role played by those who provide care to children deprived of liberty, which is 'a social service of great importance' (Havana Rule 8), while evaluation and research is considered integral to successful interventions with children in conflict with the law (European Rules 136–8).

A review of the media coverage on Oberstown Children Detention Campus in recent years highlights frequent and at times intense coverage of incidents on campus, reports of developments and opinion or analysis pieces from commentators. Newspaper articles and broadcast features relayed the details of the many serious incidents that took place, especially during 2016 and 2017, frequently setting out the views and concerns of staff and other stakeholders (for example, *The Irish Times*, 29 August 2016; *RTE*, 30 May 2017). Industrial relations, including strike action during 2016, were particularly prominent (for example, Bergin, 2016; Hennessy, 2016) along with expressions of concern, from politicians and trade unions, about the safety of the work environment (for example, MacNamee, 2016; Baker, 2017a). The publication of HIQA reports has also attracted publicity, with attention drawn to deficits in the use of single separation in particular (for example, *Newstalk*, 13 August 2017; Manning, 2018). Court reports documented the litigation against Oberstown in the area of single separation (for example, Carolan, 2017) as well as the criminal proceedings involving children charged with respect to the various incidents on campus (*Sunday World*, 4 May 2017; Tuite, 2017, 2018). Proactive media from the campus increased during 2017 and 2018 with, for instance, the launch of the Oberstown Strategy (Baker, 2017b), the publication of the Oberstown annual report (for example, Manning, 2019), release of statistical data on the characteristics of children detained in Oberstown (for example, Holland, 2017, 2020) and occasional thought leadership (for example, Kilkelly, 2017, 2018).

Radio and print features increased from this time also, seeking to raise awareness about the progress being made in the implementation of the child-centred model and the challenges that remain in this regard (for example, Meagher, 2017; Grittens, 2018; O'Keefe, 2019). Media coverage addressed the decision not to publish a review into the operations commissioned by Oberstown's Board of Management in 2016, a matter that attracted significant criticism from across civil society groups and political representatives (for example, Fagan, 2018; Hillard, 2019). As progress has continued to be made in Oberstown, however, the coverage has become more positive. Throughout 2019, for instance, the media addressed developments such as the introduction of vocational training opportunities for young people (for example, *RTE Drivetime*, 2019), the achievement of President's Awards (Gaisce) by children in Oberstown (O'Loughlin, 2019) and the wellbeing programme for staff (for example, *Fingal Independent*, 9 February 2019). In 2020, media coverage was largely confined to the HIQA report (for example, Bowers, 2020) and the implications for the campus of the COVID-19 pandemic (for example, Gallagher, 2020).

In addition to the role of the media, Oberstown is also subject to parliamentary scrutiny and both the Director and the Chairperson of the

Board of Oberstown have appeared before the Oireachtas (Parliament) Committee on Children and Youth Affairs on several occasions. These meetings are an important way to promote accountability with respect to child detention as they provide an opportunity for in-depth dialogue and information exchange on issues of public concern and interest. It is established practice that the incoming chairperson of a state board appears before the relevant Oireachtas committee prior to their appointment, and this took place with regard to the appointment of the Oberstown Board of Management chairperson in 2012 and 2016 respectively (Joint Committee on Health and Children, 2012, 2016). The Committee on Children and Youth Affairs also requested the Director and Chairperson to appear before the committee in 2016, 2017 and 2019 to provide information about the care of children and related matters (Joint Committee on Children and Youth Affairs, 2016, 2017, 2019). Committee members visited Oberstown in 2015 and 2017, while the Minister for Children and Youth Affairs has responded to written and oral parliamentary questions and attended the committee relating to Oberstown on multiple occasions (Oberstown, 2019b; 2020).

Media coverage of incidents in child detention and on developments, such as the findings of inspection reports, is to be expected, along with parliamentary scrutiny. While naturally, this interest will fluctuate with levels of activity or concern, public and parliamentary interest is not only legitimate, but also important. A retrospective analysis of media coverage since 2015 both indicates the scale of the challenges experienced by Oberstown in the implementation of national policy, especially during 2016 and 2017, and also highlights the extent to which these reforms took place in the public eye, with local and national media documenting events and developments, sometimes daily. According to the international children's rights standards, it is important that education and other campaigns are undertaken to counter negative publicity faced by children in conflict with the law given the discriminatory and negative stereotyping they experience (CRC Committee, 2019a, p 18). As Chapter 8 indicates, this is a responsibility that Oberstown has increasingly taken on, putting statistical and other factual information into the public domain to inform the debate about children deprived of liberty. A particularly relevant development in this regard was the publication in 2017 of a language guide, to encourage the media to use neutral terms such as 'young people' when referring to those detained in Oberstown (*Irish Examiner*, 2017; Oberstown, 2017d). Aside from the public interest in child detention, the media has a very important role to play in scrutinizing and reporting on the treatment of children deprived of liberty. However uncomfortable this can be for those responsible for the care of children in detention, it can have a knock-on effect on the internal environment, impacting negatively on the morale of staff and unwittingly perhaps further labelling the children sent there. The Irish experience has been that media coverage and political interest has waned when concerns about the standards of care provided to children in detention and those who care for them fade. In this regard, it is notable that in 2021, when the most positive HIQA report to date was published, the event attracted no media coverage at all. Nonetheless, in Ireland's case at least, media and political scrutiny has played an important role in advancing the public interest, not only in transparency around the treatment of children in detention but also in the actual care that children receive. It is important that this scrutiny of children's rights in detention is maintained on a consistent and regular basis into the future.

Conclusion

It is evident from this chapter that advancing the rights of children in detention is a collective endeavour, which is enhanced by varied and sustained external influences. As the CRC Committee has made clear, civil society, human rights bodies and parliamentary committees all have a role in monitoring implementation of the CRC, while the media can be a 'valuable partner' as well (CRC Committee, 2003, p 14). In Ireland's case, national and international bodies influenced law and policy and its implementation, with regular scrutiny by human rights treaty bodies, national human rights institutions, civil society, the media and Oireachtas (Parliament). The analysis in this chapter illustrates that the approaches used ranged from advocating constructively for rights-based reform on the one hand, to criticizing the failure to achieve the necessary reforms or the pace of those reforms on the other. The legitimacy of public scrutiny is self-evident especially in light of the vulnerability of children deprived of their liberty. At the same time, it is perhaps fair to say that the intensity of the scrutiny that Oberstown received did not always serve the reform agenda well. Few argued, like the CPT for instance, that the scale and complexity of change warranted more haste and less speed. At the same time, the pressure of external monitoring and concern undoubtedly helped to sustain the momentum.

As the preceding chapters illustrate, the Oberstown experience is rich with lessons for Ireland, highlighting the many measures and stages necessary to achieve reform within the national context. But it is our view that this experience transcends the Irish context and has implications internationally for the global issues concerning children's rights in detention. To widen the relevance of our shared learning and experience, we articulate those lessons in our concluding chapter, Chapter 10.

Reflections: Enablers and Barriers to Reform

Introduction

This final chapter aims to draw together the book's analysis of the experience of implementing children's rights in detention. To recap, Chapter 1 explained the imperative for a children's rights approach to detention and, drawing on a range of international instruments including the United Nations Convention on the Rights of the Child (CRC), proposed an integrated model of child detention that advances children's rights. Under this rights-based model, child detention must be child-centred and fulfil the child's rights to provision, protection, participation, preparation and partnership. As Chapter 2 illustrated, children's rights are routinely breached and ignored in detention around the world, although proposals for more radical, rights-based reforms are beginning to emerge. Many of the issues highlighted internationally were concerns in Ireland as well – use of adult prisons, inadequate standards of care, high levels of restrictive practices, insufficient focus on the child's complex needs and a marginalization of children within the process – when the commitment was set out in law and policy to establish a specialist, child-centred model for all children under 18 years of age in detention. Ireland's experience is thus highly relevant to the global context and Chapters 3 to 9 explored how the commitment to advance a children's rights approach to detention has been implemented in Oberstown. It began in Chapter 3 by tracing changes to law and policy that followed Ireland's ratification of the CRC in 1992, before focusing, in Chapter 4, on the specific requirement, set by government policy, to establish a child-centred model of detention for all children under 18 years of age. These chapters provided the foundation for the more in-depth analysis that followed. Chapter 5 presented an analysis of how this mandate was taken forward to create a single, national facility for the care of children deprived of liberty, describing elements of the disruptive and at times difficult change process. As Chapters 6 and 7 showed, however, the steps taken have now begun to bear fruit in numerous ways, most notably improving children's experiences of their rights in detention through the implementation of the rights-based model. Chapters 8 and 9 complemented these developments by demonstrating how vital it is to support the staff who provide care to children, while reinforcing the role of communication, engagement and external advocacy and scrutiny as crucial enablers in the process. The goal of this last chapter, therefore, is to draw key conclusions from the implementation of a rights-based model of detention in practice, highlighting the enablers that are essential to its success.

The chapter has five sections. The first section summarizes the application of the rights-based model in Oberstown, highlighting the significant achievements and developments in this process and the gaps that remain. The second section identifies the measures that, in Oberstown's experience, enable a rights-based approach to child detention. The final three sections offer learning, reflections and some conclusions on the process of achieving the standards of rights-based detention, identifying both the barriers that hindered or slowed the process in Ireland and the supports that facilitated its achievement.

Application of the rights-based model

As Chapter 1 illustrates, a model that advances the rights of children in detention has several important elements, including child-centred care and the five Ps of provision, protection, participation, preparation and partnership. This section summarizes the progress made in each of these areas in Oberstown Children Detention Campus, drawing attention to where progress has been achieved, where it is not yet complete and, in some cases, where the standard has been exceeded. The section concludes with some observations about the challenges associated with the implementation of children's rights standards in practice.

Child-centred care

In line with children's rights standards, child-centred care requires policies, procedures and practices designed to provide the child with the best possible care, in line with their rights. The Oberstown Children's Rights Policy Framework 2020 frames the approach to care as child-centred, involving an individual assessment of need on admission and placement plans that are personalized to meet those needs. The integrated model of care is provided in partnership with multi-disciplinary services and supports, and the process of meeting the child's needs is monitored through Placement Planning Meetings that are inclusive of the child and their family, and attended by care staff, teachers and relevant professionals. Oberstown has therapeutic services on site, providing care in the areas of psychology, speech and language, social work, counselling and psychiatry, and although it was challenging to establish a multi-disciplinary and interagency approach, this is now firmly in place. An electronic case management system promotes good record-keeping and decision-making that is increasingly informed by evidence pertaining to the child's needs and circumstances. New approaches continue to be found to embed evidence-based decision-making into children's day-to-day care.

In Oberstown, child-centred care recognizes the importance of relationships with the child and emphasizes the development of positive and mutually respectful relationships between children and staff. Through good role modelling, every formal and informal interaction with the child is used to influence positive attitudes and behaviours. More work needs to be done to roll out this approach across the campus so that this is the consistent experience of every child, every day. In this respect, the child-centred approach needs to be further embedded in all residential units. Gaps also remain with regard to children on remand, who currently do not enjoy placement planning in the same way, nor do they have access to the same quality of education or leisure, as children on detention orders. The short and unpredictable nature of their detention requires a bespoke model of care to be put in place so that their needs are met, notwithstanding that placement planning can be difficult. This is now a priority.

The new Oberstown facilities are bright and airy, and accommodation is child-centred with opportunities to personalize bedrooms and experience shared living. The Campus promotes the least restrictive living environment for children within the obvious confines of a place of detention (HIQA, 2020, p 19), visitor facilities are family-friendly and there are ample opportunities for leisure, sport and other creative afterschool activities. To this point, children on remand orders are accommodated separately in the older buildings, although this is currently being addressed.

Provision

In terms of provision of the child's basic needs, children in Oberstown have access to excellent healthcare facilities and the vocational and educational provision has many strengths. While a strong integrated placement planning process ensures that children's basic needs are met, it is important to evaluate this approach to understand how it can best support the fulfilment of individual children's needs. A longitudinal study, to map the outcomes of children, is currently a gap although doctoral research currently under way will address this issue.

In Oberstown, children's medical, health and wellbeing needs are assessed and addressed by an in-house, full-time, health team with dedicated nursing staff and access to a community-based general practitioner, and dental and physiotherapy care as required. Specialist therapeutic services are available on site, including psychology and psychiatry, as an integral part of children's care, ensuring that children's mental health or substance misuse needs are addressed as part of their care. Programmes of special importance to adolescents, including sexuality, relationships and parenting education, are available. Care staff are also trained in emergency care and a holistic approach is promoted.

Education in Oberstown is provided on site in a large, well-resourced school building with a minimum 1:3 teacher:pupil ratio. Primary and post-primary teachers, employed by the Education and Training Board, deliver the national curriculum and children are supported to take state examinations. The academic curriculum is combined with vocational education that helps to provide skills-based learning that is independently accredited. Partnerships with enterprise have supported the delivery on campus of fitness and barista training. Work is still required to develop a tailored approach to education that combines academic and vocational education with skills-based learning and qualifications that meet children's needs and interests. In general, the extent to which the education meets the needs of each individual child, from those with academic strengths to others who have more vocational interests, needs to be evaluated so that children's life chances are truly enhanced. Improvements to the quality of teaching and education planning and the development of a varied and relevant curriculum, which meets children's own needs, are key. The lack of integration of the school with the rest of the campus, arising from historical institutional and governance arrangements, has hindered efforts to develop a more collaborative approach. This is now being addressed through closer working relationships and legislative change, which will enable children's rights to education to be advanced both in Oberstown and in the community when they leave.

Through formal and informal interactions with children, staff work to nurture positive attitudes and behaviours that will promote their reintegration. The Oberstown relationship model of care was supported by research commissioned in 2015, which identified the different levels at which such interventions are possible – informal, structured and specialist interactions (Bamber et al, 2016a, 2016b). This project enhanced staff awareness about the opportunities they have to support change in the child's behaviour and attitudes, in line with their prosocial development.

The rights-based approach is also evident in the shift from a model of discipline towards one that emphasizes positive behaviour. In this regard, the new Oberstown Children's Rights Policy Framework commits to 'supporting young people to understand and develop positive behaviour, to internalize and adhere to the norms of good behaviour and to supporting young people to sustain long-term positive outcomes' (8.2.1). Importantly, the fact that the courts rejected the case for enhanced remission in Oberstown, which would have brought with it a statutory disciplinary framework at odds with the more developmentally appropriate, child-centred approach, had the positive effect of underscoring this approach.

In addition to education and healthcare, significant strides have been made in the development of Oberstown's activities programme in recent years, with the inclusion of a variety of sports, the creative arts and inspiring guest speakers. The association with Gaisce, the President's Awards, has been a welcome development in providing children with opportunities for self-motivated personal development through target-setting and achievement. They include a range of activities and initiatives including artwork, to brighten the wards of the children's hospital, seasonal gifts for local community residents, and the completion of restorative workshops to help build better relationships. One 'Gold' award involved the research and creation of a mural in the Oberstown visitor centre, depicting the wildlife from a local estuary. As these awards are completed by children all over Ireland, are externally awarded and presented to children on campus by Michael D. Higgins, the President of Ireland and patron of the programme, children are motivated to be part of a programme that connects their achievements to their peers in the community.

More generally, the activities programme has developed from an ad hoc range of events to a coherent programme that seeks to stimulate children's development in a range of areas and ways. This ran as an all-day summer programme in 2021 for the first time. One way this could be developed in line with the children's rights approach is to promote a more integrated approach where the activity programme, children's school-based learning and their accredited vocational training join up to pursue the child's developmental goals. Children's experiences must be central to this approach.

Protection

The child's right to protection from harm is central to a rights-based approach to child detention both with regard to keeping them safe and in addressing past trauma. This is enabled through a multi-disciplinary approach that responds to meet children's needs assessed on admission. Children are entitled to be safeguarded from injury or harm caused by staff or by other children while in detention and they are equally entitled to protection from self-harm. They are to be kept safe from the harm that interventions, designed to protect them from themselves or from others, may cause. Given the adversity many children in detention have experienced prior to admission, this is not an insignificant challenge and children are also entitled to treatment to support their recovery.

Oberstown complies with the national Children First legislative and policy framework that comprises Ireland's safeguarding and mandatory reporting requirements. A full-time social worker acts as the designated liaison person both to support children who have experienced harm or trauma and to ensure that this is reported, as appropriate, to Tusla, the Child and Family Agency. More complex, perhaps, is the more general necessity to keep children safe from harm, to provide an environment in which they can live and interact safely with staff and with each other. There has been a deliberate and sustained focus in Oberstown to ensure children's behaviour is managed in an appropriate and safe manner. As Chapter 7 explains, there has been a dramatic reduction in the use of restrictive practices in the past three years, with single separation, where children are separated from their peers for their safety or that of others, substantially reduced in both frequency and length. The exceptional case of four young people separated for long periods, which was the subject of High Court litigation in 2016, has not been repeated, and what is evident now is the gradual shift in culture towards the use of proactive intervention that prevents children's behaviour escalating to the point of concern. This has come about through multi-faceted sustained efforts, including training, staff supervision, a focus on learning and development, enhanced recording systems, more strict approval systems and strong oversight. Good relationships with staff, based on mutual respect and communication, combines with robust placement planning to ensure not only that children's needs are met but also that children's behaviour is better understood, so that triggers or concerns can be identified before they escalate. Limiting the use of physical intervention to exceptional circumstances only in the Children's Rights Policy Framework helps to reinforce the risks to the child of such practices (9.2.4). Ongoing systematic training, regular oversight and a review of incidents when they occur, internally and externally, together with a culture of learning and accountability all help to keep children safe. Ensuring children are heard before, during and after such practices is also vital to their protection and as the systems and approaches are reviewed by management and the Board of Management, it is vital that children's voices are heard in that context also.

Children's sense of their own safety in Oberstown has improved, although there is clearly more to be done. Heightened and continued vigilance is required to keep children safe in detention and while some known risks can be mitigated or treated, others are difficult to predict. Ensuring children are heard is essential to their protection and the appointment of an advocacy officer has been critical to the emerging children's rights culture in this regard. Comprehensive needs assessments and holistic placement plans that are effectively implemented and carefully monitored are key to ensuring children's needs are met. Robust recruitment, training and supervision of staff must combine with strong systems of data management and effective communication to ensure signs of trauma or distress are picked up early. Trust between children and the adults they rely on is vital. And even with all of this in place, it may not be enough to protect every child from harm. And if injury occurs, it is important, in line with the children's rights approach, to put in place the supports to advance the child's dignity, care and recovery, and indeed the wellbeing of staff.

Participation

It is fundamental to the protection of children's rights in detention that they are supported to participate in decision-making at all levels, with the right to be active agents in their own care, informed and supported to participate in individual and collective decision-making on matters that affect them. A children's rights approach means that children have the right to information about their rights, and about their care, and to access effective complaints mechanisms in respect of their treatment.

The adoption of the Participation Strategy in 2017 was a significant moment in the advancement of children's rights in Oberstown and the appointment of an advocacy officer, as guardian of the policy, has accelerated its implementation, promoting the voice of children across the campus in decision-making at individual, residential unit and campus levels and, now, with the Board of Management. These steps have influenced the culture shift towards a child-centred approach in Oberstown, as children raise their concerns and have them addressed at all levels, with the ability to have recourse to both internal and external complaints mechanisms, in which they have increasing confidence. Regular dialogue between their own representative body, the Campus Council, and both management and the Board of Management, has meant that children's views now inform decision-making at the highest levels.

Children's formal participation in 2021 in the process to appoint the new Director of the Campus evidences the advances that have been made in this area, with children gathering the views from their peers and being supported, by the Chief People Officer, to interview the candidates for the role. It is now proposed that children will have a say in all senior recruitment as well as in management matters that impact on their lives such as, for example, the make-up of their residential units. Further initiative in this area might include the appointment of a former resident to the Board of Management. More immediately, while progress has been significant, further embedding of child participation into everyday practice needs to continue, so that this right is not just the priority of the advocacy officer, but of every member of staff. Partnership with young people – in the development of the Health Information and Quality Authority (HIQA) inspection process and in the development of an advocacy strategy, which enables them to have a say as to how best to address the matters that impact on them – will also broaden what Oberstown can achieve in this space. The new National Framework for the Children and Young People's Participation in Decision-Making will support this process (Department of Children, 2021).

Preparation

Preparing a child for when they leave detention is integral to the rights-based approach and the children's rights standards highlight the supports and programmes that must be in place internally to prepare the child for leaving and externally to facilitate their reintegration when they leave. Ensuring children's needs are met while in detention is central to their ability to enjoy a constructive life afterwards. In Oberstown, planning for leaving begins the day the child arrives and an interagency process enables recourse to community-based services and supports that can help to support children and indeed parents through what can be a difficult transition. The measures in the Children Act 2001 that support this process – mobility trips, temporary leave and permitted absence – are used to beneficial effect and their endorsement by the Court of Appeal in 2020 heightens their standing. The absence of a statutory entitlement to aftercare, however, means that external bodies cannot be compelled to support a child leaving detention and this can limit the measures in place for an individual child. Given that successful reintegration is absolutely key not only to maximizing the potential of children who have spent time in detention but also to not undoing the progress made in that time, it is critical that this lacuna is addressed in the review of the Children Act 2001 (Forde, 2014). Similarly, while arrangements are in place to smooth a child's transition to prison, the absence of a formalized regime for emerging adults in the prison system means that children must sometimes go directly from the child-centred care in Oberstown to the adult regime when they reach the age of 18. While it is welcome that these priorities are identified in the Youth Justice Strategy 2021–2027, closing the gap will require legislative reform. Oberstown, meanwhile, will need to give particular attention to how children who receive long sentences can avoid becoming institutionalized and are supported to live independently while in detention.

Partnership

Partnership, as a theme of the rights-based approach to child detention, recognizes the importance of collaboration, coordination and a shared multi-disciplinary and interagency approach. Parents must be central to the child's care and the child's relationship with their family must be supported and strengthened while in detention. Regular contact with community-based agencies, services and individuals should take place in a manner designed to fulfil the child's rights and promote their reintegration. Approaches to youth detention must be connected to children's policy and linkages between secure and community-based services strengthened.

A flexible approach to visits enables children in Oberstown to have regular contact with family, something that has continued over videoconference through COVID-19 restrictions (Lynch and Kilkelly, 2021). Parents are regularly updated on their child's wellbeing and, when they can, attend placement planning meetings (PPMs) so that they participate fully in the decision-making around their child's care. It is important now to formalize the relationship with parents, through a representative group for instance, to ensure their views and experiences are taken into account in the development and operation of the campus.

Collaboration is at the heart of the Oberstown approach, in recognition that the complex needs of children in detention can only be met through an integrated, interagency process. Engaging services and supports from across the community, which has been the subject of deliberate and sustained effort, helps to ensure that children's holistic needs are met, in a way that enables continuity after they leave detention. The multi-professional approach to care, highlighted by the children's rights standards, is provided with the range of services based on campus, with community organizations providing augmented support through mentoring, advocacy and family-based services. This work is hampered, as highlighted earlier, by the absence of a suitable statutory framework for aftercare and consideration also needs to be given to ensuring continuity of care, including through the Probation Service and other community groups, so that the developments achieved in detention are sustained afterwards.

Measures that enable rights-based detention

The last section presented the key elements of the rights-based approach to child detention, applying them to practice in the context of Oberstown. The analysis here and in previous chapters explains the complex range of measures that must be taken to advance children's rights in detention. While the lessons from this complex process are outlined later in this chapter, this section identifies the measures that are essential to support, promote and help deliver the rights-based model. The international standards highlight the importance of the various supporting actions that enable a rights-based approach to child detention. Experience indicates that these legal and non-legal measures fall into several categories, are situated at various levels and may take place at different stages of the implementation process. They include measures that ground children's rights standards in law and policy, that support and enable staff to deliver rights-based care, that promote accountability and public scrutiny of implementation and, finally, that help the children's rights approach to be understood.

Grounded

International children's rights standards are clear that their integration into national law and policy is important to advance implementation, and research suggests a strong link between the incorporation of children's rights and their enjoyment by children in practice (Kilkelly et al, 2021). The Irish experience strongly supports this conclusion with regard to both national law and policy. The Children Act 2001 established the principle, as a matter of national law, that detention should be a measure of last resort and it prescribed the model of child-centred care and education for all children under 18 years of age. The existence of a clear statutory basis for a specialist, holistic model of child detention provided an important reference point for the reform. Government policy – to provide a single unified service in a custom-built facility for children – added clarity and urgency to the achievement of these goals. The decision to draw on the legislation in the development of the **C**are, **E**ducation, **H**ealth, **O**ffending behaviour and **P**reparation for leaving (CEHOP) model of care gave it added weight. Together, the national law and policy, and the expectation to deliver on their implementation, created a momentum from the top down, for change.

In addition to the expectation of law and policy with regard to child detention, the legislation provided elements that helped enable the delivery of the rights-based approach. For instance, the fact that the legislation framed the role of Director of Oberstown as one of quasi-parent, distinguishing the approach from prison, helped to create a unique identity for Oberstown. It also provided a level of discretion within which 'parental authority' could be exercised. This is most pertinent with regard to placement planning in which Oberstown is largely autonomous in drawing in other services and supports to ensure the child's needs are met. It is also very significant in the context of managing behaviour where in recent court judgments on both remission and single separation, the courts have reinforced that Oberstown is distinct from prison, drawing a strong connection between the loco parentis role of the Director and Oberstown's developmentally appropriate approach. In all of these respects, the legislation has been key to supporting the child-centred model.

However, reliance on legislation has been a hindrance a times. First, the legislation required to create the single child-centred model from the previous Children Detention Schools took longer to enact than anticipated, only coming into force in June 2016, whereas the new service began to take shape from 2014. This had a knock-on effect on the change process as staff wanted the new framework to be in place before committing to the new organization. Second, the current legislative framework, where the school is the responsibility of the Department of Education, rather than Oberstown or the Department of Children, has at times frustrated efforts to create an integrated approach to education. This is now being addressed with the proposal to add an additional member from the Education and Training Board to the Board of Management, which will enhance the further integration of the service. Finally, due to the absence of statutory provision for aftercare, children's access to supports when they leave detention is not a matter of right and this means that community services and supports are not always available to support children so that they are prepared for leaving notwithstanding the role of Tusla, the Child and Family Agency, here.

Supported

The international standards are explicit that detention being provided by suitable, qualified, trained and supervised staff is important to the implementation of children's rights. The Oberstown experience bears this out in two ways. First, it has been crucial both to improving the quality of care and to expanding the service to accommodate children under 18 years of age. Neither goal would have been delivered without recruitment, which brought new staff into the organization, with fresh perspectives, to work alongside more experienced staff. Separately, the Oberstown experience reinforces the view that staff who provide care in the challenging environment of secure care, must themselves be supported. In addition to resourcing health and safety, therefore, priority must be given to the development of staff wellbeing. In Oberstown, the appointment of a full-time organizational psychologist, and more recently a chief people officer, put down important markers in this respect and the resourcing of a range of initiatives to develop resilience and improve staff learning helped to achieve significant staff buy-in. Positive employee engagement internally, where staff feel heard and valued, as well as favourable external validation, are both important measures of the progress that has been achieved in this area.

Accountability

The international children's rights standards are explicit that rights-compliant detention can only be assured through independent and robust oversight delivered through rigorous, regular and transparent inspection. Public scrutiny is also important, with valuable roles played by the media, civil society and parliament. External inspection bodies such as HIQA and international bodies such as the European Committee for the Prevention of

Torture and Inhuman or Degrading Treatment or Punishment (CPT) visit the campus announced and unannounced to inspect the care provided and to make recommendations for improvements. While these processes bring deficits and progress to public attention, accountability must also be delivered internally. In Oberstown, this operates with the Director reporting to the Board of Management on how care is being provided, providing regular and comprehensive information to the board on the operation of the campus in key areas, and attending monthly board meetings as part of a robust system of governance and oversight. Holding individual staff to account is also critical, but much more difficult. International standards have an expectation of sanction when rules are breached with regard to children's care and while this must be part of any contract of employment, the threshold for determining when sanction should apply rather than a process of learning and improvement is a delicate and sensitive matter. Regardless, it is the Oberstown experience that systems to promote individual and collective accountability within the setting of child detention, while assuring on behalf of the public through external systems of inspection and scrutiny, are integral to the rights-based approach.

Understood

The international standards are clear that public awareness and understanding about the rights of children deprived of liberty and the importance of a rights-based approach to their care are vital to its implementation. They require that data collection, research and regular evaluation of practices and approaches are continuous and involve children at every stage. The value of creating awareness about the rights-based approach to the care of children in detention was evident from an early stage in Oberstown. The adoption of a Communications and External Engagement Strategy in 2017 gave important direction, helping to connect stakeholders internally and externally and to create a shared sense of purpose. Improved data collection and information systems enabled Oberstown to contribute to public debate and understanding about children in detention, and to convene events that brought together those with shared interest and expertise. Information strategies internally have also been important in creating a shared identity among staff and, in line with international standards, children have been part of this process, receiving timely and appropriate information about their rights, and about internal and external complaints mechanisms and advocacy supports.

Learning

The analysis in the last section explains the structural and supportive measures that have been found to be influential in the introduction of a rights-based approach to child detention in Ireland. It highlights the importance of law and policy, of an emphasis on staff needs and wellbeing, of robust accountability internally and externally and of research, evaluation and public awareness about children's rights in detention. Bearing in mind the process to implement the children's rights standards in Oberstown, this section contains some reflections on this experience, identifying the factors that have hindered and enabled the reform.

Extensive literature documents the management of change, and numerous models exist to inform and support the process. As Shacklady-Smith (2006, p 384) notes, 'there is no one right theory or approach to change management, rather there are multiple perspectives and lenses through which to view organizations and from which to develop ideas, actions and technologies for approaching change'. The creation of a rights-based approach to child detention was a process of 'planned' as opposed to 'emergent' change and, in this regard, Lewin's (1958) three-stage approach is relevant insofar as it prescribes a period of 'unfreezing the organisation from a presumed steady and stable state', followed by a move towards a new goal and view of the future and, finally, a refreezing or stabilizing of norms, values and behaviours, creating a new steady state (Shacklady-Smith, 2006, p 386). Kotter (1996) identified eight reasons why corporate change efforts fail, translating them into his Leading Change model, with eight steps of successful change management. Elements from both Kotter and Lewin's change models can be found in this evaluation of the process of change undertaken in Oberstown.

'Planned' change and its implications for staff

In Oberstown's case, the change was a planned and top-down process, which began with the setting of expectations by government policy for Oberstown to deliver with regard to the merger of three detention schools into one, the completion of a new building and accepting responsibility for 16- and 17-year-olds into the child-centred model. One of the significant challenges this presented was the clear perception among staff that this change was being done 'to them' and employee relationships were thus an important focus throughout the reform process. In 2014, agreement was reached between management and trade unions on a list of 99 historical industrial relations issues that stemmed from the different arrangements that had been in place across the different children detention schools over two decades. While reaching agreement paved the way for a new unified approach to employee relations, there was no provision in government pay policy at the time to offer redundancy for those staff who did not want to be part of the new campus. The small number of staff who did not want to stay had thus no option and although some long-term staff did make the personal decision to leave, when new staff were appointed, for the first time in many years, the work environment was at times quite unfamiliar. In addition, some staff suffered a loss of identity (having been strongly associated with 'their' individual school previously) and were anxious about the ability to cope in the new organization. The imperative to create new teams, as the new organization was established from several distinct entities, was also disruptive and unsettling. The expectation that Oberstown would take responsibility for 17-year-olds from prison as quickly as possible added pressure to expedite the reform and expansion process, compounding anxiety levels among staff, some of whom doubted their ability to cope with older offenders and who were already struggling with the scale of change and the demands of the newly professionalized service.

Creation of a vision and strategy

An added complication was the fact that while the 'what' of national policy was clear – a unified and specialist child detention organization was to be established – there had been little articulation of 'how' this was to be achieved. A Public Appointments Service report (IYJS, 2012) had identified the priority steps to be taken, the appointment of a campus manager to provide leadership and the creation of a change management resource to steer the process, for instance, but there was otherwise no blueprint for what needed to be done. Although work was ongoing to create a new identity for Oberstown, including a logo devised by the young people (Figure 10.1), the tumultuous events of 2016 prompted the Board of Management to adopt an Action Plan in January 2017 to articulate a new vision and purpose for the short-term future of the organization. This clarity provided some room to consult more widely as part of a strategic planning process, and with input from children, staff and external stakeholders, the first Oberstown Strategy 2017–2020 was adopted and launched by the Minister for Children in 2017. The Action Plan and subsequently the Strategy, brought clarity and set the direction and priorities for the organization at a time of great upheaval. Its adoption and widespread communication brought comfort and

Figure 10.1: Oberstown Children Detention Campus - logo

confidence, internally and externally, ultimately supporting organizational stability. The fact that implementation of the strategy was also tracked and monitored, including through published updates and stakeholder engagement sessions, helped to improve transparency and ownership in relation to Oberstown's progress.

Autonomy and engineering solutions

The fact that Oberstown is Ireland's only child detention facility means that it has no comparators or peer organizations nationally. Its unique character, which is underpinned by the legislation, gave leadership a degree of flexibility and autonomy with regard to the development of the new model and approach. As historical traditions and practices were shed and new ones emerged (in line with Lewin's unfreezing and freezing methodology), there was a significant opportunity to take 'bold' decisions. These involved acquiring or assuming responsibility – for bed management, human resources or the management of facilities – from others across government departments and agencies who had previously (always) had ownership of these areas. They also involved forging new partnerships, such as with the Department of Justice on the case management system, to create new ways of working that would benefit the new campus. Engineered solutions had to be found to the problems encountered, and workarounds and creative approaches were essential.

Political support

All successful change models propose the importance of forming alliances and creating coalitions to lead and act as an ambassador for the new vision. Kotter (1996) identified the importance of the guiding coalition comprising those in positions of power and authority but also those having expertise, reputation and relationships to deliver on the new ambition. The articulation in national policy of the rights-based model of child detention clearly gave impetus and urgency to its introduction. This meant that the unified, specialist service, including the transfer of older offenders from adult prisons, had government support, with two positive effects. The first was the confidence that the Minister for Children, in particular, supported efforts under way to implement the changes required. Public expressions of support, visits to the campus to meet the children and staff and attendance at Oberstown events all helped to boost staff morale during a difficult change process. Regular and direct access to the Minister and their officials allowed for the timely resolution of concerns, through mediation, consultation or the allocation of resources. For instance, throughout the change process the Minister convened a meeting with neighbours of the campus to hear their concerns, attended a meeting with civil society groups to update them on developments and helped coordinate resources at a cross-departmental level. The second practical effect was that government ensured the necessary resources were allocated to the project – for staffing, for completion of the capital project or to develop the service to the standard required. Strong practical support was also provided by government departments and agencies and although the pace and scale of change presented a challenge for the civil service, great care was taken to balance the competing dimensions of government responsibility for the project. Altogether, this helped to create strong practical support for the change agenda.

Governance

Oberstown's unique model of governance, whereby a statutory Board of Management has responsibility for the management of child detention, provided leadership to the change process. Independently chaired, the board comprises representatives from the main government departments, from staff and from the local community, together with five independent people with expertise in areas of relevance to the campus. The first unified board was appointed in 2012 when, for the first time, consideration was given to equipping the board with the particular expertise and experience required for steering Oberstown through the changes required. This board evolved further when, in 2016, the first board of the newly amalgamated facility was appointed, with the Public Appointments Service supporting the nomination of individuals who had applied with expertise in finance, governance and law, and the essential criterion of a commitment to improving the lives of children in conflict with the law. This process matured further in 2019 when the current Board of Management was appointed, bringing further fresh perspectives and expertise onto the board. The evolution of board membership through the years took place in parallel with a national agenda to professionalize state boards and promote their compliance with the highest standards of governance set out in the Code of Practice for the Governance of State Bodies (Department of Public Expenditure and Reform, 2016). The appointment in 2019 of a full-time board secretary has further enhanced the board's professional capacity to provide rigorous oversight, support and challenge to the management of the campus and to ensure that in governance, as in other areas, Oberstown achieves high standards in public accountability.

Stakeholder relationships

Oberstown has a complex set of stakeholders internally and externally, all of which need to be kept informed, supported and managed depending on their level of interest or influence. The reporting relationship with the Department of Children has always been very important and during the change process it was vital to have good relationships with department officials, as well as other government agencies such as the Office of Public Works (which managed the capital project) and the Department of Public Expenditure and Reform (responsible for government pay policy), whose support was regularly required to resolve issues. The neighbouring community, two members of which are represented on the Board of Management, is also an important stakeholder and early on in the change process regular meetings were established to keep the community informed about developments on campus and to ensure communication flowed at critical times. These strong relationships paid dividends, for instance, when a snowstorm cut Oberstown off from emergency services. New traditions have supplemented old ones, with an annual Christmas lunch for older people, with wreaths and other gifts made for the community by the children. The third set of stakeholders comprises civil society groups, statutory agencies and community organizations with an interest in child detention and, since 2017, Oberstown has convened an annual event to provide an update on developments, to provide context to the changes under way and raise awareness about both the operational challenges of the environment and the needs of children in detention. These events also provide the opportunity for consultation on strategic planning and other developments so that the communication is two-way. Through a difficult process, these events helped to develop relationships and trust between Oberstown and its stakeholders and to increase awareness about the complexity of the work under way, providing context to media coverage when it arose. It is important to sustain these relationships even when the intensity of public interest wanes and to evolve them so that they continue to advocate on behalf of the children in Oberstown, in line with their own perspectives and views.

Reviews and professional supports

Engaging external support and advice became commonplace during the challenges of the change process towards a national child-centred approach to detention. Professionals with expertise in change management, governance, emergency planning and team building came on board to assist with the process. Whether these were pro bono connections that arose from serendipity or were part of formal tendering processes for professional services, requests for advice and support were rarely refused and many displayed loyalty to the mission and people in Oberstown long after their formal relationship ended.

Formal mechanisms were also used to broker solutions or to mediate compromise. For example, a series of reviews was negotiated between management and trade unions under the auspices of the Workplace Relations

Commission in 2016, commissioning independent parties to review matters of concern around health and safety and security, for instance. A similar independent review mechanism was used to tease out staff demands for personal protective equipment (for example, riot gear), a request that was made routinely by employee representatives concerned that older offenders would present a greater physical challenge to staff. This was also addressed by a behaviour management review, which advised against care staff being armed or trained to use such equipment, but recommended instead that recourse to the local police (An Garda Síochána) should be in place in such circumstances.

At the same time, the reviews were not themselves without complexity and in some cases took on an importance beyond their intended purpose. The Review Implementation Group (RIG) was an important vehicle to analyse and structure their recommendations and it also enabled reflection on the obstacles to their successful implementation. According to the RIG, these included limitations on time, resources and the capacity of the campus for further change (RIG, 2017). In particular, the RIG noted that, notwithstanding the need for further improvements in the care being provided, there was a limit to the amount of 'new learning, new practices and new training' that could be undertaken in light of the ability of individuals and groups 'to sustain the knowledge and expertise acquired through training and to incorporate that into practice' (RIG, 2017, p 17). The RIG also cautioned about the pressure being created by the continuing pace and nature of change. Noting that the progress to date had been 'substantial', there was a need to 'normalise operations and to slow down the rate of change so that it forms part of the day-to-day normal rhythm of Campus operations' (RIG, 2017, p 17). In a final comment, the RIG reflected that 'while external oversight and inspection is vital to ensure public accountability, it is the staff and management of the Campus that must now take responsibility for the implementation of the reviews' recommendations' (RIG, 2017, p 24). It concluded that 'the considerations highlighted in this report should be taken into account in giving the Campus the time, capacity and resources to ensure implementation of the reviews' recommendations'. In this regard, it noted, 'providing the best possible care to young people in Oberstown must remain the overriding priority' (RIG, 2017, p 24).

Resilient leadership

During 2016 and 2017, the impact of the significant change process on the campus brought it to public attention through regular media reports of serious incidents. This in turn generated concern among stakeholders in a way that brought the challenges being experienced by the campus into the public domain in a very real way. A particularly grave incident took place on 29 August 2016 when, during strike action by staff, a number of children secured access to the roof of one of the older residential units, ultimately setting a fire that destroyed it. But there were other incidents too as the campus struggled with the mounting pressure for reform. The obstacles that arose throughout the transition period were significant, complex, unexpected and at times appeared insurmountable. While the enablers set out in this chapter served to advance the direction set by government policy, it was of significant importance that this policy was itself designed to provide better protection of children's rights. Notwithstanding the resistance and opposition and the intense public criticism at times, the motivation to overcome the various challenges came from the fact that the objective itself – to implement a rights-based approach to detention for children – was one with which no-one could disagree. It also depended, however, on the resilient leadership of a small number of people who, perhaps as luck would have it, had the expertise, the capacity and the determination to persist, at times against the odds.

Final observations on the challenges of implementing children's rights in detention

Notwithstanding the detailed nature of children's rights standards and the guidance as to how best to implement those standards in detention, significant gaps remain between these standards and the reality of children's experiences of their rights when they are deprived of liberty (Nowak, 2019). While we argue that this gap can be bridged through the adoption of a range of strategies and approaches in line with children's rights, it is important to acknowledge the challenges that can be associated with the protection of children's rights in detention.

First, it is a matter of general concern with regard to the application of children's rights in practice that the standards do not always provide a mechanism for balancing conflicting rights, such as the rights of one child as against those of another, or for justifying interferences with such rights when necessitated by other legitimate considerations. For instance, in detention settings, the obvious requirements of security and good order may at times necessitate placing limits on the rights of an individual or group of children. A risk to security may require a child's movements to be restricted, by the wearing of handcuffs; a risk that parents may pass drugs to a young person might justify the visit taking place through a screen rather than in person; or a young person displaying angry behaviour, posing a threat to themselves or others, may need to be separated from the group for a period, denying them the right to socialize. While these measures are not entirely divorced from those designed to protect the rights of the children detained – to protection from harm, to health and to associate with their peers – there are nonetheless situations where the rights of children are limited in the interests of others, including the safe and secure operation of the institution. Despite their detail, international children's rights standards offer little guidance as to how these different interests are to be balanced and such difficult situations to be managed, and they offer no explicit framework for ensuring that a proportionate balance is stuck between the limitations placed on the exercise of the child's rights and the legitimate aim that such restrictions seek to achieve. What can be argued from children's rights principles, however, is that any decision to interfere with a child's rights must be supported by a robust and fair decision-making process, in which the young person themselves has a say, and must be guided by what is in the child's best interests, with maximum protection of their rights a key goal. This is what the children's rights model of detention as implemented in Oberstown seeks to secure. It is also evident from the international standards that the staff taking these decisions must be appropriately trained, with their discretion tightly bounded, in either law or policy, and its exercise subjected to approval, inspection and review. This reflects the ancillary supports that the rights-based model of child detention requires.

A second factor relevant to the implementation of children's rights standards in detention is the complexity of the secure setting and its relationship to the external environment, including other agencies of the justice system. Those responsible for detention services do not decide who is referred to them by the courts or for how long, meaning that the size, make-up and complexity of the population are subject to change, often with little notice. This is particularly the case with respect to children detained on remand, whose time in detention can be short and unsettled. Detention services are thus required to be highly flexible and responsive, capable of meeting the complex and varying needs of each individual referred to them, often at short notice, with varying ages, backgrounds and levels of vulnerability. At the same time, while it is important that national law provides for the use of detention as a measure of last resort, it is equally important, as part of a national youth justice strategy, that there is good communication, coordination and cooperation between child detention services and those responsible for the child's care both before and after their detention. In this regard, no matter how successful detention or any other part of the youth justice system is in meeting the rights of the child, the indivisibility of the child's rights means that this will be of limited success if all parts do not work together, with a uniform approach.

The third factor relevant to the implementation of children's rights in detention relates to the complex nature of the setting itself. It is well known that young people who end up in detention have often suffered challenges and trauma in their lives, leading to complex and acute unmet needs in the areas of education, health and wellbeing (Nowak, 2019). The implementation of the requirement of Article 37 of the CRC, that detention must be a measure of last resort, means that young people who spend time in detention will be those for whom no alternative service or support was appropriate. This often means that children who are deprived of liberty will be those with the most complex set of needs, often unmet, whose behaviour can at times evolve quickly from frustration into aggression. Responding appropriately in a closed environment that runs on a 24/7 basis, where staff can themselves experience high levels of mutual dependency and stress, should not be underestimated. Although the international standards highlight that staff in detention must be appropriately recruited and trained professionals, they say little about how to ensure that the staff are themselves supported to undertake what can be challenging work. Nor do they contemplate the reality that it might be difficult, if not impossible, to attract highly qualified staff and to retain these staff when burnout may be the reality.

Finally, the standards recognize the importance of ensuring that the treatment of children deprived of liberty is subject to high levels of accountability and scrutiny, through regular robust inspections and effective complaints mechanisms. They do not recognize, however, the intense public and media gaze in which detention services tend to work, at both the progressive and the punitive end of the spectrum. Even where youth crime is not politicized, the legitimate demands of accountability, including through campaigns of litigation and investigative reporting for instance, can create a difficult environment in which to protect the rights of children in detention. While these external pressures play a vital role in improving the transparency around child detention, they can add to the challenge of creating the conditions in which children's rights are protected, impacting negatively on staff and morale and labelling the children whose rights they are seeking to promote. This is especially the case when reforms are required and those observing are impatient to see progress. Perhaps not surprisingly, this situation may be compounded by the fact that the public understanding of the challenge of providing care to an extremely vulnerable group of children within a complex secure environment is often weak, while the desire for reform is strong. Ironically, perhaps, this imperative to improve the treatment of children is counterbalanced with the reality that children, often convicted of serious offences, can be seen as less worthy.

Conclusion

The aim of this book was to identify, through illustration, one country's experience of translating children's rights into the practice of detention. It is not possible to do justice in a single book to the body of work comprising the scale and complexity associated with the Oberstown experience. Nor is it posited that the Oberstown experience will be capable of replication elsewhere given that detention centres come in different shapes and forms and not all may be suited to the kind of change and reform that compliance with children's rights demands. Nonetheless, the aim of this book was to describe the key elements of a change process for those who want to make it happen.

Of all the lessons here, one is clear: detention cannot be viewed in isolation from other parts of the youth justice system or indeed from the child welfare and protection systems of the state. What is known is that as the numbers of children in detention fall, the needs of those who end up there will continue to intensify, towards profound and complex adversity. Over-representation – of Traveller children in the Irish context, as with other minority ethnic groups elsewhere – asks questions of detention even if they are beyond its control. Similarly, the involvement of girls or transgender youth, in small numbers, can make it difficult to elaborate programmes and approaches that meet their very specific needs. The duty must always be that, regardless of background or circumstance, every individual child's needs must be met, while they serve out the ultimate punishment for their offending behaviour. This is the state's responsibility, while other measures are required to ensure that reform of detention does not take place in isolation from the wider system. Doing this in a child-centred manner, in line with international children's rights standards, is vital if the state's duties to all children are to be fulfilled. Even if it is not without challenge, the rewards for getting it right – giving a child the chance to fulfil their potential – are significant. For that, every effort must be exhausted.

Afterword

It is an African proverb that it takes a village to raise a child – a community must share its resources, its knowledge and its wisdom if the potential of the child is to be fulfilled. The same is true of Oberstown in that it took a myriad of influences and influencers over many, many years, to create, shape and implement the vision of rights-based detention for children in Ireland. This book demonstrates that it is possible to put in place a model of child-centred care for children deprived of liberty by explaining the measures, actions and steps required to make it happen. However, we are not naïve enough to think that the Oberstown 'job' is done. It will take many more years of hard work and commitment before the change we document here is embedded and the potential of the rights-based approach fulfilled. Nor do we suggest in documenting Ireland's experience, that this is a case study capable of being replicated anywhere. There are simply too many variables to do justice to a comparative analysis, but we do want to conclude this book with a reflection on where else this could happen. In what circumstances could such a project be a success?

Although it is difficult to say with certainty, we consider the following factors to be important. First, we know that the most important starting point is a political commitment to children's rights, to high standards, to wanting something better than prison-like conditions for children. Building consensus around rights-based detention is difficult without a strong, informed civil society, a respect for international instruments, which reflect consensus on these issues, and the work of international organizations that can be leveraged for reform at a national level. But it is impossible without political will and a long-term vision. Culture change requires a disruptive creativity and an almost mission-like desire to challenge orthodox thinking and question approaches that are mainstream. At the same time, vision has to come with substance. The vision has to be thought through so that the solution to the problem being solved is the right one, not the simplest. This kind of project requires architects *and* builders, both motivated by the desire to create something transformative for children at the margins of society.

Second, and related, it is our experience, and Ireland's experience, that leadership is absolutely essential. By this we mean people prepared at every level to lead, but also those who have the skill, the tenacity and the charisma to be followed and to create successors to pursue what might be a decade-long goal when they themselves are gone. Leadership comes in many forms – from the subtle influence of quiet diplomacy to the shaming effects of broadcast political statements – and all are important. Many parties have a role to play and can lead in different ways, at different times. We think it is vitally important to have leadership among political representatives, especially those seasoned enough to weather a storm or to champion an unpopular cause. We also know that leadership and, at times, steely determination among the public officials who advise them are equally, if not more, important. Finally, we have learnt that the professionals given the task of delivering must also be leaders, capable of delivering their part, ensuring ultimately that the job gets done despite the obstacles that might end up in their way.

The third essential element for international application of the rights-based model is partnership. No one individual, organization or sector can achieve reform of this complexity or scale alone and building alliances and networks for support across disciplinary, government and budgetary boundaries is crucial so that the reforms are seen as a win–win. Rights-based detention requires a comprehensive and holistic service for the child – just having the criminal justice agencies on board for instance, will not ensure that psychiatric or educational specialization is available in the detention service. Developing the service in-house, but without the partners in the community, will only get the job half done. Advocating among civil liberty groups who are already on board, but failing to persuade victim organizations of the value of the rights-based approach for children who have often caused harm, could jeopardize success. This highlights the importance of objective and informed advocacy, and the power of making friends and influencing people.

The final element we believe is critical to replicating the model elsewhere is flexibility. While this is Ireland's story of creating child-centred detention, it will not be what works everywhere. Shaping your own approach and creating your own solution are vital to ensuring a good fit with the prevailing legal, political, economic and social conditions. And flexibility is also required to adapt to changing circumstances as they evolve. In Ireland, for instance, the continuing falling numbers of children in detention mean that a facility built for 90 children now accommodates less than one third of those numbers, requiring us to reimagine the next phase of our development. And who knows what long-term impact the global COVID-19 pandemic will have on criminal justice, on state budgets and on children? Change has new meaning and we must all be agile enough to respond.

So, in conclusion then, this is but Ireland's story of reform, as it happened, and as we experienced it, from our perspective. What will we take away now that this part of it is done, that others might learn? Above all else, it will be that in the midst of change and challenge, operational and strategic, young people were always central. Amidst the different circumstances and variables, across borders and systems, this is the one constant, the one value that we can share, replicate and translate without question, from one country, from one person to another.

References

Baidawi, S. and Sheehan, R. (2020) *"Cross-over" Children in the Youth Justice and Child Protection Systems*, London: Routledge.

Baker, N. (2017a) '7 staff a week absent at Oberstown Detention Centre – 1,668 days lost', *Irish Examiner*, [online] 16 February, Available from: https://www.irishexaminer.com/news/arid-20443008.html [Accessed 28 April 2021].

Baker, N. (2017b) 'Three-year strategic plan for youth detention centre', *Irish Examiner*, [online] 14 December, Available from: https://www.irishexaminer.com/news/arid-20464400.html [Accessed 28 April 2021].

Bamber, J., Brolly, C., Mills, E. and Farrar, C. (2016a) *Lessons from Literature: Building Relationships with Young People to Improve Pro-social Outcomes*, Dublin: Oberstown Children Detention Campus.

Bamber, J., Brolly, C., Mills, E. and Farrar, C. (2016b) *Building Relationships with Young People in Oberstown to Improve Pro-social Outcomes*, Dublin: Centre for Effective Services.

Barn, R., Feilzer, M. and Hardwick, N. (2018) 'Black and minority ethnic boys and custody in England and Wales: understanding subjective experiences through an analysis of official data', *Social Sciences*, 7(11): 226.

Bergin, P. (2016) 'Reform at Oberstown in the interests of all, says director Pat Bergin', *Irish Examiner*, [online] 3 September, Available from: https://www.irishexaminer.com/opinion/commentanalysis/arid-20419172.html [Accessed 28 April 2021].

Berkery, S. (2018) 'Diversion as a core principle in the Irish youth justice system', *Irish Journal of Family Law*, 21(2): 27–35.

Bishop, D. and Feld, B. (eds) (2012) *The Oxford Handbook of Juvenile Crime and Juvenile Justice*, New York: Oxford University Press.

Bohan, C. (2013) 'Seven young offenders released as judge rules kids should get remission too', *The Journal*, [online] 10 December, Available from: https://www.thejournal.ie/remission-young-offenders-oberstown-1216359-Dec2013/ [Accessed 28 April 2021].

Bowers, S. (2020) 'Significant use of restriction in Oberstown, report says', *The Irish Times*, [online] 7 January, Available from: https://www.irishtimes.com/news/ireland/irish-news/significant-use-of-restriction-in-oberstown-report-says-1.4132809?mode=sample&auth-failed=1&pw-origin=https%3A%2F%2Fwww.irishtimes.com%2Fnews%2Fireland%2Firish-news%2Fsignificant-use-of-restriction-in-oberstown-report-says-1.4132809 [Accessed 28 April 2021].

Bradley, K., Logan, A. and Shaw, S. (2009) 'Youth and crime: centennial reflections on the Children Act 1908', *Crimes and Misdemeanours: Deviance and the Law in Historical Perspective*, 3(2): 1–17.

Brennan, A.M. (2012) 'The Garda diversion programme and the juvenile offender: the dilemma of due process rights', *Irish Criminal Law Journal*, 22(2): 46–53.

Calvin, E., Kysel, I. and Parker, A. (2012) *Against All Odds: Prison Conditions for Youth Offenders Serving Life Without Parole Sentences in the United States*, New York: Human Rights Watch.

Campaign for Youth Justice (2007) *Jailing Juveniles: The Dangers of Incarcerating Youth in Adult Jails in America*, Washington DC: Campaign for Youth Justice.

Carolan, M. (2017) 'Oberstown teens awarded €100 damages each by High Court', *The Irish Times*, [online] 6 November, Available from: https://www.irishtimes.com/news/crime-and-law/courts/high-court/oberstown-teens-awarded-100-damages-each-by-high-court-1.3281638 [Accessed 28 April 2021]

Carr, N. and Mayock, P. (2019) *Care and Justice: Children and Young People in Care and Contact with the Criminal Justice System*, Dublin: Irish Penal Reform Trust.

Cesaroni, C., Grol, C. and Fredericks, K. (2019) 'Overrepresentation of Indigenous youth in Canada's criminal justice system: perspectives of Indigenous young people', *Australian and New Zealand Journal of Criminology*, 52(1): 111–28.

Children's Commissioner (2018) *A Report on the Use of Segregation in Youth Custody in England*, London: Children's Commissioner for England.

Children's Commissioner (2019) *Who Are They? Where Are They? Children Locked Up*, London: Children's Commissioner for England.

Children's Rights Alliance (2013) *Report Card 2012*, Dublin: Children's Rights Alliance.

Children's Rights Alliance (2014) *Report Card 2013*, Dublin: Children's Rights Alliance.

Children's Rights Alliance (2015a) 'Closing the door on St. Patrick's Institution is a welcome move for children', [online] 3 December, Available from: https://www.childrensrights.ie/resources/closing-door-st-patricks-institution [Accessed 5 May 2021].

Children's Rights Alliance (2015b) *Report Card 2014*, Dublin: Children's Rights Alliance.

Children's Rights Alliance (2016) *Report Card 2015*, Dublin: Children's Rights Alliance.

Children's Rights Alliance (2017a) 'Use of "single separation" must be last resort for children in detention, Children's Rights Alliance responds to latest HIQA report on Oberstown Children Detention Campus', Press Release, [online] 3 August, Available from: https://www.childrensrights.ie/resources/press-release-use-single-separation-must [Accessed 5 May 2021].

Children's Rights Alliance (2017b) *Report Card 2016*, Dublin: Children's Rights Alliance.

Commission of Inquiry into the Reformatory and Industrial School System (1936) *Report of the Commission of Inquiry into the Reformatory and Industrial School System 1934–1936* (Cussen Report), Dublin: The Stationery Office.

Commission to Inquire into Child Abuse (2009) *Report of the Commission to Inquire into Child Abuse*, vol 1–5 (Ryan Report), Dublin: The Stationery Office.

Commissioner for Human Rights (2008) *Report by the Commissioner for Human Rights Mr. Thomas Hammarberg on his Visit to Ireland 26–30 November 2007*, CommDH(2008)9, Strasbourg: Council of Europe.

Commissioner for Human Rights (2011) *Report by Thomas Hammarberg Commissioner for Human Rights of the Council of Europe Following his Visit to Ireland from 1 to 2 June 2011*, CommDH(2011)27, Strasbourg: Council of Europe.

Commissioner for Human Rights (2012) *Letter from the Council of Europe Commissioner for Human Rights, Nils Muižnieks, to the Minister for Justice, Equality and Defence of Ireland, Mr Alan Shatter*, CommDH(2012)35, Strasbourg: Council of Europe.

Committee of Inquiry into the Penal System (1985) *Report of the Committee of Inquiry into the Penal System* (Whitaker Report), Dublin: The Stationery Office.

Committee on Reformatory and Industrial Schools (1970) *Reformatory and Industrial Schools System Report* (Kennedy Report), Dublin: The Stationery Office.

Costello, L. (2014) *Travellers in the Irish Prison System: A Qualitative Study*, Dublin: Irish Penal Reform Trust.

Costello, L. (2015) *Turnaround Youth: Young Adults (18–24) in the Criminal Justice System – the Case for a Distinct Approach*, Dublin: Irish Penal Reform Trust.

Council of Europe Development Bank (2019) *Evaluation of CEB Loan 1888 – Cork Prison and National Children Detention Facility Republic of Ireland*, Internal Evaluation Report, Office of Evaluation, Extract available from: https://coebank.org/documents/979/EVO_WebAbstract_2019_1_JI.pdf [Accessed 7 May 2021].

Courts Service (2020) *Annual Report 2019*, Dublin: Government Publications.

Cox, A. (2017) *Trapped in a Vice: The Consequences of Confinement for Young People*, New Brunswick: Rutgers University Press.

Cunneen, C. (2006) 'Racism, discrimination and the over-representation of Indigenous people in the criminal justice system: some conceptual and explanatory issues', *Current Issues in Criminal Justice*, 17(3): 329–46.

Dáil Select Committee on Crime (1992) *Juvenile Crime, Its Causes and Its Remedies*, Dublin: Government Publications.

Dale, M.J. (1998) 'Lawsuits and public policy: the role of litigation in correcting conditions in juvenile detention centers', *University of San Francisco Law Review*, 32(4): 675–734.

Delahunt, M. (2020) 'The trial of children in the Central Criminal Court', *The Bar Review Journal of The Bar of Ireland*, 25(1): 19–22.

Dempsey, M. (2020) *Justice or Injustice: Children and the Justice System*, London: Children's Commissioner for England.

Department of Children and Youth Affairs (2014) *Better Outcomes, Brighter Futures: The National Policy Framework for Children and Young People 2014–2020*, Dublin: The Stationery Office.

Department of Children and Youth Affairs (2015) *National Strategy on Children and Young People's Participation in Decision-making 2015–2020*, Dublin: Government Publications.

Department of Children and Youth Affairs (2016) *National Policy on Single Separation Use*, Dublin: Government Publications.

Department of Children, Equality, Diversity, Integration and Youth (2021) *National Framework for Children and Young People's Participation in Decision-Making*, Dublin: Government Publications.

Department of Education (1980) *Development of Youth Work Services in Ireland* (O'Sullivan Report), Dublin: The Stationery Office.

Department of Education and Skills (2019) *Evaluation of Schools Attached to Special Care Units and Children Detention Centres: Oberstown Campus School*, Date of Inspection: 08-02-2019, Available from: https://www.education.ie/en/Publications/Inspection-Reports-Publications/inspection-of-schools-attached-to-special-care-units-and-children-detention-centres/42693V_HSU_11452_20190211.pdf [Accessed 5 May 2021].

Department of Health (1980) *Task Force on Child Care Services: Final Report*, Dublin: The Stationery Office.

Department of Justice (2021) *Youth Justice Strategy 2021–2027*, Available from: http://www.justice.ie/en/JELR/Pages/Youth_Justice_Strategy [Accessed 5 May 2021].

Department of Justice, Equality and Law Reform (2006) *Report on the Youth Justice Review*, Dublin: The Stationery Office.

Department of Public Expenditure and Reform (2016) *Code of Practice for the Governance of State Bodies*, Available from: https://govacc.per.gov.ie/wp-content/uploads/Code-of-Practice-for-the-Governance-of-State-Bodies.pdf [Accessed 28 April 2021].

Detrick, S., Abel, G., Berger, M., Delon, A. and Meek, R. (2008) *Violence Against Children in Conflict with the Law: A Study on Indicators and Data Collection in Belgium, England and Wales, France and the Netherlands*, Geneva: Defence for Children International.

District Court (2014) *DC04, Practice Direction: Children Court*, Available from: https://www.courts.ie/content/children-court [Accessed 28 April 2021].

District Court (2015) *Children Court Bench Book*, Dublin: District Court.

Doek, J.E. (2019) 'The human rights of children: an introduction', in U. Kilkelly and T. Liefaard (eds) *International Human Rights of Children*, Singapore: Springer, pp 3–29.

Dowd, N.E. (ed) (2015) *A New Juvenile Justice System: Total Reform for a Broken System*, New York: New York University Press.

Drislane, S. (2011) 'The treatment of child suspects in Garda Síochána Stations', *Irish Criminal Law Journal*, 21(1): 10–14.

European Committee for the Prevention of Torture (2003a) *Report to the Government of Ireland on the Visit to Ireland Carried Out by the European Committee for the Prevention of Torture and Inhuman or Degrading Treatment or Punishment (CPT) from 20 to 28 May 2002*, CPT/Inf (2003) 36, Strasbourg: Council of Europe.

European Committee for the Prevention of Torture (2003b) *Response of the Government of Ireland to the report of the European Committee for the Prevention of Torture and Inhuman or Degrading Treatment or Punishment (CPT) on its Visit to Ireland from 20 to 28 May 2002*, CPT/Inf (2003) 37, Strasbourg: Council of Europe.

European Committee for the Prevention of Torture (2008) *Report to the Government of Cyprus on the Visit to Cyprus Carried Out by the European Committee for the Prevention of Torture and Inhuman or Degrading Treatment or Punishment (CPT) from 8 to 17 December 2004*, CPT/Inf (2008) 17, Strasbourg: Council of Europe.

European Committee for the Prevention of Torture (2015a) *Report to the Government of Ireland on the Visit to Ireland Carried Out by the European Committee for the Prevention of Torture and Inhuman or Degrading Treatment or Punishment (CPT) from 16 to 26 September 2014*, CPT/Inf (2015) 38, Strasbourg: Council of Europe.

European Committee for the Prevention of Torture (2015b) *Response of the Government of Ireland to the Report of the European Committee for the Prevention of Torture and Inhuman or Degrading Treatment or Punishment (CPT) on its Visit to Ireland from 16 to 26 September 2014*, CPT/Inf (2015) 39, Strasbourg: Council of Europe.

European Committee for the Prevention of Torture (2015c) *Juveniles Deprived of their Liberty under Criminal Legislation, Extract from the 24th General Report of the CPT, published in 2015*, CPT/Inf(2015)1-part rev1, Strasbourg: Council of Europe.

Expert Group on Children Detention Schools (2006) *Expert Group on Children Detention Schools, First Progress Report to Mr Brian Lenihan, T.D., Minister for Children*, Dublin: Office of the Minister for Children.

Expert Group on Children Detention Schools (2007) *Final Report*, Dublin: Irish Youth Justice Service.

Fagan, M. (2018) 'Decision not to publish Oberstown review "deeply problematic"', *The Irish Times*, [online] 6 August, Available from: https://www.irishtimes.com/news/crime-and-law/decision-not-to-publish-oberstown-review-deeply-problematic-1.3587256?mode=sample&auth-failed=1&pw-origin=https%3A%2F%2Fwww.irishtimes.com%2Fnews%2Fcrime-and-law%2Fdecision-not-to-publish-oberstown-review-deeply-problematic-1.3587256 [Accessed 28 April 2021].

Fagan, M. (2020) 'Call for change on disproportionate numbers of Travellers in prison', *The Irish Examiner*, [online] 20 July, Available from: https://www.irishexaminer.com/news/arid-40018400.html [Accessed 5 May 2021].

Feld, B. (2017) *The Evolution of the Juvenile Court: Race, Politics, and the Criminalizing of Juvenile Justice*, New York: New York University Press.

Fingal Independent (2019) 'Oberstown campus in "well-being initiative"', *Fingal Independent*, [online] 9 February, Available from: https://www.independent.ie/regionals/fingalindependent/news/oberstown-campus-in-well-being-initiative-37781359.html [Accessed 28 April 2021].

Fleming, J., Hine, J. and Smith, R. (2014) *Use your Situation to Change your Destination: Evaluation of The Howard League for Penal Reform's U R Boss*, London: Howard League for Penal Reform.

Forde, L. (2014) 'Aftercare for young people leaving care and detention', *Irish Law Times*, 32(12): 180–84.

Freeman, M. (1996) 'Children's education: a test case for best interests and autonomy', in R. Davie and D.M. Galloway (eds) *Listening to Children in Education*, London: David Fulton Publishers.

Gallagher, C. (2020) 'Coronavirus: nearly all visits to children in detention suspended', *The Irish Times*, [online] 6 April, Available from: https://www.irishtimes.com/news/social-affairs/coronavirus-nearly-all-visits-to-children-in-detention-suspended-1.4222188?mode=sample&auth-failed=1&pw-origin=https%3A%2F%2Fwww.irishtimes.com%2Fnews%2Fsocial-affairs%2Fcoronavirus-nearly-all-visits-to-children-in-detention-suspended-1.4222188 [Accessed 28 April 2021].

Gallagher, L.A. (2014) 'More than a time out: juvenile solitary confinement', *UC Davis Journal of Juvenile Law and Policy*, 18(2): 244–66.

Garda Youth Diversion and Crime Prevention Bureau (2017) *Annual Report of the Committee Appointed to Monitor the Effectiveness of the Diversion Programme*, Dublin: An Garda Síochána.

Garda Youth Diversion Bureau (2019). *Annual Report of the Committee Appointed to Monitor the Effectiveness of the Diversion Programme*, Dublin: An Garda Síochána.

Goldson, B. (2005) 'Child imprisonment: a case for abolition', *Youth Justice*, 5(2): 77–90.

Goldson, B. and Kilkelly, U. (2013) 'International human rights standards and child imprisonment: potentialities and limitations', *The International Journal of Children's Rights*, 21(2): 345–71.

Goldson, B., Cunneen, C., Russell, S., Brown, D., Baldry, E., Schwartz, M. and Briggs, D. (2021) *Youth Justice and Penalty in Comparative Context*, London: Routledge.

Goodfellow, P. (2017) 'Outnumbered, locked up and over-looked? The use of penal custody for girls in England and Wales', Research Paper 2017/02, The Griffins Society.

Grittens, G. (2018) 'Santa Claus does come and everyone gets a present – inside Oberstown detention centre on Christmas Day', *Independent*, [online] 25 December, Available from: https://www.independent.ie/life/santa-claus-does-come-and-everyone-gets-a-present-inside-oberstown-detention-centre-on-christmas-day-37645231.html [Accessed 28 April 2021].

Health Information and Quality Authority (HIQA) (2009a) *Trinity House: Children Detention School*, Inspection Report ID Number: 270, Dublin: Health Information and Quality Authority, Social Services Inspectorate.

Health Information and Quality Authority (HIQA) (2009b) *Oberstown Boys' Detention School*, Inspection Report ID Number: 269, Dublin: Health Information and Quality Authority, Social Services Inspectorate.

Health Information and Quality Authority (HIQA) (2009c) *Oberstown Girls' Detention School*, Inspection Report ID Number: 282, Dublin: Health Information and Quality Authority, Social Services Inspectorate.

Health Information and Quality Authority (HIQA) (2009d) *Trinity House Detention School: Follow-up Inspection Carried Out on 7th July 2009*, Inspection Report ID Number: 331, Dublin: Health Information and Quality Authority, Social Services Inspectorate.

Health Information and Quality Authority (HIQA) (2009e) *Oberstown Girls' Detention School: Follow-up Inspection Carried Out on 15th July 2009*, Inspection Report ID Number: 326, Dublin: Health Information and Quality Authority, Social Services Inspectorate.

Health Information and Quality Authority (HIQA) (2009f) *Oberstown Boy's Detention School: Follow-up Inspection Carried Out on 21 July 2009*, Inspection Report ID Number: 336, Dublin: Health Information and Quality Authority, Social Services Inspectorate.

Health Information and Quality Authority (HIQA) (2014) *Monitoring Inspection Report: Detention Schools Services Under the Children Act, 2001 (as Amended by Section 152 of the Criminal Justice Act 2006)*, Dates of Inspection 28–30 October and 4 November, Dublin: Health Information and Quality Authority.

Health Information and Quality Authority (HIQA) (2015) *Monitoring Inspection Report: Detention Schools Services Under the Children Act, 2001 (as Amended by Section 152 of the Criminal Justice Act 2006)*, Dates of Inspection 16–17 June, Dublin: Health Information and Quality Authority.

Health Information and Quality Authority (HIQA) (2017) *Monitoring Inspection Report: Detention Schools Services Under the Children Act, 2001 (as Amended by Section 152 of the Criminal Justice Act 2006)*, Dates of Inspection 27–30 March, Dublin: Health Information and Quality Authority.

Health Information and Quality Authority (HIQA) (2018) *Monitoring Inspection Report: Detention Schools Services Under the Children Act, 2001 (as Amended by Section 152 of the Criminal Justice Act 2006)*, Dates of Inspection 7, 8, 10, 12 and 13 March, Dublin: Health Information and Quality Authority.

Health Information and Quality Authority (HIQA) (2020) *Report of the Oberstown Children Detention Campus*, Dates of Inspection 16–18 July 2019, Dublin: Health Information and Quality Authority.

Health Information and Quality Authority (HIQA) (2021) *Report of Oberstown Children Detention Campus*, Dates of Inspection 8–10 December 2020, Dublin: Health Information and Quality Authority.

Hennessy, M. (2016) 'Strike planned at juvenile detention centre over safety concerns', *The Journal*, [online] 25 May, Available from: https://www.thejournal.ie/strike-oberstown-2789144-May2016/ [Accessed 28 April 2021].

Hespel, S., Put, J. and Rom, M. (2012) 'Navigating the maze – the interrelation of international legal norms, with illustrations from international juvenile justice standards', *Human Rights and International Legal Discourse*, 6: 329–65.

Hillard, M. (2019) 'Oberstown reports' authors criticise decision not to publish findings', *The Irish Times*, [online] 30 January, Available from: https://www.irishtimes.com/news/crime-and-law/oberstown-reports-authors-criticise-decision-not-to-publish-findings-1.3776404?mode=sample&auth-failed=1&pw-origin=https%3A%2F%2Fwww.irishtimes.com%2Fnews%2Fcrime-and-law%2Foberstown-reports-authors-criticise-decision-not-to-publish-findings-1.3776404 [Accessed 28 April 2021].

HM Inspectorate of Prisons (2020) *Thematic Report by HM Inspectorate of Prisons: Separation of Children in young Offender Institutions: A Thematic Review by HM Inspectorate of Prisons*, London: Her Majesty's Inspectorate of Prisons.

HM Inspectorate of Prisons (2021) *HMYOI Feltham A 2021 Survey Results*, Available from: https://www.justiceinspectorates.gov.uk/hmiprisons/wp-content/uploads/sites/4/2021/03/2021-HMYOI-FELTHAM-SV-SURVEY-ANALYSIS-WORKBOOK-QA.pdf [Accessed 5 May 2021].

Holland, K. (2017) 'Study of children in Oberstown shows high levels of abuse or neglect', *The Irish Times*, [online] 26 October, Available from: https://www.irishtimes.com/news/social-affairs/study-of-children-in-oberstown-shows-high-levels-of-abuse-or-neglect-1.3268888 [Accessed 28 April 2021].

Holland, K. (2020) 'Most children at Oberstown were not engaged in education before being sent there', *The Irish Times*, [online] 23 July, Available from: https://www.irishtimes.com/news/social-affairs/most-children-at-oberstown-were-not-engaged-in-education-before-being-sent-there-1.4312009 [Accessed 28 April 2021].

Howard League for Penal Reform (2010) *Life Inside 2010: A Unique Insight into the Day to Day Experiences of 15–17 Year Old Males in Prison*, London: Howard League for Penal Reform.

Human Rights Watch (2003) *Cruel Confinement: Abuses Against Detained Children in Northern Brazil*, Vol. 15, No. 1 (B), New York: Human Rights Watch.

Human Rights Watch (2005) *In the Dark: Hidden Abuses Against Detained Youths in Rio de Janeiro*, Vol. 17, No. 2(B), New York: Human Rights Watch.

Human Rights Watch (2006) *'Children of the Dust': Abuse of Hanoi Street Children in Detention*, Vol. 18, No. 14(C), New York: Human Rights Watch.

Human Rights Watch (2007) *Paying the Price: Violations of the Rights of Children in Detention in Burundi*, Vol. 19, No. 4(A), New York: Human Rights Watch.

Human Rights Watch and American Civil Liberties Union (2006) *Custody and Control: Conditions of Confinement in New York's Juvenile Prisons for Girls*, New York: Human Rights Watch and American Civil Liberties Union.

Human Rights Watch and American Civil Liberties Union (2012) *Growing Up Locked Down: Youth in Solitary Confinement in Jails and Prisons Across the United States*, New York: Human Rights Watch.

Inspector of Prisons (2013) *Office of the Inspector of Prisons Annual Report 2012*, Tipperary: Office of the Inspector of Prisons.

Interdepartmental Committee on Mentally Ill and Maladjusted Persons (1974) *First Interim Report of the Interdepartmental Committee on Mentally Ill and Maladjusted Persons, Assessment Services for the Courts in Respect of Juveniles* (Henchy Report), Dublin: The Stationery Office.

Irish Examiner (2017) 'Call them "young people in conflict with the law", not "yobs", says Oberstown', *Irish Examiner*, [online] 24 August, Available from: https://www.irishexaminer.com/news/arid-30803275.html [Accessed 28 April 2021].

Irish Penal Reform Trust (2007) *The Whitaker Committee Report 20 Years On: Lessons Learned or Lessons Forgotten?*, Dublin: Irish Penal Reform Trust.

Irish Penal Reform Trust (2012) *Briefing Paper on the Detention of Children in St Patrick's Institution*, Dublin: Irish Penal Reform Trust.

Irish Penal Reform Trust (2016) 'Detention of children: international standards and best practice', [online] 20 December, Available from: https://www.iprt.ie/youth-justice/detention-of-children-international-standards-and-best-practice/ [Accessed 28 April 2021].

Irish Penal Reform Trust (2020) *IPTR Submission to the Department of Justice on the Draft Youth Justice Strategy 2020–2026*, Dublin: Irish Penal Reform Trust.

Irish Youth Justice Service (2008a) *National Youth Justice Strategy 2008–2010*, Dublin: The Stationery Office.

Irish Youth Justice Service (2008b) *Standards and Criteria for Children Detention Schools*, Dublin: Department of Justice, Equality and Law Reform.

Irish Youth Justice Service (2009) *Working Group on Children's Rights Standards for the National Children Detention Service at Oberstown, Lusk, Co. Dublin*, Available from: https://www.iprt.ie/site/assets/files/6150/report_on_standards_working_group.pdf [Accessed 5 May 2021].

Irish Youth Justice Service (2012) *Review of Senior Management Structure in the Provision of Services at the Oberstown Campus*, Report prepared by the Public Appointments Service on behalf of Irish Youth Justice Service.

Irish Youth Justice Service (2013a) *Tackling Youth Crime: Youth Justice Action Plan 2014–2018*, Dublin: Department of Justice.

Irish Youth Justice Service (2013b) *Children Detention Schools: Report on Staff Information Events October/November 2012, Bracken Court, Balbriggan, Co. Dublin*, Dublin: IYJS.

Joint Committee on Children and Youth Affairs (2016) *Operations of Oberstown Children Detention Centre* (Deb 5 October), Available from: https://www.oireachtas.ie/en/debates/debate/joint_committee_on_children_and_youth_affairs/2016-10-05/2/ [Accessed 28 April 2021].

Joint Committee on Children and Youth Affairs (2017) *HIQA Inspection of the Oberstown Children's Detention Campus: Discussion* (Deb 8 November), Available from: https://www.oireachtas.ie/en/debates/debate/joint_committee_on_children_and_youth_affairs/2017-11-08/3/ [Accessed 28 April 2021].

Joint Committee on Children and Youth Affairs (2019) *Oberstown Children Detention Campus Operational Review Report: Discussion* (Deb 30 January), Available from: https://www.oireachtas.ie/en/debates/debate/joint_committee_on_children_and_youth_affairs/2019-01-30/2/ [Accessed 28 April 2021].

Joint Committee on Health and Children (2012) *FSA and Oberstown Detention Centre: Discussion with Chairmen Designate* (Deb 8 March), Available from: https://www.oireachtas.ie/en/debates/debate/joint_committee_on_health_and_children/2012-03-08/2/#spk_10 [Accessed 28 April 2021].

Joint Committee on Health and Children (2016) *Oberstown Children Detention Campus: Chairperson Designate* (Deb 28 January), Available from: https://www.oireachtas.ie/en/debates/debate/joint_committee_on_health_and_children/2016-01-28/4/#spk_40 [Accessed 28 April 2021].

Joint Committee on Human Rights (2019) *Youth Detention: Solitary Confinement and Restraint*, Nineteenth Report of Session 2017–19, London: House of Commons and House of Lords, Available from: https://publications.parliament.uk/pa/jt201719/jtselect/jtrights/994/994.pdf [Accessed 28 April 2021].

Junger-Tas, J., Marshall, I.H., Enzmann, D., Killias, M., Sketee, M. and Gruszczynska, B. (2012) *The Many Faces of Youth Crime: Contrasting Theoretical Perspectives on Juvenile Delinquency across Countries and Cultures*, Singapore: Springer.

Kilcommins, S., O'Donnell, I., O'Sullivan, E. and Vaughan, B. (2004) *Crime, Punishment and the Search for Order in Ireland*, Dublin: Institute of Public Administration.

Kilkelly, U. (1998) 'In the best interests of the child? An evaluation of Ireland's performance before the UN Committee on the Rights of the Child', *Irish Law Times*, 16: 293–300.

Kilkelly, U. (2006) *Youth Justice in Ireland: Tough Lives, Rough Justice*, Dublin: Irish Academic Press.

Kilkelly, U. (2007) 'Reform of youth justice in Ireland: the "new" Children Act 2001 Part 2', *Irish Criminal Law Journal*, 17(1): 2–8.

Kilkelly, U. (2008a) 'Youth justice and children's rights: measuring compliance with international standards', *Youth Justice*, 8(3): 187–92.

Kilkelly, U. (2008b) 'Youth courts and children's rights: the Irish experience', *Youth Justice*, 8(1): 39–56.

Kilkelly, U. (2011) 'Policing, young people, diversion and accountability in Ireland', *Crime Law and Social Change*, 55: 133–51.

Kilkelly, U. (2014) 'Diverging or emerging from law? The practice of youth justice in Ireland', *Youth Justice*, 14(3): 212–25.

Kilkelly, U. (2017) 'Making sure Oberstown's children are kept in the picture', *Irish Examiner*, [online] 14 December, Available from: https://www.irishexaminer.com/opinion/commentanalysis/arid-30818607.html [Accessed 28 April 2021].

Kilkelly, U. (2018) 'It takes a village to raise a child in detention', *The Irish Times*, [online] 10 July, Available from: https://www.irishtimes.com/life-and-style/health-family/it-takes-a-village-to-raise-a-child-in-detention-1.3553742 [Accessed 28 April 2021].

Kilkelly, U. (2019) 'The UN Convention on the Rights of the Child: incremental and transformative approaches to legal implementation', *The International Journal of Human Rights*, 23(3): 323–37.

Kilkelly, U. (2020) '"Evolving capacities" and "parental guidance" in the context of youth justice: testing the application of Article 5 of the Convention on the Rights of the Child', *International Journal of Children's Rights*, 28(3): 500–20.

Kilkelly, U. and Casale, S. (2012) *Children's Rights and the European Committee for the Prevention of Torture*, Strasbourg: Council of Europe.

Kilkelly, U. and Forde, L. (2016) 'Human rights law and juvenile justice: emerging law and practice', in L. Weber, E. Fishwick and M. Marmo (eds) *The Routledge International Handbook of Criminology and Human Rights*, London and New York: Routledge, pp 460–9.

Kilkelly, U. and Forde, L. (2021) *Looking Back at Tackling Youth Crime: Youth Justice Action Plan 2014–2018: A Review of Progress Achieved and Lessons Learned*, Dublin: Department of Justice.

Kilkelly, U. and Liefaard, T. (eds) (2019) *International Human Rights of Children*, Singapore: Springer.

Kilkelly, U. and Logan, E. (2021) *Independent National Human Rights Institutions for Children: Monitoring, Promoting and Protecting Children's Rights*, London: Palgrave Macmillan.

Kilkelly, U., Lundy, L. and Byrne, B. (eds) (2021) *Incorporating the UN Convention on the Rights of the Child into National Law*, Oxford: Intersentia.

Kotter, J.P. (1996) *Leading Change*, Boston: Harvard Business School Press.

Lammy, D. (2017) *The Lammy Review: An Independent Review into the Treatment of, and Outcomes for, Black, Asian and Minority Ethnic Individuals in the Criminal Justice System*, London: HM Government.

Leiber, M. and Fix, R. (2019) 'Reflections on the impact of race and ethnicity on juvenile court outcomes and efforts to enact change', *American Journal of Criminal Justice*, 44: 581–608.

Lewin, K. (1958) 'Group decisions and social change', in G.E. Swanson, T.M. Newcomb and E.L. Hartley (eds) *Readings on Social Psychology*, New York: Holt, Rhinehart and Winston.

Liefaard, T. (2008) *Deprivation of Liberty of Children in Light of International Human Rights Law and Standards*, Oxford: Intersentia.

Liefaard, T. (2020) 'Juvenile justice', in J. Todres and S.M. King (eds) *The Oxford Handbook of Children's Rights Law*, New York: Oxford University Press, pp 279–310.

Liefaard, T. and Kilkelly, U. (2018) 'Child-friendly justice: past, present and future', in B. Goldson (ed) *Juvenile Justice in Europe: Past, Present and Future*, London: Routledge, pp 57–73.

Lundy, L. (2007) ' "Voice" is not enough: conceptualising Article 12 of the United Nations Convention on the Rights of the Child', *British Educational Research Journal*, 33(6): 927–42.

Lynch, N. (2019) *Youth Justice in New Zealand* (3rd edn), Wellington: Thomson Reuters.

Lynch, N. and Kilkelly, U. (2021) ' "Zooming in" on children's rights during a pandemic: technology, child justice and COVID-19', *International Journal of Children's Rights*, 29(2): 286–304.

Lynch, N. and Liefaard, T. (2020) 'What is left in the "too hard basket"? Developments and challenges for the rights of children in conflict with the law', *International Journal of Children's Rights*, 28(1): 88–110.

Macallair, D.E. (2015) *After the Doors Were Locked: A History of Youth Corrections in California and the Origins of Twenty-first Century Reform*, Maryland: Rowman and Littlefield.

MacNamee, G. (2016) ' "Regular violent assaults" lead staff to strike at Oberstown youth detention facility', *The Journal*, [online] 1 December, Available from: https://www.thejournal.ie/oberstown-violence-strike-impact-dublin-3114538-Dec2016/ [Accessed 28 April 2021].

Mallett, C. (2018) 'Disproportionate minority contact in juvenile justice: today's, and yesterdays, problems', *Criminal Justice Studies*, 31(3): 230–48.

Manning, J. (2018) 'Oberstown campus improving but work still to do, reports HIQA', *Fingal Independent*, [online] 20 October, Available from: https://www.independent.ie/regionals/fingalindependent/news/oberstown-campus-improving-but-work-still-to-do-reports-hiqa-37421676.html [Accessed 28 April 2021].

Manning, J. (2019) 'Annual report is published for the Oberstown campus', *Fingal Independent*, [online] 13 July, Available from: https://www.independent.ie/regionals/fingalindependent/news/annual-report-is-published-for-the-oberstown-campus-38293064.html [Accessed 28 April 2021].

Martynowicz, A., and Moore, L. (2018) *Behind the Door: Solitary Confinement in the Irish Penal System*, Dublin: Irish Penal Reform Trust.

Martynowicz, A. and Ní Dhrisceoil, V. (2009) *Detention of Children in Ireland: International Standards and Best Practice*, Dublin: Irish Penal Reform Trust.

McNickle, A. (2018) 'Rejuvenate juvenile justice', *The Bar Review*, 23(4): 112–14.

Meagher J. (2017) 'Young offenders: inside Ireland's teenage borstal', *Independent*, [online] 21 May, Available from: https://www.independent.ie/irish-news/special-reports/young-offenders-inside-irelands-teenage-borstal-35731829.html [Accessed 28 April 2021].

Mendel, R.A. (2011) *No Place for Kids: The Case for Reducing Juvenile Incarceration*, Baltimore, Maryland: The Annie E. Casey Foundation.

Meuwese, S. (2003) *Kids Behind Bars: A Study on Children in Conflict with the Law: Towards Investing in Prevention, Stopping Incarceration and Meeting International Standards: An International Study on the Situation of Children in Prison with Country Reports from: Albania, Argentina, Bulgaria, Burundi, Canada, Costa Rica, Ghana, Germany, Indonesia, Kenya, Kyrgyz Republic, Mauritius, The Netherlands, Palestine, Pakistan, Philippines, Romania, Spain, Tanzania, Ukraine, United Kingdom, United States of America*, Amsterdam: Defence for Children International.

Miller, J.G. (1991) *Last One Over the Wall: The Massachusetts Experiment in Closing Reform Schools*, Columbus, Ohio: Ohio State University Press.

Minister for Justice and Equality (2012) *Reply from the Minister for Justice, Equality and Defence of Ireland, Mr Alan Shatter, to Nils Muižnieks, Council of Europe Commissioner for Human Rights*, CommHR/SG/sf115-2012.

Muncie J. (2006) 'Repenalisation and rights: explorations in comparative youth criminology', *The Howard Journal of Criminal Justice*, 45(1): 42–70.

Muncie J. (2008) 'The "punitive turn" in juvenile justice: cultures of control and rights compliance in Western Europe and the USA', *Youth Justice*, 8(2): 107–21.

National Children's Office (2000) *The National Children's Strategy: Our Children - Their Lives*, Dublin: The Stationery Office.

Naughton, C., Redmond, S. and Coonan, B. (2019) *Evaluation of The Bail Supervision Scheme for Children (Pilot Scheme)*, Dublin: Department of Children and Youth Affairs.

Newstalk (2017) 'Oberstown Detention Centre in breach of national safety standards', *Newstalk*, [online] 13 August, Available from: https://www.newstalk.com/news/oberstown-detention-centre-in-breach-of-national-safety-standards-527149 [Accessed 28 April 2021].

Nowak, M. (2019) *The United Nations Global Study on Children Deprived of Liberty*, Geneva: United Nations.

Oberstown Children Detention Campus (2017a) *Combined Annual Report 2012–2016*, Dublin: Oberstown Children Detention Campus.

Oberstown Children Detention Campus (2017b) *Communications and Engagement Strategy 2017–2020*, Dublin: Oberstown Children Detention Campus.

Oberstown Children Detention Campus (2017c) *Key Characteristics of Young People in Detention: A Snapshot* (Q1, 2017), Dublin: Oberstown Children Detention Campus.

Oberstown Children Detention Campus (2017d) 'Not Just Language', News and Media [online], Available from: https://www.oberstown.com/2017/08/23/not-just-language/ [Accessed 6 May 2021].

Oberstown Children Detention Campus (2017e) *Oberstown Children Detention Campus Strategy 2017–2020*, Dublin: Oberstown Children Detention Campus.

Oberstown Children Detention Campus (2017f) *Oberstown Strategy for the Participation of Young People in Decision-Making*, Dublin: Oberstown Children Detention Campus.

Oberstown Children Detention Campus (2018) *Annual Report 2016/2017*, Dublin: Oberstown Children Detention Campus.

Oberstown Children Detention Campus (2019a) *Key Characteristics of Young People in Detention: A Snapshot* (Q1, 2019), Dublin: Oberstown Children Detention Campus.

Oberstown Children Detention Campus (2019b) *Annual Report 2018*, Dublin: Oberstown Children Detention Campus.

Oberstown Children Detention Campus (2020) *Annual Report 2019*, Dublin: Oberstown Children Detention Campus.

Oberstown Children Detention Campus (2021) *Annual Report 2020*, Dublin: Oberstown Children Detention Campus.

O'Dwyer, K. (2019) 'Reducing youth crime: the role of mentoring', *Irish Probation Journal*, 16: 153–67.

Office of the Minister for Children and Youth Affairs (2010) *Office of the Minister for Children and Youth Affairs Annual Report 2009*, Dublin: Government Publications.

O'Keefe, C. (2019) 'Special report: planting the seeds of change in young offenders at Oberstown', *Irish Examiner*, [online] 24 February, Available from: https://www.irishexaminer.com/lifestyle/arid-30906804.html [Accessed 28 April 2021].

O'Loughlin, B. (2019) 'Young offenders given President's Awards for positive contributions', *Dublin's 98FM*, [online] 1 August, Available from: https://www.98fm.com/news/young-offenders-given-presidents-awards-positive-contributions-889636 [Accessed 28 April 2021].

Ombudsman for Children (2011) *Young People in St. Patrick's Institution*, Dublin: Ombudsman for Children's Office.

Ombudsman for Children (2015) *Report of the Ombudsman for Children to the UN Committee on the Rights of the Child on the Occasion of the Examination of Ireland's Consolidated Third and Fourth Report to the Committee*, Dublin: Ombudsman for Children's Office.

Ombudsman for Children (2018) *Annual Report 2017*, Dublin: Ombudsman for Children's Office.

Ombudsman for Children (2019) *Annual Report 2018*, Dublin: Ombudsman for Children's Office.

Ombudsman for Children (2020a) *Annual Report 2019*, Dublin: Ombudsman for Children's Office.

Ombudsman for Children (2020b) *Submission to the UN Committee on the Rights of the Child on the List of Issues Prior to Reporting for the Fourth Periodic Examination of Ireland*, Dublin: Ombudsman for Children's Office.

Osborough, W.N. (1975) *Borstal in Ireland: Custodial Provision for the Young Adult Offender, 1906–1974*, Dublin: Institute for Public Administration.

O'Sullivan, E. and O'Donnell, I. (2012) *Coercive Confinement in Ireland: Patients, Prisoners and Penitents*, Manchester: Manchester University Press.

Peleg, N. (2019) 'International children's rights law: general principles', in U. Kilkelly and T. Liefaard (eds) *International Human Rights of Children*, Singapore: Springer, pp 135–57.

Penal Reform International (2014) *Neglected Needs: Girls in the Criminal Justice System*, London: Penal Reform International.

Perkins, D. and O'Rourke, M. (2018) *Behavioural Management Review 2017: Oberstown Children Detention Campus*, Dublin: Oberstown Children Detention Campus.

Pinheiro, P.S. (2006) *World Report on Violence Against Children*, Geneva: United Nations Secretary-General's Study on Violence against Children.

Regional Juvenile Justice Observatory (2014) *Monitoring Report on Juvenile Justice Systems in Latin America*, Geneva: Defence for Children International.

Review Implementation Group of Oberstown Children Detention Campus (2017) *Final Report of the Review Implementation Group of Oberstown Children Detention Campus: December 2017*, Available from: https://www.gov.ie/en/publication/34bea6-final-report-of-the-review-implementation-group-of-oberstown-childre/ [Accessed 28 April 2021].

Review Implementation Group of Oberstown Children Detention Campus (2018) *First Report on the Implementation of Review Recommendation Action Plan*, Available from: https://www.gov.ie/en/press-release/b15aa2-publication-of-second-report-on-the-implementation-of-review-recomme/ [Accessed 28 April 2021].

Review Implementation Group of Oberstown Children Detention Campus (2019) *Second Report on the Implementation of Review Recommendation Action Plan*, Available from: https://www.gov.ie/en/press-release/b15aa2-publication-of-second-report-on-the-implementation-of-review-recomme/ [Accessed 28 April 2021].

Robinson, B. and D'Aloisio, J. (2009) *'Education in Chains: Gaps in Education Provision to Children in Detention': An Overview of the Right to Education of Children in Detention*, Geneva: Defence for Children International.

Roush, D.W. (2019) *Recalibrating Juvenile Detention: Lessons Learned from the Court-ordered Reform of the Cook County Juvenile Temporary Detention Centre*, London: Routledge.

RTE (2017) 'Oberstown director hurt as three youths abscond', *RTE*, [online] 30 May, Available from: https://www.rte.ie/news/2017/0530/878893-oberstown/ [Accessed 28 April 2021].

RTE Drivetime (2019) 'Training young offenders', *RTE Radio 1*, [online] 25 February, Available from: https://www.rte.ie/radio/radioplayer/html5/#/radio1/21517565 [Accessed 28 April 2021].

Sargent, P. (2016) *Wild Arabs and Savages: A History of Juvenile Justice in Ireland*, Manchester: Manchester University Press.

Sawyer, W. (2019) *Youth Confinement: The Whole Pie 2019*, Prison Policy Initiative [online], Available from: https://www.prisonpolicy.org/reports/youth2019.html [Accessed 28 April 2021].

Shacklady-Smith, A. (2006) 'Appreciating the challenge of change', in K. Walshe and J. Smith (eds) *Healthcare Management*, Maidenhead: Open University Press, pp 381–98.

Sherman, F.T. (2005) *Detention Reform and Girls: Challenges and Solutions: JDAI Pathways to Juvenile Detention Reform #13*, Baltimore, Maryland: The Annie E. Casey Foundation.

Singer, W. (2012) 'Judicial intervention and juvenile corrections reform: a case study of Jerry M. v District of Colombia', *Journal of Criminal Law and Criminology*, 102(3): 901–64.

Sloth-Nielsen J. (2019) 'Monitoring and implementation of children's rights', in U. Kilkelly and T. Liefaard (eds) *International Human Rights of Children*, Singapore: Springer.

Smyth, P. (2011) 'Diverting young offenders from crime in Ireland: the need for more checks and balances on the exercise of police discretion', *Crime, Law and Social Change*, 55(2–3): 153–66.

Stein, L.A.R., Clair, M., Rossi, J.S., Martin, R.A., Cancilliere, M.K. and Clarke, J.G. (2015) 'Gender, ethnicity and race in incarcerated and detained youth: services and policy implications for girls', *Psychiatric Rehabilitation Journal*, 38(1): 65–73.

Sutherland, E. and Barnes Macfarlane, L.A. (2018) *Implementing Article 3 of the United Nations Convention on the Rights of the Child: Best Interests, Welfare and Well-being*, Cambridge: Cambridge University Press.

Swirak K. (2016) 'Problematising advanced liberal youth crime prevention: the impacts of management reforms on Irish Garda youth diversion projects', *Youth Justice*, 16(2): 162–80.

Taylor, C. (2016) *Review of the Youth Justice System in England and Wales*, Ministry of Justice, UK: Williams Lea Group on behalf of the Controller of Her Majesty's Stationery Office, Available from: https://assets.publishing.service.gov.uk/government/uploads/system/uploads/attachment_data/file/577105/youth-justice-review-final-report-print.pdf [Accessed 28 April 2021].

The Irish Times (2016) 'Oberstown youth detention centre staff to strike today', *The Irish Times*, [online] 29 August, Available from: https://www.irishtimes.com/news/ireland/irish-news/oberstown-youth-detention-centre-staff-to-strike-today-1.2771381 [Accessed 28 April 2021].

The Lord Carlile of Berriew QC (2006) *An Independent Inquiry into the Use of Physical Restraint, Solitary Confinement and Forcible Strip Searching of Children in Prisons, Secure Training Centres and Local Authority Secure Children's Homes*, London: Howard League for Penal Reform.

The Traveller Movement (2016) *Overlooked and Overrepresented: Gypsy, Traveller and Roma Children in the Youth Justice System: An Analysis of 12–18-Year-Old Gypsy, Traveller and Roma Perceptions of their Experiences in Secure Training Centres and Young Offender Institutions*, London: The Traveller Movement.

Tilley, L. and Jones, R.L. (2013) 'Managing change in health and social care' in S. McKian and J. Simons (eds) *Leading, Managing, Caring: Understanding Leadership and Management in Health and Social Care*, London: Routledge, pp 89–112.

Tobin, J. (ed) (2019) *The UN Convention on the Rights of the Child: A Commentary*, New York: Oxford University Press.

Tuite, T. (2017) 'Youths with metal poles cause €26,000 of damage at Oberstown', *Independent*, [online] 10 August, Available from: https://www.independent.ie/irish-news/courts/youths-with-metal-poles-cause-26000-of-damage-at-oberstown-36017581.html [Accessed 28 April 2021].

Tuite, T. (2018) 'Teen with 50 convictions pleads guilty to Oberstown rampage', *Independent*, [online] 4 January, Available from: https://www.independent.ie/irish-news/courts/teen-with-50-convictions-pleads-guilty-to-oberstown-rampage-36459072.html [Accessed 28 April 2021].

United Nations Committee against Torture (2017) *Concluding Observations on the Second Periodic Report of Ireland*, 31 August, CAT/C/IRL/CO/2.

United Nations Committee on the Rights of the Child (1998) *Concluding Observations of the Committee on the Rights of the Child: Ireland CRC/C/15. Add 85*, adopted by the Committee at the 453rd meeting, held on 23 January.

United Nations Committee on the Rights of the Child (2003) *General Comment No 5, General Measures of Implementation of the Convention on the Rights of the Child*, CRC/GC/2003/5.

United Nations Committee on the Rights of the Child (2006) *Concluding Observations: Ireland*, CRC/C/IRL/CO/2, adopted by the Committee on 29 September.

United Nations Committee on the Rights of the Child (2007) *General Comment No 10, Children's rights in juvenile justice*, CRC/C/GC/10.

United Nations Committee on the Rights of the Child (2014a) *Concluding Observations on the Combined Second to Fourth Periodic Reports of Fiji*, CRC/C/FJI/CO/2-4, adopted by the Committee at its 67th session (1–19 September).

United Nations Committee on the Rights of the Child (2014b) *Concluding Observations on the Combined Third and Fourth Periodic Report of Portugal*, CRC/C/PRT/CO/3-4, adopted by the Committee at its 65th session (13–31 January).

United Nations Committee on the Rights of the Child (2014c) *Concluding Observations on the Combined Third, Fourth and Fifth Periodic Reports of Hungary*, CRC/C/HUN/CO/3-5, adopted by the Committee at its 67th session (1–19 September).

United Nations Committee on the Rights of the Child (2014d) *Concluding Observations on the Combined Fourth and Fifth Periodic Reports of the Russian Federation*, CRC/C/RUS/CO/4-5, adopted by the Committee at its 65th session (13–31 January).

United Nations Committee on the Rights of the Child (2014e) *Concluding Observations on the Combined Third to Fifth Periodic Reports of the Bolivarian Republic of Venezuela*, CRC/C/VEN/CO/3-5, adopted by the Committee at its 67th session (1–19 September).

United Nations Committee on the Rights of the Child (2014f) *Concluding Observations on the Combined Third and Fourth Periodic Reports of Kyrgyzstan*, CRC/C/KGZ/CO/3-4, adopted by the Committee at its 66th session (26 May–13 June).

United Nations Committee on the Rights of the Child (2014g) *Concluding Observations on the Combined Third and Fourth Periodic Reports of Croatia*, CRC/C/HRV/CO/3-4, adopted by the Committee at its 67th session (1–19 September).

United Nations Committee on the Rights of the Child (2014h) *Concluding Observations on the Combined Fourth and Fifth Periodic Reports of Jordan*, CRC/C/JOR/CO/4-5, adopted by the Committee at its 66th session (26 May–13 June).

United Nations Committee on the Rights of the Child (2014i) *Concluding Observations on the Combined Second to Fourth Periodic Reports of the Congo,* CRC/C/COG/CO/2-4, adopted by the Committee at its 65th session (13–31 January).

United Nations Committee on the Rights of the Child (2015a) *Concluding Observations on the Combined Third to Fifth Periodic Reports of Uruguay,* CRC/C/URY/CO/3-5, adopted by the Committee at its 68th session (12–30 January).

United Nations Committee on the Rights of the Child (2015b) *Concluding Observations on the Combined Second to Fourth Periodic Reports of Brazil,* CRC/C/BRA/CO/2-4, adopted by the Committee at its 70th session (14 September–2 October).

United Nations Committee on the Rights of the Child (2015c) *Concluding Observations on the Combined Fourth and Fifth Periodic Reports of Honduras,* CRC/C/HND/CO/4-5, adopted by the Committee at its 69th session (18 May–5 June).

United Nations Committee on the Rights of the Child (2015d) *Concluding Observations on the Combined Third and Fourth Periodic Reports of Jamaica,* CRC/C/JAM/CO/3-4, adopted by the Committee at its 68th session (12–30 January).

United Nations Committee on the Rights of the Child (2015e) *Concluding Observations on the Combined Second to Fourth Periodic Reports of Iraq,* CRC/C/IRQ/CO/2-4, adopted by the Committee at its 68th session (12–30 January).

United Nations Committee on the Rights of the Child (2015f) *Concluding Observations on the Combined Third to Fifth Periodic Reports of Mauritius,* CRC/C/MUS/CO/3-5, adopted by the Committee at its 68th session (12–30 January).

United Nations Committee on the Rights of the Child (2015g) *Concluding Observations on the Combined Fourth and Fifth Periodic Reports of Chile,* CRC/C/CHL/CO/4-5, adopted by the Committee at its 70th session (14 September–2 October).

United Nations Committee on the Rights of the Child (2016a) *Concluding Observations on the Combined Third to Fifth Periodic Reports of Bulgaria,* CRC/C/BGR/CO/3-5, adopted by the Committee at its 72nd session (17 May–3 June).

United Nations Committee on the Rights of the Child (2016b) *Concluding Observations on the Second Periodic Report of South Africa,* CRC/C/ZAF/CO/2 (reissued for technical reasons on 9 November 2016), adopted by the Committee at its 73rd session (13–30 September).

United Nations Committee on the Rights of the Child (2016c) *Concluding Observations on the Initial Report of Nauru,* CRC/C/NRU/CO/1, adopted by the Committee at its 73rd session (13–30 September).

United Nations Committee on the Rights of the Child (2016d) *Concluding Observations on the Fifth Periodic Report of the United Kingdom of Great Britain and Northern Ireland*, CRC/C/GBR/CO/5, adopted by the Committee at its 72nd session (17 May–3 June).

United Nations Committee on the Rights of the Child (2016e) *Concluding Observations on the Fifth Periodic Report of France*, CRC/C/FRA/CO/5, adopted by the Committee at its 71st session (11–29 January).

United Nations Committee on the Rights of the Child (2016f) *Concluding Observations on the Combined Third to Fifth Periodic Reports of Kenya*, CRC/C/KEN/CO/3-5, adopted by the Committee at its 71st session (11–29 January).

United Nations Committee on the Rights of the Child (2016g) *Concluding Observations on the Fifth Periodic Report of Pakistan*, CRC/C/PAK/CO/5, adopted by the Committee at its 72nd session (17 May–3 June).

United Nations Committee on the Rights of the Child (2016h) *Concluding Observations on the Combined Third and Fourth Periodic Reports of Ireland*, CRC/C/IRL/CO/3-4, adopted by the Committee at its 71st session (11–29 January).

United Nations Committee on the Rights of the Child (2017a) *Concluding Observations on the Combined Second and Third Periodic Reports of Serbia*, CRC/C/SRB/CO/2-3, adopted by the Committee at its 74th session (16 January–3 February).

United Nations Committee on the Rights of the Child (2017b) *Concluding Observations on the Combined Second to Fourth Periodic Reports of Estonia*, CRC/C/EST/CO/2-4, adopted by the Committee at its 74th session (16 January–3 February).

United Nations Committee on the Rights of the Child (2017c) *Concluding Observations on the Second Periodic Report of Barbados*, CRC/C/BRB/CO/2, adopted by the Committee at its 74th session (16 January–3 February).

United Nations Committee on the Rights of the Child (2018a) *Concluding Observations on the Combined Fifth and Sixth Periodic Reports of Argentina,* CRC/C/ARG/CO/5-6, adopted by the Committee at its 78th session (14 May–1 June).

United Nations Committee on the Rights of the Child (2018b) *Concluding Observations on the Combined Fifth to Seventh Periodic Reports of Angola*, CRC/C/AGO/CO/5-7, adopted by the Committee at its 78th session (14 May–1 June).

United Nations Committee on the Rights of the Child (2018c) *Concluding Observations on the Combined Fifth and Sixth Periodic Reports of Sri Lanka*, CRC/C/LKA/CO/5-6, adopted by the Committee at its 77th session (14 January–2 February).

United Nations Committee on the Rights of the Child (2019a) *General Comment No 24 on Children's Rights in the Child Justice Sys*tem, CRC/C/GC/24.

United Nations Committee on the Rights of the Child (2019b) *Concluding Observations on the Combined Third to Sixth Periodic Reports of Guinea*, CRC/C/GIN/CO/3-6, adopted by the Committee at its 80th session (14 January–1 February).

United Nations Committee on the Rights of the Child (2019c) *Concluding Observations on the Combined Fifth and Sixth Periodic Reports of the Republic of Korea*, CRC/C/KOR/CO/5-6, adopted by the Committee at its 82nd session (9–27 September).

United Nations Committee on the Rights of the Child (2019d) *Concluding Observations on the Combined Fifth and Sixth Periodic Reports of Australia*, CRC/C/AUS/CO/5-6 (reissued for technical reasons on 29 November 2019), adopted by the Committee at its 82nd session (9–27 September).

United Nations Committee on the Rights of the Child (2019e) *Concluding Observations on the Combined Fourth to Sixth Periodic Reports of Bahrain*, CRC/C/BHR/CO/4-6, adopted by the Committee at its 80th session (14 January–1 February).

United Nations Committee on the Rights of the Child (2019f) *Concluding Observations on the Combined Third to Sixth Periodic Reports of Malta*, CRC/C/MLT/CO/3-6, adopted by the Committee at its 81st session (13–31 May).

United Nations Committee on the Rights of the Child (2020a) *Concluding Observations on the Combined Fifth and Sixth Periodic Reports of Bosnia and Herzegovina*, CRC/C/BIH/CO/5-6, adopted by the Committee at its 82nd session (9–27 September).

United Nations Committee on the Rights of the Child (2020b) *Concluding Observations on the Combined Third and Fourth Periodic Reports of Mozambique*, CRC/C/MOZ/CO/3-4, adopted by the Committee at its 82nd session (9–27 September).

United Nations Committee on the Rights of the Child (2020c) *Concluding Observations on the Initial Report of the State of Palestine*, CRC/C/PSE/CO/1, adopted by the Committee at its 83rd session (20 January–7 February).

United Nations Committee on the Rights of the Child (2020d) *Concluding Observations on the Combined Fifth and Sixth Periodic Reports of Rwanda*, CRC/C/RWA/CO/5-6, adopted by the Committee at its 83rd session (20 January–7 February).

United Nations Committee on the Rights of the Child (2020e) *Concluding Observations on the Combined Fifth and Sixth Periodic Reports of Portugal*, CRC/C/PRT/CO/5-6 (reissued for technical reasons on 13 January 2020), adopted by the Committee at its 82nd session (9–27 September).

United Nations Committee on the Rights of the Child (2020f) *Concluding Observations on the Combined Fifth and Sixth Periodic Reports of Costa Rica*, CRC/C/CRI/CO/5-6, adopted by the Committee at its 83rd session (20 January–7 February).

United Nations Committee on the Rights of the Child (2020g) *Concluding Observations on the Second Periodic Report of Côte d'Ivoire*, CRC/C/CIV/CO/2, adopted by the Committee at its 81st session (13–31 May).

United Nations Committee on the Rights of the Child (2020h) *Concluding Observations on the Sixth Periodic Report of Hungary CRC/C/HUN/CO/6* (reissued for technical reasons on 21 April 2020), adopted by the Committee at its 83rd session (20 January–7 February).

United Nations Committee on the Rights of the Child (2020j) *List of Issues Prior to Submission of the Combined Fifth and Sixth Reports of Ireland*, CRC/C/IRL/QPR/5-6.

Volz, A. (2010) *Stop the Violence! The Overuse of Pre-trial Detention, or the Need to Reform Juvenile Justice Systems: Review of Evidence*, Geneva: Defence for Children International.

Webster, C. (2018) ' "Race", ethnicity, social class and juvenile justice in Europe', in B. Goldson (ed) *Juvenile Justice in Europe: Past, Present and Future*, London: Routledge, pp 168–81.

Zahn, M.A., Day, J.C., Mihalic, S.F. and Tichavsky, L. (2009) 'Determining what works for girls in the juvenile justice system: a summary of evaluation evidence', *Crime and Delinquency*, 55(2): 266–93.

Zane, S. (2021) 'Have racial and ethnic disparities in juvenile justice declined over time? An empirical assessment of the DMC mandate', *Youth Violence and Juvenile Justice*, 19(2): 163–85.

Zettler H.R. (2021) 'Much to do about trauma: a systematic review of existing trauma-informed treatments on youth violence and recidivism', *Youth Violence and Juvenile Justice*, 19(1): 113–34.

Zimring, F.E. (2014) 'Minority overrepresentation: on causes and partial cures', in F.E. Zimring and D.S. Tanenhaus (eds) *Choosing the Future for American Juvenile Justice*, New York: University Press, pp 169–86.

Index

Page numbers in *italics* refer to figures.